P9-DIJ-429

BEGINNING
DIRECTX®9

WENDY JONES

ISBN: 1-59200-349-4
Library of Congress Catalog Card Number: 2004090736
Printed in the United States of America

06 07 08 PH 10 9 8 7 6 5 4 3

THOMSON

COURSE TECHNOLOGY

Professional ■ Technical ■ Reference

Course PTR, a division of Course Technology
25 Thomson Place
Boston, MA 02210
http://www.courseptr.com

Senior Vice President, Course PTR Group:
Andy Shafran

Publisher:
Stacy L. Hiquet

Senior Marketing Manager:
Sarah O'Donnell

Marketing Manager:
Heather Hurley

Manager of Editorial Services:
Heather Talbot

Senior Acquisitions Editor:
Emi Smith

Associate Marketing Manager:
Kristin Eisenzopf

Project/Copy Editor:
Karen A. Gill

Technical Reviewer:
Joseph Hall

Retail Market Coordinator:
Sarah Dubois

Interior Layout:
Marian Hartsough

Cover Designer:
Steve Deschene

CD-ROM Producer:
Brandon Penticuff

Indexer:
Sharon Shock

Proofreader:
Sean Medlock

To my children,
Virginia, Elizabeth, and Ian
and my forever, Ilene.

Acknowledgments

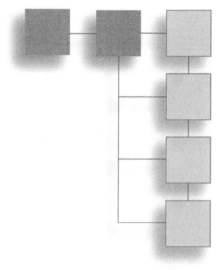

I'd definitely like to thank Emi Smith and Karen Gill for working so patiently with me in the writing of this book. I'm very grateful to Joseph Hall for agreeing to do the technical editing. His comments regarding the code samples kept me sane.

I'd also like to thank Course PTR for giving me the opportunity to present such a wonderful topic as DirectX.

Finally, I'd like to send a heartfelt thank you to Albert James, my friend and mentor, who helped me embrace my love for programming and allow it to grow.

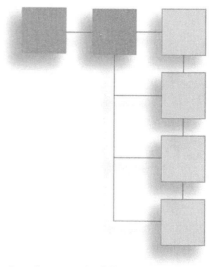

ABOUT THE AUTHOR

WENDY JONES devoted herself to computers the first time her eyes befell an Apple IIe in elementary school. From that point on, she spent every free moment learning BASIC and graphics programming, sketching out her ideas on graph paper to type in later. Other computer languages followed, including Pascal, C, Java, and C++.

As Wendy's career in computers took off, she branched out from DOS, teaching herself Windows programming and then jumping into the dot-com world for a bit. Although Internet companies provided cash, they didn't provide fulfillment, so Wendy started expanding her programming skills to games, devoting any extra energy to its pursuit.

Wendy's true passion became apparent when she got the opportunity to work for Atari's Humongous Entertainment as a game programmer. During her time at Atari, she worked on both PC and console titles, thrilled with the challenge they provided.

Wendy is currently working with PocketPC software and handheld gaming devices.

If you have any comments or questions about this book, you can reach Wendy at gadget2032@yahoo.com.

CONTENTS AT A GLANCE

CONTENTS

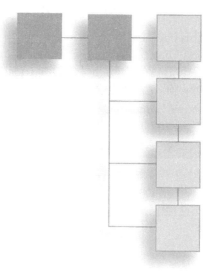

INTRODUCTION

G ame programming is an exciting job in the computing world. Where else do you get the chance to create virtual worlds that encompass creatures or places normally found only in dreams? You give people the ability to become anyone they want, and provide them with environments that bring their fantasies to life.

The game industry is growing by leaps and bounds, and the technology is expanding right along with it. Just a few years ago, video cards with 3D hardware on the consumer level were unheard of. Only expensive SGI workstations were capable of real-time 3D, and OpenGL was in its infancy. As PCs became more popular, OpenGL was ported to this expanding platform, bringing 3D rendering to the masses for the first time.

Windows was still an unpopular platform for games, but that began to change when Microsoft introduced DirectX. DirectX slowly gained popularity until it surpassed OpenGL as the standard way to create 3D graphics under Windows. Today, most PC games on the market are built on DirectX, enabling gamers to experience the latest graphics technologies and the most realistic worlds.

How Much Should You Know?

A relatively decent understanding of C++ and object-oriented concepts can help you understand all the lessons presented in this book. Basic math skills are a plus, although most math concepts are explained in detail. Working knowledge of Visual Studio .NET 2003 or any product in the Visual Studio family is helpful. The opening chapters explain what you need to get started.

How to Use This Book

This book is divided into three parts. The first part describes DirectX and how to get your first DirectX program up and running. The second part gives you the basics you need for designing and building 3D worlds, with an introduction to 3D concepts and Direct3D. The third and final part rounds out your DirectX knowledge with an introduction to sound processing with DirectSound and getting input from the user with DirectInput. The book wraps up everything with a final project that shows you how to apply the concepts you've learned.

If you're already familiar with DirectX and have already written a few applications, you can easily skip Part I. Anyone who's just getting into game programming and DirectX should read this book straight through to gain a full understanding of what DirectX can do.

PART I

GETTING DOWN THE BASICS

CHAPTER 1

THE WHAT, WHY, AND HOW OF DIRECTX

DirectX is the premier game Application Programming Interface (API) for the Windows platform. Just a few years ago, game makers were struggling with problems stemming from hardware incompatibilities, making it impossible for everyone to enjoy their games. Then Microsoft came along with DirectX. It provided game makers with a single, clean API to write to that would almost guarantee compatibility across different sets of PC hardware. Over the years since DirectX's release, the number of games that are running under Windows has increased dramatically.

Here's what you'll learn in this chapter:

- What DirectX is
- Why DirectX is useful
- Which components make up the DirectX API

What Is DirectX?

DirectX is the Microsoft collection of APIs that are designed to give game developers a low-level interface to the PC hardware that is running Windows. Currently on version 9.0, each DirectX API component provides access to different aspects of the hardware, including graphics, sound, and networking, all through a standard interface. This interface allows developers to write their games using one set of functions and run on any hardware that supports DirectX.

The Components

The DirectX API is split into multiple components, each one representing a different aspect of the system. Each API can be used independently, thereby adding only the functionality that your game requires. Here are the components:

- **DirectX Graphics.** This is the component that handles all graphics output. This API provides functions for handling 2D and 3D graphics drawing, as well as initializing and setting the resolution for your game.

- **DirectInput.** All user input is handled through this API. This component includes support for devices such as the keyboard, mouse, gamepad, and joysticks. DirectInput also now adds support for force-feedback.

- **DirectPlay.** Network support for your games is added through DirectPlay. The networking functions provide communication with other machines, allowing more than one person to play. DirectPlay gives you a high-level interface for networking, keeping you from having to implement every aspect of network communication.

- **DirectSound.** When you need to add sound effects or background music, this is the API to use. DirectSound's functionality allows for the loading and playing of one or more WAV files, while providing complete control over how they're played.

- **DirectMusic.** This component allows you to create a dynamic soundtrack. Sounds can be played back on a timed schedule or adapted to the gameplay using pitch, tempo, or volume changes.

- **DirectShow.** You access cut scenes and streaming audio through this component. AVI, MP3, MPEG, and ASF files are just a few of the formats that DirectShow allows to be played. With DirectShow, the entire file doesn't have to be loaded into memory; you can stream the file from the hard drive or CD-ROM.

- **DirectSetup.** After your game is complete, you'll want to show it to others. DirectSetup gives you the functionality to install the latest version of DirectX on the user's computer.

note

The DirectX Graphics component includes all the functionality of both DirectDraw and Direct3D. Version 7 of DirectX was the last version to separate DirectDraw into its own interface.

Why Is DirectX Needed?

Before the release of the Windows operating system, developers wrote games for DOS. This single-threaded, non-GUI operating system provided developers with a direct path between their application code and the hardware it was running on. This had both advantages and problems. For example, because there was a direct path between the game code and the hardware, developers could pull every ounce of power out of the machine, giving them complete control over how their games performed. The downside to this included the need to write device drivers for any hardware they wanted their game titles to support. This even included common hardware, such as video and sound cards.

At the time, not all video cards followed the same standard. This made drawing to the screen difficult if you wanted to support a resolution above 320 × 240. Each card manufacturer had a specific way that video memory could be accessed. The complexity caused by not having a common standard restricted the amount of video cards games could support. Developers were definitely looking for a better and easier way.

When Windows 3.1 was released, it carried with it the same limitations that DOS had. Because Windows ran on top of DOS, it severely limited the resources available to games and took away the direct access that developers had enjoyed for so long. Most games that were written to support Windows at the time consisted mainly of card games and board games, whereas action games continued to support only DOS.

Previously, Microsoft had attempted to give developers a faster way to access the video adapter through a library called WinG. It predated DirectX and offered only a few functions. WinG was a nice attempt, but it still didn't give developers the much-needed access to the system they enjoyed under DOS.

Microsoft did address a lot of these issues with the release of DirectX 1, called the Game Software Development Kit (SDK). DirectX gave developers a single library to write to, placing a common layer between their games and the PC hardware. Drawing graphics to the screen became easier. The first version of DirectX still didn't give support for all the hardware out there, but it was a great starting point in giving game developers what they had been waiting for. Over the years, there have been nine releases of DirectX, each one improving and adding support for new technologies such as network play, streaming audio and video, and new kinds of input devices.

How Is DirectX Put Together?

DirectX made life a bit easier for developers who wanted to write games under Windows. Developers had a clear set of libraries and support from Microsoft, who had finally realized the importance and market potential of games.

Through the years, DirectX has evolved and improved, building on previous versions to offer updated and faster support for new hardware. Microsoft wanted to make sure that each subsequent release of DirectX allowed games written for previous versions to run without problems. To accomplish this goal, Microsoft based DirectX on COM.

The Component Object Model

The DirectX API is based on the *Component Object Model* (COM). *COM* objects consist of a collection of interfaces that expose methods that developers use to access DirectX. COM objects are normally DLL files that have been registered with the system. For DirectX COM objects, this happens during the installation of DirectX. Although they're similar to C++ objects, COM objects require the use of an interface to access the methods within them. This is actually an advantage over standard objects because multiple versions of an interface can be present within a COM object, allowing for backward compatibility.

For instance, each version of DirectX includes a new DirectDraw interface that is accessible through the API, while still containing the previous version so it doesn't break existing code. Games that were created using DirectX 7 can work with DirectX 9 with no problems.

An additional advantage to COM objects is their ability to work with multiple languages beyond just C++. Developers can use Visual Basic, C++, or C# and still use the same DirectX libraries.

The Architecture

DirectX is based on two layers: the API layer and the Hardware Abstraction Layer (HAL). The API layer communicates with the hardware in the machine by talking to the HAL. The HAL provides a standardized interface to DirectX, while also being able to talk directly to the hardware through its specific device driver. Because the HAL needs to know how the hardware and device driver actually work, the hardware manufacturer writes it. You never interact with the HAL directly while writing your game, but you do access it indirectly through functions that DirectX provides. Figure 1.1 displays how the HAL is layered between Direct3D and the hardware device driver.

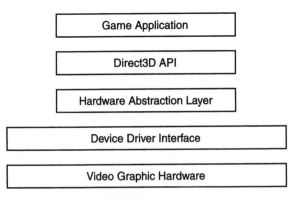

Figure 1.1 DirectX integration.

In previous versions, DirectX was split into both the HAL and another layer called the Hardware Emulation Layer (HEL) or RGB device. The HEL emulated some missing functionality of the hardware. This allowed both low-end and high-end video cards to seamlessly provide the same functionality to the DirectX API. Although the functionality of the HEL was the same, the performance was not. Because the HEL did all its rendering in software, normally the frame rate was significantly lower than with hardware acceleration.

The HEL has since been replaced with the pluggable software device. This device performs software rendering and must be written by the application developer. Most games on the market do not use software rendering anymore and require a video card with 3D hardware.

note

The Direct3D Device Driver Kit (DDK) provides information you need to write your own pluggable software device.

Chapter Summary

You've now learned the behind-the-scenes details of what DirectX is and why you need it. The next chapter dives into how to create your first application using DirectX.

CHAPTER 2

YOUR FIRST DIRECTX PROGRAM

I t's time to get into writing some actual code now. I'm going to take you step-by-step through the process of creating your very first DirectX application. Most examples that come with the DirectX Software Development Kit (SDK) rely on the sample framework, a collection of source files that take care of a lot of the tedious programming for you. In my explanations and examples that follow, however, I will not be using this framework so that you get an idea of everything that's needed for an actual game.

Here's what you'll learn in this chapter:

- How to create a project
- How to set up a Windows application
- How to initialize DirectX
- How to clear the screen
- How to present your scene
- How to take your game full screen
- How to determine the video modes the system supports

Creating the Project

The first step to any application is the creation of the Visual Studio project. Start by running Visual Studio .NET with no project loaded.

1. Select New, Project from the File menu to bring up the New Project dialog box, shown in Figure 2.1.

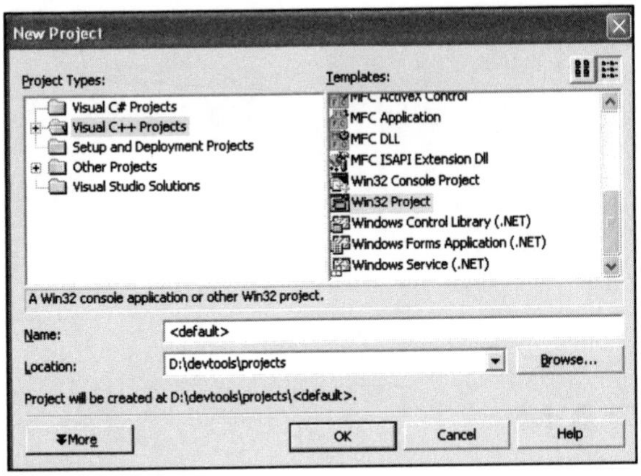

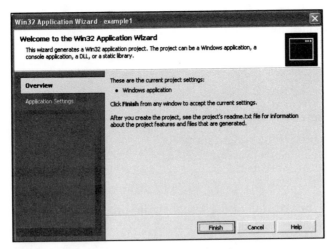

Figure 2.1 Creating a new project.

2. Change the project name to `example1` and select Win32 Project from the list of project templates. Click on the OK button when this is complete. The Application Wizard dialog box appears with two option tabs available: Overview and Application Settings. This dialog box is shown in Figure 2.2.

3. Select the Application Settings tab and make sure the Empty Project option is checked, as shown in Figure 2.3.

4. Click the Finish button.

Figure 2.2 The Application Wizard dialog box.

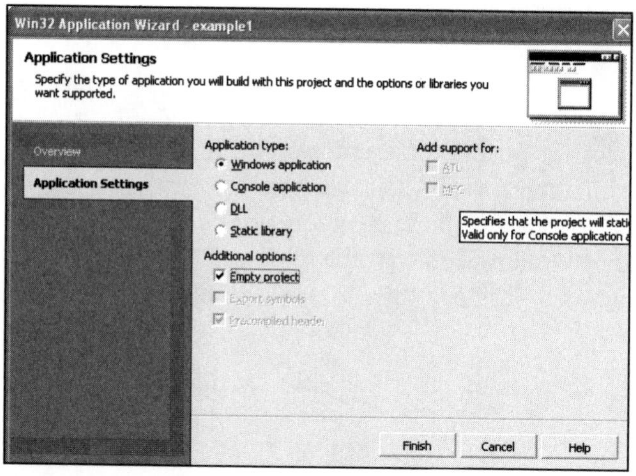

Figure 2.3 The Application Settings dialog box.

Adding the Windows Code

At this point, Visual Studio will have created an empty project. The next step is to create the source code to initialize the main application window. You start off by adding a blank source file to the project.

1. Select Add New Item from the Project menu. This brings up the Add New Item dialog box, as shown in Figure 2.4.

2. Select the C++ File (.cpp) from the Templates list.

3. Change the name of the file to winmain.cpp.

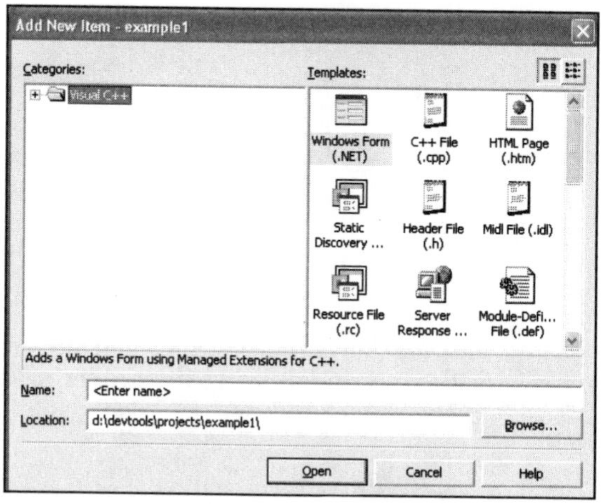

Figure 2.4 The Add New Item dialog box.

4. Click the Open button.

WinMain

The first part of any Windows application is always the entry point. In console applications, for example, the entry point function is called main, whereas the entry point function for Windows applications is called WinMain. The WinMain function is used to initialize your application, create the application window, and start the message loop. At this point, you can either type the code that follows or just load the winmain.cpp file from the chapter2\example1 directory.

```cpp
// Include the Windows header file that's needed for all Windows applications
#include <windows.h>

HINSTANCE hInst;              // global handle to hold the application instance
HWND wndHandle;              // global variable to hold the window handle

// forward declarations
bool initWindow( HINSTANCE hInstance );
LRESULT CALLBACK WndProc( HWND, UINT, WPARAM, LPARAM );

// This is winmain, the main entry point for Windows applications
int WINAPI WinMain( HINSTANCE hInstance, HINSTANCE hPrevInstance,
                    LPTSTR lpCmdLine, int nCmdShow )
{
    // Initialize the window
    if ( !initWindow( hInstance ) )
        return false;

    // main message loop:
    MSG msg;
    ZeroMemory( &msg, sizeof( msg ) );
while (GetMessage(&msg, NULL, 0, 0) )
{
    TranslateMessage( &msg );
    DispatchMessage( &msg );
}
```

The most important part of this function is the main message loop. This is the part of the application that receives messages from the rest of the system, allowing the program to run in the Windows environment. The GetMessage function checks the application's message queue and determines whether user input or system messages are waiting. If messages are available, the TranslateMessage and DispatchMessage functions are called.

After the WinMain function is complete, it's time to create the application window.

InitWindow

Before Windows allows an application to create a window on the desktop, the application must register a window class. After the class is registered, the application can create the needed window. The following code example registers a generic window with the system and then uses this class to create a default window.

```
/*****************************************************************************
* bool initWindow( HINSTANCE hInstance )
* initWindow registers the window class for the application, creates the window
*****************************************************************************/
bool initWindow( HINSTANCE hInstance )
{
    WNDCLASSEX wcex;

    // Fill in the WNDCLASSEX structure. This describes how the window
    // will look to the system
    wcex.cbSize             = sizeof(WNDCLASSEX);  // the size of the structure
    wcex.style              = CS_HREDRAW | CS_VREDRAW; // the class style
    wcex.lpfnWndProc        = (WNDPROC)WndProc;    // the window procedure callback
    wcex.cbClsExtra         = 0;       // extra bytes to allocate for this class
    wcex.cbWndExtra         = 0;       // extra bytes to allocate for this instance
    wcex.hInstance          = hInstance;    // handle to the application instance
    wcex.hIcon              = 0;   // icon to associate with the application
    wcex.hCursor            = LoadCursor(NULL, IDC_ARROW);// the default cursor
    wcex.hbrBackground      = (HBRUSH)(COLOR_WINDOW+1);    // the background color
    wcex.lpszMenuName   .   = NULL;    // the resource name for the menu
    wcex.lpszClassName      = "DirectXExample"; // the class name being created
    wcex.hIconSm            = 0;       // the handle to the small icon
    RegisterClassEx(&wcex);

    // Create the window
    wndHandle = CreateWindow(
                "DirectXExample",          // the window class to use
                "DirectXExample",          // the title bar text
                WS_OVERLAPPEDWINDOW,       // the window style
                CW_USEDEFAULT,       // the starting x coordinate
```

```
            CW_USEDEFAULT,      // the starting y coordinate
            640,                // the pixel width of the window
            480,                // the pixel height of the window
            NULL,               // the parent window; NULL for desktop
            NULL,               // the menu for the application; NULL for
                                // none
            hInstance,          // the handle to the application instance
            NULL);              // no values passed to the window
    // Make sure that the window handle that is created is valid
    if (!wndHandle)
        return false;

    // Display the window on the screen
    ShowWindow(wndHandle, SW_SHOW);
    UpdateWindow(wndHandle);
    return true;
}
```

The preceding function is documented in every Windows programming book. I'll just give a short rundown of what this code does.

Every application that will display a window must first register a window class with the system. The window class describes certain characteristics of the window, such as the background color, the mouse cursor to use, and the icon to associate with the application. The window class is represented by the WNDCLASSEX structure. After the WNDCLASSEX structure is properly filled in, it is passed as a parameter to the function RegisterClassEx.

The RegisterClassEx function takes the information provided within the WNDCLASSEX structure and registers a window class with the system. Now that you have a valid window class registered, you are ready to create the window that your application will use.

Next, the window needs to be created, which is handled through a call to CreateWindow.

The CreateWindow function requires 11 parameters, each one assisting in telling the system what the window will look like when it's created. Each parameter is documented in the previous code sample.

WndProc

The window procedure is the final part required for a working windows application. The window procedure, shown as WndProc in the code sample that follows, handles events from the system that relate to your application. For instance, when a mouse click occurs within your application window, the system sends a mouse click event to your windows procedure. Your windows procedure can then decide whether it needs to handle the event or ignore it.

The window procedure in the following example contains only the bare minimum of code needed to end the application.

```
/*************************************************************************
* LRESULT CALLBACK WndProc(HWND hWnd, UINT message, WPARAM wParam,
*                                                     LPARAM lParam)
* The window procedure
*************************************************************************/
LRESULT CALLBACK WndProc(HWND hWnd, UINT message, WPARAM wParam, LPARAM lParam)
{
    // Check any available messages from the queue
    switch (message)
    {
        case WM_DESTROY:
            PostQuitMessage(0);
        break;
    }
    // Always return the message to the default window
    // procedure for further processing
    return DefWindowProc(hWnd, message, wParam, lParam);
}
```

You should be able to compile this application and get a blank window with a white background, as shown in Figure 2.5. You will find this simple application in the chapter2\ example1 directory on the CD-ROM.

Figure 2.5 The blank window application.

Time for DirectX

Before DirectX 8, drawing was split into two separate interfaces: DirectDraw and Direct3D. DirectDraw, which was used for all 2D rendering, is no longer being updated. All 2D rendering must now be handled through the Direct3D API.

You're going to take the new path and do all drawing through Direct3D. The following steps are needed to get Direct3D up and running:

1. Create the Direct3D object.
2. Create the Direct3D device.
3. Draw to the device.

The Direct3D Object

The *Direct3D object* provides an interface for functions used to enumerate and determine the capabilities of a Direct3D device. For example, the Direct3D object gives you the ability to query the number of video devices installed in a system and to check the capabilities of each one.

The Direct3D object is created using the following call:

```
IDirect3D9 *Direct3DCreate9( D3D_SDK_VERSION );
```

note

D3D_SDK_VERSION is the only valid parameter that can be sent to the Direct3DCreate9 function.

This function returns a pointer to an IDirect3D9 interface. If the returned value is NULL, the call has failed.

Remember when I mentioned that it's possible to query the number of video devices or adapters in the machine? As an example of the functionality provided by the Direct3D object, you're going to do just that.

The GetAdapterCount function, defined next, allows you to count the number of video adapters.

```
UINT IDirect3D9::GetAdapterCount(VOID);
```

This function requires no parameters to be passed to it and returns the number of video adapters in the system. The GetAdapterCount function returns a value of 1 on most end user systems.

note

If a system has only one video adapter installed, this device is referred to as the primary adapter. If more than one adapter is available, the first card is the primary adapter.

Creating the Rendering Device

The *Direct3D device*, through the IDirect3DDevice9 interface, provides the methods that applications use to render to the screen. It's through this interface that all drawing for your game must be done.

The Direct3D device is created with a call to CreateDevice.

```
HRESULT CreateDevice(
    UINT Adapter,
    D3DDEVTYPE DeviceType,
    HWND hFocusWindow,
    DWORD BehaviorFlags,
    D3DPRESENT_PARAMETERS *pPresentationParameters,
    IDirect3DDevice9** ppReturnedDeviceInterface
);
```

The resulting device object will be used throughout your game to access the video adapter for drawing. The CreateDevice function requires a total of six parameters and has a return value of type HRESULT. If the function call succeeds, it returns a value of D3D_OK; otherwise, there are three possible return values:

- **D3DERR_INVALIDCALL.** One of the given parameters may be invalid.
- **D3DERR_NOTAVAILABLE.** The device doesn't support this call.
- **D3DERR_OUTOFVIDEOMEMORY.** The video adapter doesn't have enough video memory to complete this call.

tip

It's always a good idea to check the return values of Direct3D functions to confirm that the objects were created correctly. Most Direct3D functions return a value of D3D_OK if the creation was successful.

Following are the parameters required by CreateDevice:

- **Adapter.** Type UINT. This is the number of the video adapter that the device will be created for. Most game applications send the value D3DADAPTER_DEFAULT, which corresponds to the primary video adapter in the machine.

- **DeviceType.** Type D3DDEVTYPE. There are three possible device types to choose from:
  - D3DDEVTYPE_HAL. The device uses hardware acceleration and rasterization.
  - D3DDEVTYPE_REF. The Microsoft reference rasterizer is used.
  - D3DDEVTYPE_SW. A pluggable software device is used.

- **hFocusWindow.** Type HWND. This is the window to which this device will belong.

- **BehaviorFlags.** Type DWORD. This parameter allows multiple flags to be passed that specify how the device should be created. The examples presented here will only be using the D3DCREATE_SOFTWARE_VERTEXPROCESSING flag, which specifies that vertex processing will be handled in software.

- **PresentationParamters.** Type D3DPRESENT_PARAMETERS. This structure controls how the device will be presented, such as whether this is a windowed application or whether this device will include a backbuffer. The D3DPRESENT_PARAMETERS structure is defined like this:

```
typedef struct _D3DPRESENT_PARAMETERS_ {
    UINT BackBufferWidth, BackBufferHeight;
    D3DFORMAT BackBufferFormat;
    UINT BackBufferCount;
    D3DMULTISAMPLE_TYPE MultiSampleType;
    DWORD MultiSampleQuality;
    D3DSWAPEFFECT SwapEffect;
    HWND hDeviceWindow;
    BOOL Windowed;
    BOOL EnableAutoDepthStencil;
    D3DFORMAT AutoDepthStencilFormat;
    DWORD Flags;
    UINT FullScreen_RefreshRateInHz;
    UINT PresentationInterval;
} D3DPRESENT_PARAMETERS;
```

Table 2.1 describes the preceding parameters in more detail.

- **ppReturnedDeviceInterface.** Type IDirect3Ddevice9**. This is the variable that will contain the valid Direct3D device.

After the device has been created, it's possible to call other Direct3D methods and get something drawn to the screen.

Table 2.1 D3DPRESENT_PARAMETERS

Member	Description
BackBufferWidth	The width of the backbuffer.
BackBufferHeight	The height of the backbuffer.
BackBufferFormat	The format for the backbuffer. This is of type D3DFORMAT. In windowed mode, passing D3DFMT_UNKNOWN uses the current display-mode format.
BackBufferCount	The number of backbuffers to create.
MultiSampleType	The levels of full-scene multisampling. Unless multisampling is being supported specifically, pass D3DMULTISAMPLE_NONE.
MultiSampleQuality	The quality level. Pass 0 to this parameter unless multisampling is enabled.
SwapEffect	The type of swapping used when switching backbuffers. Examples presented here use D3DSWAPEFFECT_DISCARD.
hDeviceWindow	The window that owns this device.
Windowed	This is TRUE for a windowed application or FALSE for full screen.
EnableAutoDepthStencil	This value controls the depth buffers for the application. Setting this to TRUE enables Direct3D to manage these buffers for you.
AutoDepthStencilFormat	The format of the depth buffers. This is of type D3DFORMAT.
Flags	Unless you're specifically setting one of the D3DPRESENTFLAG, set this to 0.
FullScreen_RefreshRateInHz	The rate at which the adapter refreshes the screen. In windowed mode, this parameter must be set to 0.
PresentationInterval	This controls the rate at which the buffers are swapped.

Clearing the Screen

Now that the Direct3D device has been created, you can render to the screen, be it with an image or a bunch of polygons. The first thing you'll have to do in your main game loop is clear the screen. Clearing the screen gives you a clean slate to render to for each frame. An updated winmain.cpp file can be found in the chapter2\example2 directory on the CD-ROM.

You can clear the frame with the function call Clear.

```
HRESULT Clear(
    DWORD Count,
    const D3DRECT *pRects,
    DWORD Flags,
    D3DCOLOR Color,
    float Z,
    DWORD Stencil
);
```

Six parameters are required for this function.

The first parameter, Count, is the number of rectangles that you will be clearing. If this value is 0, the second parameter pRects must be NULL. In this instance, the entire viewing area of the screen will be cleared, which is the most common behavior. If count is a number greater than 0, pRects must point to an array of D3DRECT structures designating the rectangular areas of the screen to be cleared.

The Flags parameter specifies the buffer to be cleared. There are three possible values for Flags:

- D3DCLEAR_STENCIL
- D3DCLEAR_TARGET
- D3DCLEAR_ZBUFFER

The value you're going to use at the moment is D3DCLEAR_TARGET, which specifies the render target.

Color is a D3DCOLOR value containing the color to clear the render target to. Multiple macros are available that can be used to specify this value, such as D3DCOLOR_XRGB.

The Z parameter is the value to store in the depth buffer. This value ranges from 0.0f to 1.0f. I'll go into more detail on the Z buffer later.

The Stencil parameter holds the value to store in the stencil buffer. When the Stencil buffer is not in use, the value should be 0.

Displaying the Scene

Now that you've cleared the frame, it's time to display it to the screen. Direct3D uses the Present function to do this. The Present function performs the page flipping of the back buffer.

All the drawing that you've been doing up to this point has been to the back buffer. The *back buffer* is the area of memory where drawing can be completed before being displayed to the screen. *Page flipping* is the process of taking the information contained in the back buffer and displaying it to the screen. Attempting to update the graphics currently being displayed results in screen flicker. To keep your graphics updates smooth, all drawing is done to an offscreen buffer and then copied to the display.

note

Page flipping refers to the swapping of the front and back buffers. For instance, drawing to the back buffer requires a page flip to occur before its contents can be seen on the screen.

```
HRESULT Present(
    CONST RECT *pSourceRect,
    CONST RECT *pDestRect,
    HWND hDestWindowOverride,
    CONST RGNDATA *pDirtyRegion
);
```

Present requires only four parameters:

- **pSourceRect** is a pointer to a RECT structure containing the source rectangle to display from the backbuffer. This value should be NULL to use the entire backbuffer, which is the most common behavior.
- **pDestRect** is another RECT that contains the destination rectangle.
- **hDestWindowOverride** is the destination window to use as the target area. This value should be NULL to use the window specified earlier in the presentation parameters structure.
- **pDirtyRegion** details the region within the buffer that needs to be updated. Again, this value should be NULL to update the whole buffer.

Cleaning Up

The final thing to do in any DirectX application is to clean up and release the objects that you've used. For instance, at the beginning of your program, you created both a Direct3D object and a Direct3D device. When the application closes, you need to release these objects so that the resources they've used are returned to the system for reuse.

COM objects, which DirectX is based on, keep a reference count that tells the system when it's safe to remove these objects from memory. By using the Release function, you decrement the reference count for an object. When the reference count reaches 0, the system reclaims these resources.

For example, to release the Direct3D device, you would use the following:

```
If ( pd3dDevice != NULL )
    pd3dDevice->Release( );
```

The if statement first checks to make sure that the variable pd3dDevice, which was assigned to the device earlier, is not NULL and then calls the device's Release function.

tip

Always check to make sure that DirectX objects are not NULL before calling Release on them. Attempting to release an invalid pointer causes your game to crash.

Updating the Code

Now that you've seen how to get DirectX up and running, it's time to add the code to do it yourself. These code additions will be made to the winmain.cpp file that was created earlier.

The first step when writing any DirectX-enabled application is adding the Direct3D header.

```
#include <d3d9.h>
```

The following two variables need to be added to the globals section at the top of the code.

```
LPDIRECT3D9              pD3D;                  // the Direct3D object
LPDIRECT3DDEVICE9        pd3dDevice;            // the Direct3D device
```

The LPDIRECT3D9 type says that you're creating a long pointer to the IDirect3D9 interface. The LPDIRECT3DDEVICE9 type is creating a pointer to the IDirect3DDevice9 interface.

Next, you add a call to the initDirect3D function, which you'll be defining a bit further down in the code. This call should be placed right after the initWindow call within the WinMain function.

```
// called after creating the window
If ( !initDirect3D(  ) )
    return false;
```

Changing the Message Loop

Here you need to replace the default Windows *message loop* with one that is useful for games. The original message loop uses a function call to GetMessage that checks whether messages are waiting for the application; if there are messages, GetMessage waits to return until the message has been posted. PeekMessage checks for messages and returns immediately, allowing your game to call its own functions in the loop.

In this instance, you will add an else clause after the call to PeekMessage to call the game's render function. The render function takes care of drawing everything to the screen. This function will be defined in a bit.

```
if( PeekMessage( &msg, NULL, 0U, 0U, PM_REMOVE ) )
{
    TranslateMessage ( &msg );
    DispatchMessage ( &msg );
}
else
{
    render( );
}
```

The Init Function

The initDirect3D function creates the Direct3D object and the device.

```
/*********************************************************************
* initDirect3D
*********************************************************************/
bool initDirect3D(void)
{
    pD3D = NULL;
    pd3dDevice = NULL;

    // Create the DirectX object
    if( NULL == ( pD3D = Direct3DCreate9( D3D_SDK_VERSION ) ) )
    {
        return false;
    }

    // Fill the presentation parameters structure
    D3DPRESENT_PARAMETERS d3dpp;
    ZeroMemory( &d3dpp, sizeof( d3dpp ) );
    d3dpp.Windowed = TRUE;
    d3dpp.SwapEffect = D3DSWAPEFFECT_DISCARD;
    d3dpp.BackBufferFormat = D3DFMT_UNKNOWN;
    d3dpp.BackBufferCount  = 1;
    d3dpp.BackBufferHeight = 480;
    d3dpp.BackBufferWidth  = 640;
    d3dpp.hDeviceWindow    = wndHandle;

    // Create a default DirectX device
    if( FAILED( pD3D->CreateDevice( D3DADAPTER_DEFAULT,
                                    D3DDEVTYPE_HAL,
                                    wndHandle,
                                    D3DCREATE_SOFTWARE_VERTEXPROCESSING,
                                    &d3dpp,
                                    &pd3dDevice ) ) )
    {
        return false;
    }
    return true;
}
```

At the beginning of this function, you're making a call to Direct3DCreate9. This creates the Direct3D object, which in turn allows you to create the device. Next, you fill out the presentation parameters structure. I'm setting this to handle a 640 × 480 window.

Then the CreateDevice function is called, and the structure you just filled in is passed as the second-to-last parameter. Here you're telling CreateDevice that you want to use the primary video adapter by passing D3DADAPTER_DEFAULT. The D3DDEVTYPE_HAL parameter tells Direct3D to use the video hardware renderer. If you had specified the value D3DDEVTYPE_REF, this would have enabled the default software renderer. You're also using D3DCREATE_SOFTWARE_VERTEXPROCESSING to ensure that your sample runs on most hardware. Hardware vertex processing is available on some of the newer video cards. The final parameter is &pd3dDevice. This is where CreateDevice stores the Direct3D device that you've created.

The Render Function

The render function is where the actual drawing takes place. As you'll recall from earlier, this function is called from within the main loop and is called once per frame.

```
/***********************************************************************
* render
***********************************************************************/
void render(void)
{
    // Check to make sure you have a valid Direct3D device
    if( NULL == pd3dDevice )
        return;// Clear the back buffer to a blue color
    pd3dDevice->Clear( 0, NULL, D3DCLEAR_TARGET,
                        D3DCOLOR_XRGB( 0,0,255 ), 1.0f, 0 );

    // Present the back buffer contents to the display
    pd3dDevice->Present( NULL, NULL, NULL, NULL );
}
```

This is a simple example of a render function. First, you check to make sure that you have a valid Direct3D device by checking it against NULL. If this object has been released before calling the render function, you don't want further code in here to execute.

Next, you need to make use of the Clear function presented earlier. Because you want to clear the entire buffer, you need to pass 0 and NULL as the first two parameters. The D3DCLEAR_TARGET parameter tells DirectX that you want the render buffer to be cleared. The next parameter calls for a type of D3DCOLOR. I'm using the macro D3DCOLOR_XRGB to clear the screen to a blue color specified by the values R=0, G=0, and B=255.

You'll also need to pass a float value of 1.0 into the depth buffer. The depth buffer, which helps Direct3D determine how far away an object is from the viewer, can hold a value anywhere from 0.0 to 1.0. The higher the value is, the farther the distance from the viewer.

The stencil buffer allows for the masking of certain areas of an image so they aren't displayed. Because the stencil buffer is not currently being used, a value of 0 is passed to this parameter.

The last thing that needs to be done during the render function is to display the contents to the screen. This happens with a call to Present. Again, because you want the whole back buffer flipped to the screen, NULL values are passed for all parameters to the Present function. It's rare that you would want to flip only a portion of the back buffer.

The cleanUp Function

Of course, after the application ends, you need to release the objects that were created. This is handled with the following code.

```
void cleanUp (void)
{
    // Release the device and the Direct3D object
    if( pd3dDevice != NULL )
        pd3dDevice->Release( );

    if( pD3D != NULL )
        pD3D->Release( );
}
```

First, you need to make sure that the objects have not been released before by checking whether they are equal to NULL. If they're not, you call their Release method. The preceding code should be added right before the return call at the end of the WinMain function.

Adding the DirectX Libraries

At last, you have all the code you need to create your first DirectX application. Before you can compile and run this, you have to do one more thing: link in the *DirectX libraries*. For this simple example, you only need to link with d3d9.lib.

1. Select the Properties option from the Project menu. The Property Pages dialog box appears. This dialog box is shown in Figure 2.6.
2. Click the Linker option in the left pane. This expands to show the included options.
3. Next, select the Input option. The dialog box changes and should reflect what's shown in Figure 2.7.

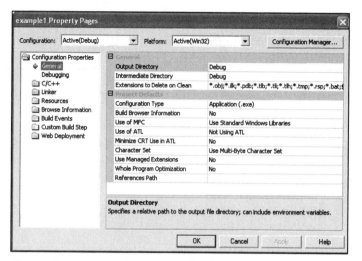

Figure 2.6 The Property Pages dialog box.

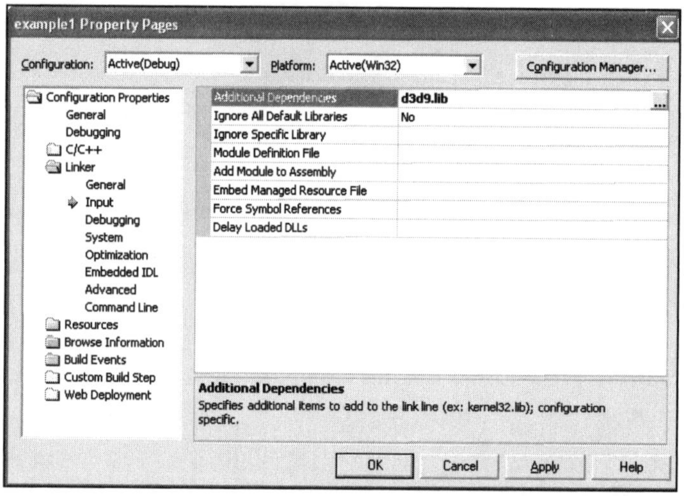

Figure 2.7 Changing the Linker option in the Property Pages dialog box.

4. Type d3d9.lib into the Additional Dependencies field and click OK.

Compile and run the application. Unlike the white window from before, this window should now display a blue background color. Although this application doesn't show the depth of what DirectX can do, it does give you the basics to start with.

note

Multiple libraries are needed for different DirectX functionality. You only need to link to those specific libraries that you are accessing functions within.

Taking the Game Full Screen

So far, the examples that you've gone through all take place in a 640 × 480 window on the desktop. Although this is fine for applications, when you're trying to immerse yourself in a virtual world, nothing but full screen will do.

You need to make just a few changes to your code to transform your game from being a window on the desktop to being full screen. One of the biggest changes is within the CreateWindow function.

If you'll recall, this is the CreateWindow function you've been using.

```
wndHandle = CreateWindow("DirectXExample",
                "DirectXExample",
                WS_OVERLAPPEDWINDOW,
                CW_USEDEFAULT,
                CW_USEDEFAULT,
                640,
                480,
                NULL,
                NULL,
                hInstance,
                NULL);
```

The third parameter, the window style, has been set to WS_OVERLAPPEDWINDOW up to this point. This is the standard style for a desktop application, which includes a title bar, a border, and the Minimize and Close buttons. Before you can create a full-screen window, the window style needs to be changed to this:

```
WS_EX_TOPMOST | WS_POPUP | WS_VISIBLE
```

The first part of this new style, WS_EX_TOPMOST, tells this window that it will be created above all other windows. WS_POPUP creates a window with no border, title bar, or system menus. The final part, WS_VISIBLE, tells the window to display itself.

The new function call for CreateWindow looks like this:

```
wndHandle = CreateWindow("DirectXExample",
                "DirectXExample",
                WS_EX_TOPMOST | WS_POPUP | WS_VISIBLE,
```

```
                    CW_USEDEFAULT,
                    CW_USEDEFAULT,
                    640,
                    480,
                    NULL,
                    NULL,
                    hInstance,
                    NULL);
```

The next step is to make a few minor changes to your initDirect3D function. Within the D3DPRESENT_PARAMETERS structure that is being passed to CreateDevice, you need to modify two items: the Windowed and BackBufferFormat variables. Currently, you're setting these variables like this:

```
d3dpp.BackBufferFormat = D3DFMT_UNKNOWN;
d3dpp.Windowed = TRUE;
```

note

Using D3DFMT_UNKNOWN for the BackBufferFormat variable causes Direct3D to use the current display format for the desktop.

To enable full-screen mode within DirectX, the Windowed and BackBufferFormat variables need to be changed to this:

```
d3dpp.BackBufferFormat = D3DFMT_X8R8G8B8;
d3dpp.Windowed = FALSE;
```

The obvious change is the d3dpp.Windowed change. Basically, setting this to FALSE lets CreateDevice know that you want full screen.

The d3dpp.BackBufferFormat change is not so obvious. When you were creating a windowed application, you didn't necessarily need to know what format the desktop was using. Passing D3DFMT_UNKNOWN automatically takes the current setting and uses it. When you want full screen, you need to specifically tell Direct3D what D3DFORMAT you want to use. The D3DFORMAT is a value that represents the bit depth of the screen. For example, I chose D3DFMT_X8R8G8B8 as a default format that most video cards should support. D3DFMT_X8R8G8B8 represents a 32-bit format that includes 8 bits for the red component, 8 bits for the green component, and 8 bits for the blue component. This format also includes 8 bits that are unused.

These changes and the full code listing can be found in the chapter2\example3 directory on the CD-ROM.

The next section explains how to query the available formats and how to determine which video modes your system supports.

Video Modes and Formats

If a game you write runs only in windowed mode on the desktop, then knowing which video modes the computer supports isn't that important; however, when you want your game running full screen, it's vital to know which modes the computer supports. Most computers support a 640 × 480 screen resolution, but what about 800 × 600 or 1024 × 768? Not all video adapters support these higher resolutions. And if they do, will they give you the bit depth you want? That's why, when you write a game that supports full screen, it's best to query the hardware to make sure that it supports what your game needs. To do this, you use the functions provided to you by Direct3D through the IDirect3D9 interface.

The first function you need was actually covered earlier:

```
UINT IDirect3D9::GetAdapterCount(VOID);
```

To recap a bit, this function returns an unsigned integer that holds the number of video adapters in the system. DirectX can support multiple video adapters, which allows games to run across multiple screens. To keep things simple, though, you're going to assume only one video adapter in the following explanations.

Gathering Video Adapter and Driver Information

Most times, it's useful to have certain information about the video adapter in a machine. For instance, you might want to know the resolutions that the video adapter supports, or the manufacturer of the device. Using the function GetAdapterIdentifier, you can gather this information and much more. GetAdapterIdentifier is defined like this:

```
HRESULT GetAdapterIdentifier(
    UINT Adapter
    DWORD Flags,
    D3DADAPTER_IDENTIFIER9 *pIdentifier
);
```

- The first parameter is an unsigned integer that specifies which video adapter you want information for. Because I'm assuming only one adapter right now, the value of D3DADAPTER_DEFAULT, which means the primary video adapter, should be passed.
- The second parameter, Flags, represents the WHQLLevel of the driver.
- The third and final parameter is a pointer to a D3DADAPTER_IDENTIFIER9 structure. This structure gets filled with the information that is returned from the display adapter.

The D3DADAPTER_IDENTIFIER9 structure provides the following information:

```
typedef struct _D3DADAPTER_IDENTIFIER9 {
    // the name of the driver
    char Driver[MAX_DEVICE_IDENTIFIER_STRING];
    // a textual description of the device
    char Description[MAX_DEVICE_IDENTIFIER_STRING];
    // a short text version of the device name
    char DeviceName[32];
    // the version of the driver installed
    LARGE_INTEGER DriverVersion;
    // This value holds the bottom 32 bits of the driver version
    DWORD DriverVersionLowPart;
    // This value holds the upper 32 bits of the driver version
    DWORD DriverVersionHighPart;
    // the ID of the manufacturer
    DWORD VendorId;
    // the ID of the particular device
    DWORD DeviceId;
    // the second part of the device ID
    DWORD SubSysId;
    // the revision level of the device chipset
    DWORD Revision;
    // a unique identifier for the device
    GUID DeviceIdentifier;
    // the level of testing that this driver has gone through
    DWORD WHQLLevel;
} D3DADAPTER_IDENTIFIER9;
```

This structure holds all the specific data concerning the adapter and the device driver that's installed. The full structure is explained in more detail in the DirectX documentation.

Getting the Display Modes for an Adapter

The next step is getting the details on the display modes that the video adapter supports. To do this, you first have to check how many display modes are available. This is done using a function called GetAdapterModeCount, which is defined as follows:

```
UINT GetAdapterModeCount(
    UINT Adapter,
    D3DFORMAT Format
);
```

The first parameter is the number of the adapter you want to query. Again, you use the value of D3DADAPTER_DEFAULT.

The second parameter is asking for the D3DFORMAT that you want to check for. Earlier I used D3DFMT_X8R8G8B8, which was 8 bits for red, 8 bits for green, 8 bits for blue, and 8 bits that were unused. You can pass in any of the formats that Direct3D defines, and GetAdapterModeCount will return the number of video modes that fit this format. Table 2.2 lists some of the D3DFORMATs that DirectX has available.

Table 2.2 D3DFORMATs

Format	Description
D3DFMT_R8G8B8	24-bit RGB pixel format with 8 bits per channel.
D3DFMT_A8R8G8B8	32-bit ARGB pixel format with alpha, using 8 bits per channel.
D3DFMT_X8R8G8B8	32-bit RGB pixel format, where 8 bits are reserved for each color.
D3DFMT_R5G6B5	16-bit RGB pixel format with 5 bits for red, 6 bits for green, and 5 bits for blue.
D3DFMT_X1R5G5B5	16-bit pixel format, where 5 bits are reserved for each color.
D3DFMT_A1R5G5B5	16-bit pixel format, where 5 bits are reserved for each color and 1 bit is reserved for alpha.
D3DFMT_A4R4G4B4	16-bit ARGB pixel format with 4 bits for each channel.
D3DFMT_R3G3B2	8-bit RGB texture format using 3 bits for red, 3 bits for green, and 2 bits for blue.

The final function that you need to make use of is EnumAdapterModes. This function fills in a D3DDISPLAYMODE structure for each of the modes available. Here's the definition of the function EnumAdapterModes:

```
HRESULT EnumAdapterModes(
    UINT Adapter,
    D3DFORMAT Format,
    UINT Mode,
    D3DDISPLAYMODE* pMode
);
```

Again, the first parameter, Adapter, can be passed D3DADAPTER_DEFAULT. The second parameter format is the D3DFORMAT you are querying modes for. The third parameter, Mode, is the number of the mode you are looking at. Remember that GetAdapterModeCount returned the number of modes this adapter has? Mode is any value from 0 up to this value. The final parameter is a pointer to a D3DDISPLAYMODE structure. This structure holds information about this video mode, such as its width, height, refresh rate, and format.

A Code Example for Querying the Video Adapter

The following bit of code is from example4, located in the chapter2\example4 directory on the CD-ROM. This code sample shows the exact steps and calls needed to display a dialog box listing the display modes available for a particular D3DFORMAT.

I took the initDirect3D function from previous examples and changed it to gather the needed information from the video adapter.

```
bool initDirect3D()
{
    pD3D = NULL;

    // Create the DirectX object
    if( NULL == ( pD3D = Direct3DCreate9( D3D_SDK_VERSION ) ) )
    {
        return false;
    }
```

First you create the Direct3D object. You'll use this to access the needed functions.

```
    // This section gets the adapter details
    D3DADAPTER_IDENTIFIER9 ident;
    pD3D->GetAdapterIdentifier(D3DADAPTER_DEFAULT, 0, &ident);
```

Here I defined a D3DADAPTER_IDENTIFIER9 structure and passed it into the GetAdapterIdentifier function. Using this, I was able to obtain the following details.

```
    addItemToList("Adapter Details");
    addItemToList(ident.Description);
    addItemToList(ident.DeviceName);
    addItemToList(ident.Driver);
```

I'm calling the addItemToList helper function to add the details to be shown in a dialog box later.

```
    // collects the modes this adapter has
    UINT numModes = pD3D->GetAdapterModeCount(
                                        D3DADAPTER_DEFAULT,
                                        D3DFMT_X8R8G8B8);
```

Next, I'm using GetAdapterModeCount to get the number of modes. I then use this number in the for loop that follows. Here you start looping through the modes and gathering the details for each one.

```
    for (UINT i=0; I < numModes; i++)
    {
        D3DDISPLAYMODE mode;      // Define the D3DDISPLAYMODE structure
```

```
char modeString[255];    // This is a temporary char array
// Get the displaymode structure for this adapter mode
pD3D->EnumAdapterModes(D3DADAPTER_DEFAULT,
                       D3DFMT_X8R8G8B8,
                       i,
                       &mode);

// Draw a blank line in the list box
addItemToList("");
// Output the width
sprintf(modeString, "Width=%d",mode.Width);
addItemToList(modeString);
// Output the height
sprintf(modeString, "Height=%d",mode.Height);
addItemToList(modeString);
// Output the refresh rate
sprintf(modeString, "Refresh Rate=%d",mode.RefreshRate);
addItemToList(modeString);
}
return true;
}
```

This is a simple helper function that takes one parameter of STL *string* and adds it to the end of a vector. By the end of the initDirect3D function, the vector will include all the details concerning the video adapter.

```
// The adapterDetails variable is a vector that contains strings; each string will
// hold the information for the different video modes
std::vector<std::string> adapterDetails;
void addItemToList(std::string item)
{
    adapterDetails.push_back(item);
}
```

Figure 2.8 shows the dialog box and the details that you should get when you run this example. Because everyone has different video cards, expect the details to vary based on the machine that this is run on.

Figure 2.8 Video modes details.

tip

The Standard Template Library (STL) provides many useful items, such as the string and vector types that you've already used, as well as others. Using STL types also eases your work when porting to additional platforms, such as UNIX or gaming consoles.

Chapter Summary

This chapter covered a lot of information, ranging from the beginnings of a project to a workable DirectX application. These examples might not show much, but they are the building blocks for everything you will do going forward.

What You Have Learned

In this chapter, you learned the following:

- How the Direct3D object and Direct3D device are created
- The proper method for clearing the screen each frame
- The changes to a standard message loop that need to be made for games
- How to add the DirectX libraries to your game projects
- How to determine the video adapter in a system and what its capabilities are

The next chapter introduces surfaces and the creation of animated sprites.

Review Questions

You can find the answers to Review Questions and On Your Own exercises in Appendix A, "Answers to End-of-Chapter Exercises."

1. What's the first DirectX object that needs to be created in any application?
2. What does the GetAdapterCount function do?
3. The D3DFORMAT of D3DFMT_A8R8G8B8 defines how many bits for each color?
4. What DirectX function is required to blank the screen to a specific color?
5. What function do you use to find the number of modes that are available on a video adapter?

On Your Own

1. Change example 2 on the CD-ROM to clear the screen to green instead of blue.
2. Update example 4 on the CD-ROM to search your system for the display modes available for another D3DFORMAT other than D3DFMT_X8R8G8B8.

CHAPTER 3

SURFACES, SPRITES, AND SALMON

Sprite-based and 2D games still have a big part to play in the game market. Not all games require the latest in 3D video hardware; fun and timeless games like *Tetris* are completely 2D and still immensely popular. This chapter introduces you to some simple ways to use DirectX for the creation of sprite-based games.

Here's what you'll learn in this chapter:

- What surfaces are and how they can be used
- How to gain access to the back buffer
- How to create offscreen surfaces
- How to load a bitmap easily
- How to create and use sprites
- How to animate sprites
- How to use timers for smooth animation

You've Just Touched the Surface

Surfaces are an integral part of DirectX. Surfaces are areas within memory that are used for the storage of image information. They store images and textures and are used to represent the display buffers. Surfaces are stored internally as a contiguous block of memory, usually residing on the video card, but occasionally in main system memory.

This chapter covers two specific types of surfaces: display buffers and offscreen surfaces.

The Display Buffers

There are two display buffers that you have to worry about: the front buffer and the back buffer. These are the areas of video memory where your game is drawn.

The *front buffer* is the surface that represents the viewable area of your game window. Everything that you can see within your application window is considered the front buffer or drawing area. In full-screen mode, the front buffer is expanded to fill the whole screen. The second buffer is the back buffer. As you'll recall from earlier, the back buffer is where you perform all the drawing. After the drawing to the back buffer is complete, you use the Present function to display its contents.

The back buffer is created during the call to CreateDevice by specifying the BackBufferCount parameter in the D3DPRESENT_PARAMETERS structure.

note

Attempting to draw directly to the front buffer results in your graphics flashing and tearing. Graphics should always be drawn to the back buffer first, and then displayed using the Present method.

Offscreen Surfaces

Offscreen surfaces are areas of video or system memory that hold the graphics that your game needs. For instance, if you're creating an overhead role-playing game, you need an area to store the tiles that represent the different terrain, as well as the graphics for your characters. An offscreen surface would be a perfect choice for this task.

Graphics for use within DirectX are usually bitmaps. Figure 3.1 shows an example bitmap that would be loaded for use in your game.

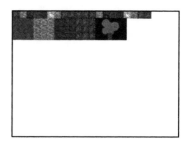

Figure 3.1 Example tiles for a 2D role playing game.

note

Some older video cards allow only for the creation of offscreen surfaces that are the same resolution as the primary buffer. Newer video cards allow for creation of larger surfaces.

Offscreen surfaces, represented by the IDirect3DSurface9 interface, are created using the function CreateOffscreenPlainSurface. You must call this function for each surface you want to create. The CreateOffscreenPlainSurface function is defined as follows:

```
HRESULT CreateOffscreenPlainSurface(
        UINT Width,                 // width of the surface
        UINT Height,                // height of the surface
```

```
                    D3DFORMAT Format,      // D3DFORMAT type
                    DWORD Pool,                    // memory pool
                    IDirect3DSurface9** ppSurface,   // resulting surface pointer
                    HANDLE* pHandle        // always NULL
);
```

`CreateOffscreenPlainSurface` has six parameters:

- **Width.** This parameter is the width in pixels that the created surface should be.
- **Height.** This is the height in pixels of the created surface.
- **Format.** This is the `D3DFORMAT` that the surface should use.
- **Pool.** This is the memory location in which the surface will be placed. You can choose from four types of memory pools:
  - **D3DPOOL_DEFAULT.** The system places the resource in the most appropriate type of memory. This can be either in video or system memory.
  - **D3DPOOL_MANAGED.** The resource is copied to the appropriate memory when needed.
  - **D3DPOOL_SYSTEMMEM.** The surface is created in system memory.
  - **D3DPOOL_SCRATCH.** Again, this is created in system memory but is not directly accessible by DirectX.
- **PpSurface.** This is a pointer to an `IDirect3DSurface9` interface. This variable holds the reference to the surface after it is created.
- **pHandle.** This is a reserved parameter and should always be `NULL`.

Next is a sample call to `CreateOffscreenPlainSurface`. This sample creates a surface that is 640 × 480 resolution and has the display format of `D3DFMT_X8R8G8B8`.

```
hResult = CreateOffscreenPlainSurface(
                            640,  // the width of the surface to create
                            480,  // the height of the surface to create
                            D3DFMT_X8R8G8B8,  // the surface format
                            D3DPOOL_DEFAULT,  // the memory pool to use
                            &surface,         // holds the resulting surface
                            NULL);            // reserved; should be NULL
// Check the return value to make sure that this function call was successful
if (FAILED(hResult))
    return NULL;
```

Loading a Bitmap to a Surface

Because bitmaps are commonly used for graphics within Windows, I'll be using this format exclusively in the examples. DirectX provides functions within the *D3DX* library that enable the easy loading and drawing of bitmaps.

D3DX Explained

The D3DX library is a collection of commonly used functions that Microsoft has provided with the DirectX SDK. Included in this collection are functions to do any of the following:

- Handle loading images
- Load and manipulate 3D meshes
- Perform shader effects
- Make transforms and rotations simpler

You can use functions within the D3DX library by including the d3dx9.h file and linking to d3dx9.lib.

note

Many image formats are used in game development today. Some companies use common formats such as bitmap or Targa, whereas others create their own proprietary formats to protect their art assets. Rarely are games released with images that are editable by the end user.

The function D3DXLoadSurfaceFromFile performs the loading of a source bitmap into an off-screen surface. The D3DXLoadSurfaceFromFile function is defined as follows:

```
HRESULT D3DXLoadSurfaceFromFile(
    LPDIRECT3DSURFACE9 pDestSurface,
    CONST PALETTEENTRY* pDestPalette,
    CONST RECT* pDestRect,
    LPCTSTR pSrcFile,
    CONST RECT* pSrcRect,
    DWORD Filter,
    D3DCOLOR ColorKey,
    D3DXIMAGE_INFO* pSrcInfo
);
```

D3DXLoadSurfaceFromFile takes eight parameters:

- **pDestSurface.** A pointer to the surface that should hold the incoming bitmap image.
- **pDestPalette.** A pointer to a PALEETTEENTRY structure. This parameter is used only for 256-color bitmaps. For 16-, 24-, and 32-bit images, this parameter should be set to the value of NULL.
- **pDestRect.** A pointer to a RECT structure that represents the rectangular area of the surface that the bitmap should be loaded to.

- **pSrcFile.** A string representing the file name of the bitmap to load.
- **pSrcRect.** A pointer to a RECT structure that represents the area of the source bitmap that should be loaded into the surface.
- **Filter.** A D3DX_FILTER type that specifies the type of filtering that should be applied.
- **ColorKey.** The D3DCOLOR format of the color that should be used for transparency. The default color value is 0.
- **pSrcInfo.** A pointer to a D3DXIMAGE_INFO structure. This structure holds information about the source bitmap file, such as width, height, and bit depth.

Here's an example of a simple call to D3DXLoadSurfaceFromFile, which loads a bitmap called test.bmp into an offscreen surface. Remember: This surface must first be created with a call to CreateOffscreenPlainSurface.

```
IDirect3DSurface9* surface;
hResult = D3DXLoadSurfaceFromFile( surface,
                                   NULL,
                                   NULL,
                                   "test.bmp",
                                   NULL,
                                   D3DX_DEFAULT,
                                   0,
                                   NULL );

if ( FAILED( hResult ) )
    return NULL;
```

Following this call, the bitmap will reside in memory and be ready for use in your game.

Using DirectX to Render a Bitmap

Now that you've seen how to create and load a bitmap to a surface, it's time to display it. To do this, you have to make some changes to the Render function that was created earlier.

The previous Render function looked like this.

```
/********************************************************************
* Render(void)
********************************************************************/
void Render(void)
{
    // Check to make sure you have a valid Direct3D device
    if( NULL == pd3dDevice )
        return;
```

```
// Clear the back buffer to a blue color
pd3dDevice->Clear( 0, NULL, D3DCLEAR_TARGET,
                    D3DCOLOR_XRGB(0,0,255), 1.0f, 0 );
// Present the back buffer contents to the display
pd3dDevice->Present( NULL, NULL, NULL, NULL );
}
```

To get the bitmap shown on the screen, you'll need to use the StretchRect function. StretchRect performs rectangular copies between two surfaces.

The StretchRect function is defined as follows:

```
HRESULT StretchRect(
    IDirect3DSurface9 *pSourceSurface,
    CONST RECT *pSourceRect,
    IDirect3DSurface9 *pDestSurface,
    CONST RECT *pDestRect,
    D3DTEXTUREFILTERTYPE Filter
);
```

StretchRect has the following parameters:

- **pSourceSurface.** A pointer to the offscreen surface that has already been created.
- **pSourceRect.** A pointer to a RECT structure that holds the area to be copied. If this parameter is NULL, the full source surface is copied.
- **pDestSurface.** A pointer to the destination surface. In most cases, this will be a pointer to the back buffer surface.
- **pDestRect.** A pointer to the RECT structure that represents the area on the destination surface where the copy will be placed. This parameter can be NULL if no destination RECT is needed.
- **Filter.** The filter type to apply to this copy. Sending the value of D3DTEXF_NONE indicates that no filtering should be applied.

You might be wondering how you get a pointer to the back buffer surface. The aptly named function GetBackBuffer does the trick. A standard call to this function would look like this:

```
GetBackBuffer( 0,      // a value that represents the swap chain
               0,      // index of the buffer chain;
                       // 0 if only one back buffer is available
               D3DBACKBUFFER_TYPE_MONO, // the only valid type
               &backbuffer); // IDirect3DSurface9 object for the back buffer
```

Including the new calls to StretchRect and GetBackBuffer, your new Render function now looks like this:

```
/*********************************************************************
* Render
*********************************************************************/
void Render(void)
{
    // This will hold the back buffer
    IDirect3DSurface9* backbuffer = NULL;
    // Check to make sure you have a valid Direct3D device
    if( NULL == pd3dDevice )
        return;

    // Clear the back buffer to a blue color
    pd3dDevice->Clear( 0, NULL, D3DCLEAR_TARGET,
                        D3DCOLOR_XRGB(0,0,255), 1.0f, 0 );

    // Get the back buffer
    pd3dDevice->GetBackBuffer( 0,
                                0,
                                D3DBACKBUFFER_TYPE_MONO,
                                &backbuffer );

    // Copy the offscreen surface to the back buffer
    // Note the use of NULL values for the source and destination RECTs
    // This ensures a copy of the entire surface to the back buffer
    pd3dDevice->StretchRect( srcSurface,
                                NULL,
                                backbuffer,
                                NULL,
                                D3DTEXF_NONE );

    // Present the back buffer contents to the display
    pd3dDevice->Present ( NULL, NULL, NULL, NULL );
}
```

You can find the full source listing for this example in the chapter3\example1 directory on the CD-ROM. Compiling and running this example produces the window shown in Figure 3.2.

Figure 3.2 Background bitmap displayed using the function StretchRect.

StretchRect Revisited

Previously, you used StretchRect to copy the whole offscreen surface to the back buffer, but that only touches on the usefulness of this function. StretchRect lets you copy one or more portions of an offscreen surface, allowing the surface to contain many smaller graphics. For instance, an offscreen surface can hold multiple frames of an animation or include different pieces needed for a puzzle game. StretchRect has two parameters—pSourceRect and pDestRect—that are used to define the areas to copy. Figure 3.3 shows an example of using a source and destination rectangle area in a copy.

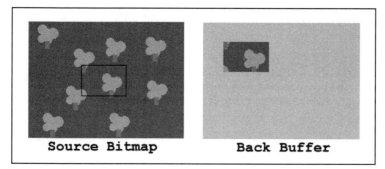

Figure 3.3 The left image represents the source bitmap with a rectangular area selected to be copied. The right image shows the resulting back buffer after the StretchRect function call.

The next example uses this functionality to display a message to the screen using the bitmapped font. Figure 3.4 shows the source bitmap that holds the font. As you can see, all the letters of the alphabet are included in one bitmap and are placed in blocks of equal size. By keeping each letter the same size, the code can predict the location of each letter in the source bitmap and make copying the needed letters much easier.

Figure 3.4 The bitmap that will hold the font you'll be using.

Because you'll need to copy more than one item per frame, you must make multiple calls to the StretchRect function. To keep things simple, I've placed all the needed calls into a for loop in the updated Render function.

```
/*************************************************************************
* Render
*************************************************************************/
void Render(void)
{
    int letterWidth=48;         // the uniform width of each letter block
    int letterHeight=48;        // the uniform height of each letter block
    int destx = 48;      // the top-left X coordinate for the first letter
    int desty = 96;      // the top-left Y coordinate for the first letter

    // This variable will hold the pointer to the back buffer
    IDirect3DSurface9* backbuffer = NULL;

    // Check to make sure you have a valid Direct3D device
    if( NULL == pd3dDevice )
        return;

    // Clear the back buffer to a blue color
    pd3dDevice->Clear( 0, NULL, D3DCLEAR_TARGET,
                    D3DCOLOR_XRGB(0,0,255), 1.0f, 0 );

    // Retrieve a pointer to the back buffer
    pd3dDevice->GetBackBuffer(0,0,D3DBACKBUFFER_TYPE_MONO, &backbuffer);

    // Set up a counter variable to hold the letter's position on the screen
    int count=0;

    // Loop through the message one character at a time
    for ( char *c = message; c != " "; c++ )
    {
```

```
// source and destination rectangles
RECT src;
RECT dest;

// Set the source rectangle
int srcY = ( ( ( *c - 'A' ) / 6 ) ) * letterHeight;
int srcX = ( ( ( *c - 'A' ) %7 ) * letterWidth );
src.top = srcY ;
src.left = srcX;
src.right = src.left + letterWidth;
src.bottom = src.top + letterHeight;

// Set the dest rectangle
dest.top = desty;
dest.left = destx + ( letterWidth * count );
dest.right = dest.left + letterWidth;
dest.bottom = dest.top + letterHeight;

// Increase the letter count by one
count++;

// Copy this letter to the back buffer
pd3dDevice->StretchRect( srcSurface,        // the source surface
                         src,               // the source rectangle
                         backbuffer,        // the destination surface
                         dest,              // destination rectangle
                         D3DTEXF_NONE);     // the filter to apply
    }

    // Present the back buffer contents to the display
    pd3dDevice->Present( NULL, NULL, NULL, NULL );
}
```

The resulting output from this example displays the text "HELLO WORLD" and gives you the feeling that you are looking at a ransom letter. The output is shown in Figure 3.5. You can find the full code listing in the chapter3\example2 directory on the CD-ROM. Some future projects on the CD-ROM have split the DirectX functions into a file called dxManager to make the code easier to follow.

The previous code loops through each letter in the message variable, which was defined outside the Render function as follows:

```
char *message = "HELLO WORLD";
```

Each time through the loop, you are working with only one letter. For example, the first time through the code, you're handling only the *H* from the word "HELLO". The code then computes the source rectangle by getting the top-left X and Y coordinates for this letter.

```
int srcY = ( ( ( *c - 'A' ) / 6 ) ) * letterHeight;
int srcX = ( ( ( *c - 'A' ) %7 ) * letterWidth);
```

After you have the top-left coordinates, you can get the bottom-right ones by adding the width and height of the letter.

```
src.top = srcY ;
src.left = srcX;
src.right = src.left + letterWidth;
src.bottom = src.top + letterHeight;
```

Next you'll want to figure out where on the back buffer this letter should be copied.

```
dest.top = desty;
dest.left = destx + ( letterWidth * count );
dest.right = dest.left + letterWidth;
dest.bottom = dest.top + letterHeight;
```

I set up a variable called count to keep track of how many letters have already drawn to the screen. Using count, you can figure out what the top-left X coordinate should be. The top-left Y coordinate remains the same throughout. Again, you determine the bottom-right coordinates by adding the width and height of the letters.

Figure 3.5 Using your bitmapped font, Hello World!

note

You can also use the `StretchRect` function to stretch or shrink an image during a copy. If the destination rectangle is larger or smaller than the source rectangle, the image will be adjusted appropriately.

Sprites

As was covered in the previous section, you can copy small rectangles between surfaces. You did this in example two to display a bitmapped font. Using the same method, you can create a system to display sprites.

Sprites are 2D graphical objects that are commonly used in games to represent the player characters or any range of objects within your game. For example, in a platform game, a sprite displays the character you move around the screen. Sprites normally have multiple frames of animation, can be moved about by the player, and can interact with the game world. I'm going to cover what it takes to create a sprite and how to use one in a game.

note

A *frame* is a single still image of an animation. Quickly displaying multiple frames in succession creates the illusion of movement.

What Do Sprites Need?

The first thing all sprites need is an image to display. This image will be the sprite's one or more frames of animation.

A sprite also needs a location. The location is where the sprite is currently on the screen. Two numbers normally represent this value: the X and the Y coordinates.

To be usable in a game, the sprites need to be able to hold a bit more information, but these two items are the core requirements for any sprite and serve as a good starting point.

Representing a Sprite in Code

This will be your first attempt at creating a sprite structure. This structure will hold all the information for each sprite that you want to create. Here's the sprite structure:

```
struct {
        RECT sourceRect;
        // position
        int X;              // the X coordinate
        int Y;              // the Y coordinate
} spriteStruct ;
```

In the spriteStruct structure, the image needed is being represented by a RECT variable. The sourceRect holds the location of the sprite within the source bitmap.

The X and Y coordinates are represented by integers. Because this example only needs to be able to support a resolution of 640 × 480, a standard integer has plenty of space to hold your data.

As I stated before, this is just a simple starting point for a sprite. For now, let's get something on the screen.

Creating Your First Sprite

To create your first sprite, you're going to need to use some of the functions that were covered earlier.

- D3DXLoadSurfaceFromFile
- CreateOffscreenPlainSurface
- StretchRect

Each of these functions has its own benefits when using sprites. D3DXLoadSurfaceFromFile assists you in the loading of your source art, CreateOffscreenPlainSurface gives you an area of memory to store your artwork, and StretchRect displays your sprites on the screen.

Loading the Sprite Images

You load the sprite image using the D3DXLoadSurfaceFromFile function and place it into an IDirect3DSurface9 object created, as before, with the CreateOffscreenPlainSurface function.

To encompass the needed functionality into a single function, I have created getSurfaceFromBitmap.

This function has only a single parameter: a string to hold the file name of the bitmap to load.

```
/**********************************************************
 * getSurfaceFromBitmap
 **********************************************************/
IDirect3DSurface9* getSurfaceFromBitmap(std::string filename)
{
    HRESULT hResult;
    IDirect3DSurface9* surface = NULL;
    D3DXIMAGE_INFO imageInfo;        // holds details concerning this bitmap

    // Get the width and height info from this bitmap
    hResult = D3DXGetImageInfoFromFile(filename.c_str(), &imageInfo);
    // Make sure that the call to D3DXGetImageInfoFromFile succeeded
```

```
      if FAILED (hResult)
         return NULL;


      // Create the offscreen surface that will hold the bitmap
      hResult = pd3dDevice->CreateOffscreenPlainSurface( width,
                                                         height,
                                                         D3DFMT_X8R8G8B8,
                                                         D3DPOOL_DEFAULT,
                                                         &surface,
                                                         NULL )
      // Make sure that this function call did not fail; if it did,
      // exit this function
      if ( FAILED( hResult ) )
         return NULL;


      // Load the bitmap into the surface that was created earlier
      hResult = D3DXLoadSurfaceFromFile( surface,
                                         NULL,
                                         NULL,
                                         filename.c_str( ),
                                         NULL,
                                         D3DX_DEFAULT,
                                         0,
                                         NULL );

   if ( FAILED( hResult ) )
      return NULL;


   return surface;
}
```

The getSurfaceFromBitmap function is used in the following manner:

```
IDirect3DSurface9* spriteSurface;
spriteSurface = getSurfaceFromBitmap( "sprites.bmp");
If (spriteSurface == NULL)
        return false;
```

First you create a variable to hold the new surface, and then you call getSurfaceFromBitmap with the name of the bitmap to load.

Always check the return value of the getSur-faceFromBitmap call to make sure that the bitmap was loaded correctly and that you have a valid surface. Figure 3.6 shows a sample bitmap that contains multiple sprites.

Figure 3.6 Bitmap containing multiple sprite graphics.

The getSurfaceFromBitmap function will be used throughout the rest of this book as needed.

Initializing the Sprites

After you have your sprite graphic loaded, it's time to fill the sprite structures with the correct information. Because you're going to be using a single surface that contains all the graphics for the sprites, it's a good idea to place the code to initialize each sprite into a for loop. The initSprites function that follows demonstrates this technique.

```
#define SPRITE_WIDTH 48
#define SPRITE_HEIGHT 48
#define SCRN_WIDTH 640
#define SCRN_HEIGHT 480
/********************************************************************************
* bool initSprites(void)
********************************************************************************/
bool initSprites(void)
{
    // Loop through 10 sprite structures and initialize them
    for (int i = 0; i < 10; i++ )
    {
        spriteStruct[i].srcRect.top = 0;
        spriteStruct[i].srcRect.left = i * SPRITE_WIDTH;
        spriteStruct[i].srcRect.right = spriteStruct[i].srcRect.left +
                                                            SPRITE_WIDTH;
        spriteStruct[i].srcRect.bottom = SPRITE_HEIGHT;
        spriteStruct[i].posX = rand()% SCRN_WIDTH - SPRITE_WIDTH;
        spriteStruct[i].posY = rand()% SCRN_HEIGHT - SPRITE_HEIGHT;
    }
    return true;
}
```

First, the for loop is set up. It iterates through the loop 10 times, resulting in 10 different sprites.

Within the loop, the srcRect must be set. This tells the sprite where within the source bitmap it should find its graphic. The final two lines set the X and Y coordinate position of the sprite. In this case, they are being set to a random position that guarantees they will be visible on the screen.

Displaying the Sprites

You're almost there! Only one more step to go, and your sprites will be on the screen. Again, you need to change the Render function. This time, a for loop is created that will call StretchRect multiple times, once for each sprite being rendered.

```
/****************************************************************************
* Render(void)
****************************************************************************/
void Render(void)
{
    // This will hold the back buffer
    IDirect3DSurface9* backbuffer = NULL;

    if( NULL == pd3dDevice )
        return;

    // Clear the back buffer to a black color
    pd3dDevice->Clear( 0,
                       NULL,
                       D3DCLEAR_TARGET,
                       D3DCOLOR_XRGB(0,0,0),
                       1.0f,
                       0 );

    // Retrieve a pointer to the back buffer
    pd3dDevice->GetBackBuffer(0,0,D3DBACKBUFFER_TYPE_MONO, &backbuffer);

    // Loop through all the sprites
    for ( int i = 0; i < 10; i++ )
    {
        RECT destRect;            // Create a temporary destination RECT
        // Fill the temporary RECT with data from
        // the current sprite structure
        destRect.left = spriteStruct[i].posX;
        destRect.top = spriteStruct[i].posY;
        destRect.bottom = destRect.top + SPRITE_HEIGHT;
        destRect.right = destRect.left + SPRITE_WIDTH;

        // Draw the sprite to the back buffer
         pd3dDevice->StretchRect(spriteSurface,
                            srcRect,
                            backbuffer,
                            destRect,
                            D3DTEXF_NONE);
    }
    // Present the back buffer contents to the display
    pd3dDevice->Present( NULL, NULL, NULL, NULL );
}
```

The previous code segment again loops through all 10 sprites. Within the loop, it creates and sets a temporary destination RECT variable. StretchRect uses the RECT structure you created to tell DirectX where the sprite should be drawn. Finally, the StretchRect function is called. One by one, the sprites should be drawn to the back buffer. Figure 3.7 shows how all 10 sprites might look when rendered on the screen.

You can find the full code for this example in the chapter3\example3 directory on the CD-ROM.

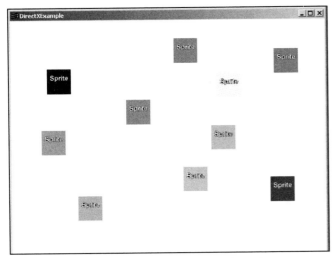

Figure 3.7 Ten sprites being drawn in random places.

Moving Your Sprite

Your sprites are on the screen and everyone's happy, right? Probably not. One of the advantages of a sprite is that it can move around. I'm sure *Sonic the Hedgehog* wouldn't have been very much fun if Sonic couldn't move. Sprites need a way of tracking how far and in what direction they need to move in each frame.

To fix this problem, you need to add a few more variables to the sprite structure that was defined earlier.

```
struct {
    RECT srcRect;               // holds the location of this sprite
                                // in the source bitmap

    // position
    int posX;                   // the sprite's X position
    int posY;                   // the sprite's Y position

    // movement
    int moveX;                  // how many pixels to move in the X direction
```

```
                                    // per frame
        int moveY;                  // how many pixels to move in the Y direction
                                    // per frame
} spriteStruct;
```

As you can see, two variables—moveX and moveY—have been added. These two variables will be used to hold a value that corresponds to the number of pixels per frame that you want to move your sprite. The moveX and moveY variables will then be added to the posX and posY values in the spriteStruct for each sprite. For example, for each frame, the following would take place:

```
for (int i = 0; i < 10; i++)
{
    spriteStruct[ i ].posX += spriteStruct[ i ].moveX;
    spriteStruct[ i ].posY += spriteStruct[ i ].moveY;
}
```

The sprites would then be sent to the Render function to be drawn. For each frame, their position variables (posX, posY) would be updated, resulting in the sprite's movement across the screen.

Of course, you'll have to check the posX and posY variables against the screen resolution if you want them to stay on the screen. For example, the previous code sample could be changed to keep the sprites within the 640 × 480 boundary of your window.

```
for (int i = 0; i < 10; i++)
{
    // Add the moveX to posX
    spriteStruct[ i ].posX += spriteStruct[ i ].moveX;
    // Check to make sure that posX is not greater than 640
    if (spriteStruct[ i ].posX > SCRN_WIDTH)
    {
        // If posX has become greater than 640, change the moveX value
        // to a negative value by multiplying it by -1
        // This causes the sprite, on the next frame, to start
        // moving backward away from the side of the screen
        spriteStruct[ i ].moveX *= -1;
    }

    // Add the moveY to posY
    spriteStruct[ i ].posY += spriteStruct[ i ].moveY;
    // Check again to make sure that posY doesn't go bigger than 480
    if (spriteStruct[ i ].posY > SCRN_HEIGHT)
    {
        // If posY is bigger than 480, multiply the moveY value by -1
```

```
            // This causes the sprite, on the next frame, to start moving
            // away from the bottom of the screen
            spriteStruct[ i ].moveY *= -1;
        }


        // Because the sprites will also be traveling backward now, it's a
        // good idea to check 0 again as well; this allows the sprites to
        // bounce off the left and top sides of the screen
        if (spriteStruct[ i ].posX < 0)
        {
            // Reverse the direction of the sprite if it has reached the left
            // side of the screen
            spriteStruct[ i ].moveX *= -1;
        }


        // Check to make sure the sprite has hit the top of the screen
        if (spriteStruct[ i ].posY < 0)
        {
            // If the sprite has reached the top of the screen, reverse
            // its direction
            spriteStruct[ i ].moveY *= -1;
        }
    }
}
```

The previous code causes the sprites to bounce around the screen, staying within the 640 × 480 area. The fish will appear to seamlessly swim over the black background. If you change the color of the background to another color though, you will notice a black box around each of the fish. Because of the way surfaces work, they don't support transparency.

note

If you change the resolution of the window, you must make sure to change the values that the posX and posY variables check against to ensure that the sprites stay contained.

Animating Your Sprite

The previous version of the sprite structure allowed for the movement of the sprites around the screen, but the sprites still aren't that exciting. The sprites are constantly displaying the same static image the whole time. In this section, you're going to add multiple frames of animation and bring your sprites to life.

To accomplish your goal of lifelike sprites, you're going to use the updated sprite structure, shown next, and the new bitmap, shown in Figure 3.8.

Figure 3.8 Bitmap showing the needed frames for a sprite animation.

```
struct {
    RECT srcRect;               // holds the location of this sprite
                                // in the source bitmap
    // position data
    int posX;                   // the sprite's X position
    int posY;                   // the sprite's Y position

    // movement data
    int moveX;                  // how many pixels to move in the X direction
                                // per frame
    int moveY;                  // how many pixels to move in the Y direction
                                // per frame
    // animation data
    int numFrames;              // number of frames this animation has
    int curFrame;               // the current frame of animation
} spriteStruct;
```

To include support for animation to the sprite structure, you must add two new variables:

- **numFrames.** The number of frames within the sprite's animation.
- **curFrame.** The current frame the animation is displaying.

The two new variables help you to keep track of which frame of the animation is currently being shown and allow you to loop your animation.

Because you now have new information added to the sprite structure, you must change the initSprites function to support this.

The new initSprites function is shown next.

```
/*****************************************************************************
* bool initSprites(void)
*****************************************************************************/
bool initSprites(void)
{
    // Loop through all the sprite structures and initialize them
    for (int i=0; i < 10; i++)
    {
        // Set the sprite position data
        spriteStruct[i].srcRect.top = 0;
        spriteStruct[i].srcRect.left = i * 64;
        spriteStruct[i].srcRect.right = spriteStruct[i].srcRect.left + 64;
        spriteStruct[i].srcRect.bottom = 23;
        spriteStruct[i].posX = rand()%600;       // places the sprite in a
                                                 // random position
        spriteStruct[i].posY = rand()%430;
```

```
        // Set the animation data
        spriteStruct[i].curFrame = 0;    // Start at frame 0
        spriteStruct[i].numFrames = 4;   // The animation has four frames

        // Set the move data
        spriteStruct[i].moveX = 1;       // Move the sprite 1 pixel per frame
                                         // in a left-right direction
        spriteStruct[i].moveY = 0;       // The sprite will not move up and down
    }

    return true;
}
```

Now that the sprites have been initialized with their position and animation data, they're ready to be displayed.

Displaying the Animated Sprites

The Render function again needs to be updated to support the new data. Each time through this function, the curFrame variable is incremented. This variable controls which frame of the sprite animation is being shown. When this number becomes greater than the number of frames in the animation, represented by the numFrames variable, the curFrame variable is reset to zero and the process starts over again. This causes the animation to loop indefinitely. A new version of the Render function follows.

```
/**************************************************************************
* Render(void)
**************************************************************************/
void Render(void)
{
    // This holds the back buffer
    IDirect3DSurface9* backbuffer = NULL;

    // Check to make sure you have a valid D3DDevice pointer
    if( NULL == pd3dDevice )
        return;

    // Clear the back buffer to a black color
    pd3dDevice->Clear( 0,
                       NULL,
                       D3DCLEAR_TARGET,
                       D3DCOLOR_XRGB(0,0,0),
                       1.0f,
                       0 );
```

```
// Retrieve a pointer to the back buffer
pd3dDevice->GetBackBuffer(0,0,D3DBACKBUFFER_TYPE_MONO, &backbuffer);

// Loop through all the sprite structures
for ( int i = 0; i < 10; i++ )
{
    // Increment the sprite animation frame
    if (spriteStruct[ i ].curFrame < spriteStruct[ i ].numFrames - 1)
        spriteStruct[ i ].curFrame++;
    else
        // You have reached the last frame; reset to first frame
        spriteStruct[ I ].curFrame = 0;

    // Set the source rectangle to the correct frame position
    spriteStruct[ i ].srcRect.left = spriteStruct[ i ].curFrame * 64;
    spriteStruct[ i ].srcRect.right = spriteStruct[ i ].srcRect.left + 64;

    // Create a temporary destination RECT
    RECT destRect;
    // Fill the temporary RECT with data
    destRect.left = spriteStruct[i].posX;
    // from the current sprite structure
    destRect.top = spriteStruct[i].posY;
    // The fish sprite is 23 pixels tall
    destRect.bottom = destRect.top + SPRITE_HEIGHT;
    // The fish sprite is 64 pixels wide
    destRect.right = destRect.left + SPRITE_WIDTH;

    // Draw the sprite to the back buffer
    pd3dDevice->StretchRect (spriteSurface,
                             srcRect,
                             backbuffer,
                             destRect,
                             D3DTEXF_NONE);
}
// Present the back buffer contents to the display
pd3dDevice->Present( NULL, NULL, NULL, NULL );
}
```

If you compile and run the previous changes, you should see a couple of fish swimming back and forth on the screen. Figure 3.9 shows the fish you should see. You can find the full source code listing for the sprite animation example in the chapter3\example4 directory on the CD-ROM. The code in the Render function in example4 has been modified from above slightly for full functionality.

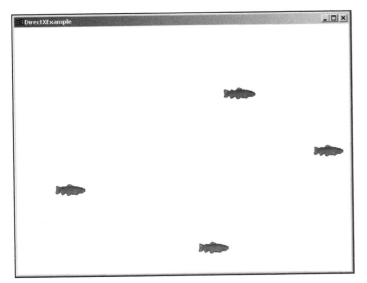

Figure 3.9 Swimming fish with nowhere to go.

Why Is It So Fast?

You've probably noticed that the fish tend to go through their four frames of animation and move rather quickly about the screen. This is because of the frame-based animation technique that was used. Because there is no way to speed up or slow down the animations, they are completely system dependent. On faster computers, the fish move about rapidly, whereas on slower machines, the fish movement might be sluggish.

In the next section, you're going to learn how to slow down your animations and keep them at a constant rate by using a timer.

Timers: How to Animate on Time

Creating smooth animations within your game should be a top priority. Using a timer, animation movement can be set up to occur at fixed intervals. For example, if you want to run an animation at 30 frames per second (fps) but your game's current frame rate is 60 fps, you need to slow down the updating of animation to keep it from playing through twice in one second. In this instance, you would use a timer to update the animation only half as often, maintaining your 30 fps rate.

Timing Under Windows

You can track time under Windows using GetTickCount and QueryPerformanceCounter.

GetTickCount, based on the system timer, is limited in its usefulness when it comes to game programming. GetTickCount retrieves the number of milliseconds that has elapsed since the system was started. It has a limited granularity and is updated every 10 milliseconds. Because of GetTickCount's limitations, a higher performance timer is needed. The QueryPerformanceCounter function fills that need.

QueryPerformanceCounter has a higher resolution than its GetTickCount counterpart. The QueryPerformanceCounter function, being based on a hardware counter instead of a software solution, allows for timing in microseconds. This is useful in games where functions for animation normally require a more detailed timer to keep the animation smooth.

Using QueryPerformanceCounter

The QueryPerformanceCounter function is defined as follows:

```
BOOL QueryPerformanceCounter(
    LARGE_INTEGER *lpPerformanceCount
);
```

The previous function takes only one parameter: a pointer to a LARGE_INTEGER type. After this function is completed, the lpPerformanceCount variable contains the current value from the hardware performance counter.

Following is a small code example using the QueryPerformanceCounter function.

```
LARGE_INTEGER timeStart;
QueryPerformanceCounter(&timeStart);
```

Here, the timeStart variable is holding the value returned from the QueryPerformanceCounter function.

Getting the Time for Each Frame

To accurately time your animations, you need to call the QueryPerformanceCounter function twice within the game loop: once before you start a drawing, and once after all drawing has been completed. Both values returned contain the number of counts from the system at the time the function was called. Because the performance counter has such a high resolution, both of these values should be unique. You can use the difference between these two values to determine the number of counts that has passed between the calls.

For example, you could write the following code:

```
LARGE_INTEGER timeStart;
LARGE_INTEGER timeEnd;
QueryPerformanceCounter(&timeStart);
Render( );
QueryPerformanceCounter(&timeEnd);
LARGE_INTEGER numCounts = ( timeEnd.QuadPart - timeStart.QuadPart )
```

After this code is executed, the numCounts variable contains the number of timer counts that have elapsed between the two calls to QueryPerformanceCounter. The QuadPart portion of the LARGE_INTEGER type tells the system that you want the full 64-bit value to be returned from the counter.

When you have the number of counts stored in a variable, you need to perform one more step before you have a useful number to help time your animations with. You must divide the value in numCounts by the frequency of the performance counter.

note

The *performance counter frequency* is a value that represents the number of times per second the counter is incremented.

The function QueryPerformanceFrequency obtains the frequency of the counter from the system.

The QueryPerformanceFrequency function takes only one parameter: a pointer to a LARGE_ INTEGER that holds the returned frequency. A sample call to this function is shown next:

```
LARGE_INTEGER timerFrequency;
QueryPerformanceFrequency(&timerFrequency);
```

After you have the frequency of the timer, you can use it along with the value in the numCounts variable to calculate a rate of movement for your animation. You can find the animation rate by dividing the number of counts that has passed by the frequency of the timer. The code sample that follows performs this task:

```
float anim_rate = numCounts / timerFrequency.QuadPart;
```

Now that you have the animation rate, you can change the timing code to give a smoother animation rate.

Changing the Animation to Be Time Based

I'm going to show you how to take the information you learned in the previous section and apply it by changing example 4 to use time-based animation.

The first step is making a few changes to the sprite structure. Originally, the movement variables—moveX and moveY—were integer values. They must change to float values so that you can update the sprite's movement more accurately. Here's an updated version of the sprite structure.

```
struct {
    RECT srcRect;                // holds the location of this sprite
                                 // in the source bitmap
```

```
    float posX;                    // the sprite's X position
    float posY;                    // the sprite's Y position

    // movement
    float moveX;
    float moveY;

    // animation
    int numFrames;                 // the number of frames this animation has
    int curFrame;                  // the current frame of animation
} spriteStruct[MAX_SPRITES];
```

As you can see, the position variables—posX and posY—were changed to floats to help more accurately depict their location in the game world.

Next, you need to update the value used in the initSprites function for the moveX variable. The moveX variable was previously set to 1, but you must change it to a new value to reflect the time-based animation. The new value needs to be the number of pixels you want the sprite to travel in a one-second time frame. In this case, let's set it to 30.0. This should allow the fish to swim across the screen at a decent rate.

The final piece of the sprite code you must change is within the drawSprite function. Inside this function, you'll see the following bit of code:

```
spriteStruct[whichOne].posX += spriteStruct[whichOne].moveX;
```

This line of code controls the movement of each sprite across the screen. You'll see that the X position variable—posX—is being incremented by the value within the moveX variable. To allow this to be based on the animation rate determined earlier, you need to change this line of code as follows:

```
spriteStruct[whichOne].posX += spriteStruct[whichOne].moveX * anim_rate;
```

Here, the moveX variable is being multiplied by the value stored in the anim_rate variable. Because the anim_rate variable is updated each frame based on the counter, this should produce a smooth-moving sprite that won't speed up on fast machines.

Now that you've updated the sprite code, you have to add in the timer code. The timer code requires three new global variables:

```
LARGE_INTEGER timeStart;           // holds the starting count
LARGE_INTEGER timeEnd;             // holds the ending count
LARGE_INTEGER timerFreq;           // holds the frequency of the counter
```

Next, you need to make a call to QueryPerformanceFrequency to get the frequency of the counter. You should call this function right before the main message loop:

```
QueryPerformanceFrequency(&timerFreq);
```

Finally, you need to add the calls around the Render function to QueryPerformanceCounter. The first one should go right *before* the call to Render.

```
QueryPerformanceCounter(&timeStart);
```

The second call should go *after* the call to Render.

```
QueryPerformanceCounter(&timeEnd);
```

Immediately following the last QueryPerformanceCounter function, you must determine the new animation rate.

```
anim_rate = ( (float)timeEnd.QuadPart - (float)timeStart.QuadPart ) /
timerFreq.QuadPart;
```

You can now compile the updated example to see how the changes you made have affected the smoothness of the animation. View the full source listing in the chapter3\example5 directory on the CD-ROM.

Chapter Summary

At this point, you should have a basic understanding of how DirectX works and how it creates and uses surfaces.

You should now understand how timers work within the Windows environment and how to use them to smooth out your animations. You'll continue to use timers throughout this book, so you're not done with them quite yet.

In the next chapter, you'll dive into the world of 3D.

What You Have Learned

In this chapter, you learned the following:

- How to load a bitmap using the D3DX Utility Library
- How to draw an image to the screen using DirectX
- What sprites are and how to use them
- How to animate a sprite using frame- and time-based animation techniques

Review Questions

You can find the answers to Review Questions and On Your Own exercises in Appendix A, "Answers to End-of-Chapter Exercises."

1. Offscreen surfaces are created using which function?

2. What is the StretchRect function used for?

3. What sort of data can be stored in an offscreen surface?

4. Why is it a good idea to clear the back buffer each frame?

5. What is the difference between the QueryPerformanceCounter and GetTickCount functions?

On Your Own

1. Write a small example of how you can use the StretchRect function to shrink a section of an image.

2. Write a program using what you've learned in this chapter to scroll a text message across the screen using sprites.

PART II

IT'S A 3D WORLD AFTER ALL

CHAPTER 4

3D PRIMER

You've probably noticed that 2D games have been on the decline for the past few years. Recently, games have been all about pushing the power of the latest 3D video cards, trying to bring more reality to the games being played. Direct3D is a key component in the 3D wave. It allows millions of Microsoft Windows users to experience the latest technologies in games.

Here's what you'll learn in this chapter:

- How 3D space is used
- What coordinate systems are
- How to plot the points of a polygon
- How Direct3D defines vertices
- What a vertex buffer is
- How to define a 3D scene
- The different primitive types available to you

3D Space

Previously, I talked about games that only allowed movement in two directions, which created a rather flat world. The sprites you created before resided in a world with width and height but no depth; the sprites existed in a two-dimensional world.

Direct3D gives you the power to take your game world one dimension further with the addition of depth. *Depth* is the ability for objects to move farther away or closer to the viewer. Characters within a three-dimensional world are more realistic than their 2D counterparts.

3D space is the area in which your three-dimensional world exists. 3D space enables your characters to move around in a way that is similar to the real world. Before you can take advantage of 3D space, you need to know how that space is constructed and how objects are placed into it.

Coordinate Systems

Coordinate systems are a way of defining points within a space. They consist of a set of imaginary grid-like lines—called axes—that run perpendicular to one another. A 2D coordinate system contains only two axes, whereas a 3D system adds one more. The center of a coordinate system, where the axes intersect, is called the *origin*. Figure 4.1 shows what a standard 2D coordinate system looks like. The two axes in a 2D coordinate system are referred to by the letters X and Y. The X axis is horizontal, whereas the Y axis is vertical.

You'll notice in Figure 4.1 that the center X and Y lines are darker than the rest. These lines define the center for each axis and have a value of 0.

Defining a Point in 2D Space

A *point* is defined as a single position along an axis. A point in 1D space, which consists of a single line, would be referred to by a single value. Figure 4.2 shows a single point plotted on a line. The origin of the line is represented by the value of 0. Points to the right of the origin have a positive value, whereas those to the left of the origin have a negative value. In Figure 4.2, the point has a value of positive 4.

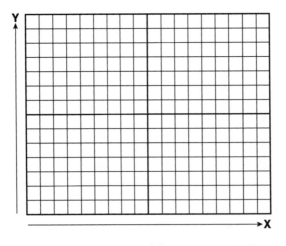

Figure 4.1 How a 2D coordinate system is laid out.

Figure 4.2 A 1D coordinate system.

2D coordinate systems, because they have two axes, require a second value to plot a point. To plot a point within 2D space, you need to define a position along both the X and Y axes. For instance, a single point in a 2D coordinate system would be referred to by two numbers—an X value and a Y value—each number referring to the point's position on that axis.

Like the 1D example shown in Figure 4.2, the values on the X axis continue to increase to the right of the origin, but the values on the Y axis increase as you go up from the origin.

Figure 4.3 shows a 2D coordinate system with a point plotted at an X value of 3 and a Y value of 5. You'll commonly see points shown as (X, Y). In this instance, the point would be shown as (3, 5).

Defining a Point in 3D Space

As I mentioned earlier, a 3D coordinate system adds an extra axis, called the Z axis. The Z axis is perpendicular to the plane created by the X and Y axes. Figure 4.4 shows how a 3D coordinate system would look.

Notice that the coordinate system has the Z axis pointing off into the distance. Commonly, the X and Y axes describe width and height, and the Z axis describes depth.

The Z axis can have either a positive or negative value as it moves away from the origin based on the layout of the coordinate system. Coordinate systems are commonly laid out in either a left-handed or right-handed manner.

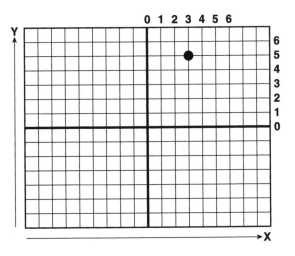

Figure 4.3 A point plotted on a 2D coordinate system.

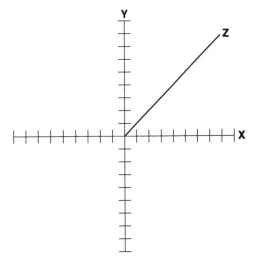

Figure 4.4 A 3D coordinate system layout.

Left-Handed Systems

A left-handed coordinate system extends the positive X axis to the right and the positive Y axis upward. The major difference is the Z axis. The Z axis in a left-handed system is positive in the direction away from the viewer, with the negative portion extending toward him. Figure 4.5 shows how a left-handed coordinate system is set up. This is the coordinate system used in Direct3D.

Right-Handed Systems

The right-handed coordinate system, which is the system used by OpenGL, extends the X and Y axes in the same direction as the left-handed system, but it reverses the Z axis. The positive Z values extend toward the viewer, whereas the negative values continue away. Figure 4.6 shows a right-handed system.

Vertices Explained

A vertex is similar to the idea of the point that I described earlier. A vertex includes information such as location along the X, Y, and Z axes, but it can include other information as well, such as color or texture.

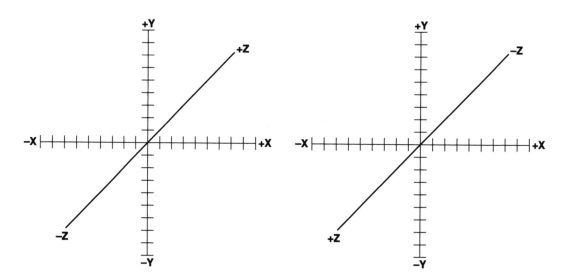

Figure 4.5 A left-handed coordinate system.   **Figure 4.6** A right-handed coordinate system.

When describing a vertex in code, you can use a structure similar to this:

```
struct {
        float x;
        float y;
        float z;
} vertex;
```

This vertex structure contains three variables—each one of type float—that describe the vertex's location along each axis.

Creating a Shape

You can create shapes by using two or more vertices. For instance, in the creation of a triangle, three vertices would be needed to define the three points of the triangle. Plotting a shape with vertices is similar to playing connect the dots. Figure 4.7 shows how to create a triangle by using three vertices.

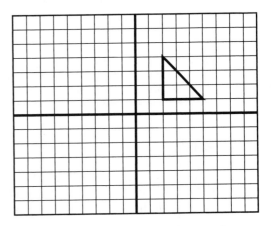

Figure 4.7 Three vertices create a triangle.

Defining this triangle in code requires three vertex structures.

```
struct {
        float x;          // the X coordinate
        float y;          // the Y coordinate
        float z;          // the Z coordinate
} vertex [ 3 ];
```

Here, I've changed the vertex structure to define an array of three vertices. The next step is setting each of the vertices to the positions found in Figure 4.7.

```
// Set the first vertex
vertex[0].x = 2.0;          // Set the X coordinate
vertex[0].y = 4.0;          // Set the Y coordinate
vertex[0].z = 0.0;          // Set the Z coordinate

// Set the second vertex
vertex[1].x = 5.0;          // Set the X coordinate
vertex[1].y = 1.0;          // Set the Y coordinate
vertex[1].z = 0.0;          // Set the Z coordinate
```

```
// Set the final vertex
vertex[0].x = 2.0;                      // Set the X coordinate
vertex[0].y = 1.0;                      // Set the Y coordinate
vertex[0].z = 0.0;                      // Set the Z coordinate
```

Notice that the Z coordinate of all three vertices was set to 0.0. This triangle has no depth, so the Z coordinate remains at 0.

note

Triangles are the simplest closed shapes that you can plot with vertices. You can create more complex shapes, such as squares or spheres, but they are broken down into triangles before rendering.

Adding Color

Previously, the vertex structure only included information that related to the position of each vertex. However, vertices can also contain color information. This color information can be held in four additional variables called R, G, B and A.

- **R.** The red component of the color
- **B.** The green color component
- **B.** The blue color component
- **A.** The alpha color component

Each of these values helps to define the final color of the vertex. You can see the updated vertex structure next.

```
struct {
        // position information
        float x;
        float y;
        float z;

        // color information
        float R;
        float G;
        float B;
        float A;
} vertex;
```

Using the R, G, B, and A variables, you can set the color of the vertex. For instance, if you want your vertex to be white in color, the R, G, and B variables should be set to 1.0.

Setting the vertex to a pure blue color requires R and G to be set to 0.0, whereas the B variable is set to 1.0.

note

The alpha component of a color determines its transparency level. If the value of an alpha component is 0, the color specified in the R, G, and B values is completely opaque. If the alpha value is greater than 0, the color specified has a level of transparency. The alpha component can be any value between 0.0f and 1.0f.

Vertex Buffers

Vertex buffers are areas of memory that hold the vertex information needed to create 3D objects. The vertices contained within the buffer can contain different kinds of information, such as position information, texture coordinates, and vertex colors. Vertex buffers are useful for storing static geometry that needs to be rendered repeatedly. Vertex buffers can exist in either system memory or the memory on the graphics adapter.

A vertex buffer is created by first declaring a variable of type IDirect3DVertexBuffer9. The resulting pointer refers to the vertex buffer that DirectX will create for you.

Next, your game must create the vertex buffer and store it in the variable you created. After you have a valid vertex buffer available, you need to fill it with vertices. You can do this by locking the vertex buffer and copying the vertices.

Creating a Vertex Buffer

You can create vertex buffers by using a call to CreateVertexBuffer. The CreateVertexBuffer function, defined next, requires six parameters.

```
HRESULT CreateVertexBuffer(
        UINT Length,
        DWORD Usage,
        DWORD FVF,
        D3DPOOL Pool,
        IDirect3DVertexBuffer9** ppVertexBuffer,
        HANDLE* pHandle
);
```

- **Length.** Variable containing the length of the vertex buffer in bytes.
- **Usage.** Flags that determine the behavior of the vertex buffer. This value should commonly be 0.
- **FVF.** The flexible vertex format that the vertex buffer uses.
- **Pool.** The memory pool where the vertex buffer resides. This value is an enumerated value of type D3DPOOL.

- **ppVertexBuffer.** An address to a pointer of a variable of type IDirect3DVertexBuffer9. This variable holds the newly created buffer.
- **pHandle.** A reserved value, this should always be NULL.

The vertices within a vertex buffer can contain flexible vertex information. Basically, this means that the vertices in the buffer can include just position information, or they can include colors or texture coordinates. The type of data contained within the vertices of the buffer is controlled by the Flexible Vertex Format (FVF) flags.

Flexible Vertex Format

The Flexible Vertex Format allows for customization of the information stored in the vertex buffer. By using a set of FVF flags, the buffer can be made to contain any number of vertex properties. Table 4.1 describes the FVF flags in move detail.

Table 4.1 Flexible Vertex Format Flags

Flag	Description
D3DFVF_XYZ	Vertex format includes the X, Y, and Z coordinate of an untransformed vertex.
D3DFVF_XYZRHW	Vertex format includes the X, Y, and Z coordinates, but this time they are already transformed.
D3DFVF_XYZW	Vertex format contains transformed and clipped vertex data.
D3DFVF_NORMAL	Vertex format contains normal information.
D3DFVF_PSIZE	Format includes the point size of the vertex.
D3DFVF_DIFFUSE	Diffuse color is part of the vertex buffer.
D3DFVF_SPECULAR	Specular information is part of the vertex buffer.
D3DFVF_TEX0	Texture coordinate 0.
D3DFVF_TEX1	Texture coordinate 1.
D3DFVF_TEX2	Texture coordinate 2.
D3DFVF_TEX3	Texture coordinate 3.
D3DFVF_TEX4	Texture coordinate 4.
D3DFVF_TEX5	Texture coordinate 5.
D3DFVF_TEX6	Texture coordinate 6.
D3DFVF_TEX7	Texture coordinate 7.
D3DFVF_TEX8	Texture coordinate 8.

Direct3D can handle up to eight sets of texture coordinates per vertex.

The format of the vertices you use is created by defining a custom vertex structure. The following structure defines a vertex that contains untransformed position information, as well as a color component.

```
struct CUSTOMVERTEX
{
        FLOAT x, y, z, rhw;     // the untransformed, 3D position for the vertex
        DWORD color;            // the vertex color
};
```

The CUSTOMVERTEX structure consists of the standard vertex position variables X, Y, and Z, but also includes the variable RHW. The RHW value, which stands for Reciprocal of Homogeneous W, tells Direct3D that the vertices that are being used are already in screen coordinates. This value is normally used in fog and clipping calculations and should be set to 1.0.

note

The vertex color is a DWORD value. Direct3D provides a few macros to assist you in creating these colors. One such macro is the D3DCOLOR_ARGB(a, r, g, b) macro. This macro accepts four components: an alpha, a red, a green, and a blue. Each of these components is a value between 0 and 255. This macro returns a DWORD color value that Direct3D can use.

D3DCOLOR_ARGB(0, 255, 0, 0) creates a color value representing all red.

Additional macros are D3DCOLOR_RGBA and D3DCOLOR_XRGB, which are described fully in the DirectX documentation.

Now that the vertex structure is created, the next step is determining the flags that will be sent to the CreateVertexBuffer function as the FVF parameter.

Because the CUSTOMVERTEX structure requires non-transformed position information and a color component, the needed flags would be D3DFVF_XYZRHW and D3DFVF_DIFFUSE.

The sample code that follows shows a call to CreateVertexBuffer using this vertex structure.

```
// a structure for your custom vertex type
struct CUSTOMVERTEX
{
        FLOAT x, y, z, rhw;     // the untransformed, 3D position for the vertex
        DWORD color;          // the vertex color
};

// Create the variable to hold the vertex buffer
LPDIRECT3DVERTEXBUFFER9 buffer   = NULL;
```

```
// variable used to hold the return code
HRESULT hr;

// Create the vertex buffer
hr = pd3dDevice->CreateVertexBuffer(
                                3*sizeof( CUSTOMVERTEX ),
                                0,
                                D3DFVF_XYZRHW | D3DFVF_DIFFUSE,
                                D3DPOOL_DEFAULT,
                                &buffer,
                                NULL );
// Check the return code
if FAILED ( hr)
        return false;
```

As you can see, the CUSTOMVERTEX structure is created first, telling Direct3D the type of vertices to use. Next, the call to CreateVertexBuffer creates the actual buffer and stores it in the buffer variable.

The first parameter to CreateVertexBuffer, the size of the buffer in bytes, is created with enough space to hold three vertices of type CUSTOMVERTEX.

The third parameter, the FVF, is shown as having the flags D3DFVF_XYZRHW and D3DFVF_DIFFUSE being used.

The fourth parameter sets the memory pool for this vertex buffer. The value D3DPOOL_DEFAULT is used, which allows the buffer to be created in the most appropriate memory for this type.

The final parameter that you have to worry about is the fifth one. This is where you pass in the variable that holds the newly created buffer.

After the call to CreateVertexBuffer is complete, make sure to check the return code to confirm that the buffer was created successfully.

Loading Data into a Buffer

Now that you have a valid vertex buffer, you need to add vertices to it. Before you can place vertices in the buffer, you must lock the memory the buffer is using. After this memory is locked, it is freely available to be written to by your game.

Locking the Vertex Buffer

Locking the memory used by the vertex buffer allows your application to write to it. At this point, you've already defined the vertex buffer and the type of vertices it will hold. The next step is locking the buffer and copying the vertices. Locking of the buffer is accomplished with the Lock function, defined next.

```
HRESULT Lock(
        UINT OffsetToLock,
        UINT SizeToLock,
        VOID **ppbData,
        DWORD Flags
);
```

The Lock function takes four parameters:

- **OffsetToLock.** The offset into the buffer to lock. If you want to lock the entire buffer, this value should be 0.
- **SizeToLock.** The size in bytes to lock. Again, if you are locking the whole buffer, this value should be 0.
- **ppbData.** A void pointer to the buffer that holds the vertices.
- **Flags.** Flags that describe the type of lock. Following are the available flags:
  - **D3DLOCK_DISCARD.** The entire buffer is overwritten.
  - **D3DLOCK_NO_DIRTY_UPDATE.** Dirty regions of the buffer are not written to.
  - **D3DLOCK_NO_SYSLOCK.** The system keeps normal display mode changes from happening during a lock. This flag enables the system to continue processing other events.
  - **D3DLOCK_READONLY.** The buffer cannot be written to.
  - **D3DLOCK_NOOVERWRITE.** Any information currently in the buffer is not to be overwritten.

The following code sample shows a normal call to the Lock function.

```
HRESULT hr;
VOID* pVertices;

// Lock the vertex buffer
hr = g_pVB->Lock( 0, 0, ( void** ) &pVertices, 0 );

// Check the return code to make sure the lock was successful
if FAILED (hr)
return false;
```

The Lock function assumes that you've already created a valid vertex buffer. The variable g_pVB refers to this buffer.

Copying Vertices to a Vertex Buffer

After the vertex buffer is locked, you can freely copy data into the buffer. You can either copy enough vertices to fill the whole buffer, or you can selectively change vertices within the buffer. The next example shows how to use memcpy to copy an array of vertices into a vertex buffer.

```
// the customvertex structure
struct CUSTOMVERTEX
{
        FLOAT x, y, z, rhw;    // the transformed, 3D position for the vertex
        DWORD color;           // the vertex color
};

// Define the vertices to be used in the buffer
CUSTOMVERTEX g_Vertices [ ] =
{
        {320.0f, 50.0f, 0.5f, 1.0f, D3DCOLOR_ARGB (0, 255, 0, 0),},
        {250.0f, 400.0f, 0.5f, 1.0f, D3DCOLOR_ARGB (0, 0, 255, 0),},
        {50.0f, 400.0f, 0.5f, 1.0f, D3DCOLOR_ARGB (0, 0, 0, 255),},
};

// Copy the vertices into the vertex buffer
memcpy( pVertices, g_Vertices, sizeof( g_Vertices ) );
```

The sample first declares the CUSTOMVERTEX structure. As mentioned before, this structure takes a position vertex as well as a color component. Next, an array of vertices is created. The array, referred to by the g_Vertices variable, holds the vertices to be copied into the buffer. Finally, a call to memcpy is made to copy the vertices into the buffer. The first parameter to memcpy, pVertices, refers to the void pointer that was created during the call to Lock.

Unlocking the Vertex Buffer

After the vertices have been copied into the buffer, you must unlock the buffer. Unlocking the buffer allows Direct3D to continue processing normally. You can unlock the buffer through the Unlock function, defined here:

```
HRESULT Unlock (VOID);
```

The Unlock function requires no parameters and returns the value of D3D_OK on success.

After the vertex buffer is filled with vertices, it's ready to be drawn to the screen.

The SetupVB function that follows takes all the steps from earlier and places them in an easy-to-use function.

```
// variable to hold the newly created vertex buffer
LPDIRECT3DVERTEXBUFFER9 g_pVB            = NULL;


/****************************************************************************
* SetupVB
* Creates and fills the vertex buffer
****************************************************************************/
HRESULT SetupVB()
{
HRESULT hr;

// Initialize three vertices for rendering a triangle
CUSTOMVERTEX g_Vertices[] =
                        {
                        {320.0f, 50.0f, 0.5f, 1.0f, D3DCOLOR_ARGB (0, 255, 0, 0), },
                        {250.0f, 400.0f, 0.5f, 1.0f, D3DCOLOR_ARGB (0, 0, 255, 0), },
                        {50.0f, 400.0f, 0.5f, 1.0f, D3DCOLOR_ARGB (0, 0, 0, 255), },
                        };

// Create the vertex buffer
hr = pd3dDevice->CreateVertexBuffer(
                            3*sizeof(CUSTOMVERTEX),
                            0,
                            D3DFVF_XYZRHW|D3DFVF_DIFFUSE,
                            D3DPOOL_DEFAULT,
                            &g_pVB,
                            NULL );

        // Check to make sure that the vertex buffer was
        // created successfully
        if FAILED ( hr )
                return NULL;

        VOID* pVertices;

        // Lock the vertex buffer
        hr = g_pVB->Lock( 0, sizeof(g_Vertices), (void**)&pVertices, 0 );

        // Check to make sure the lock was successful
        if FAILED (hr)
                return E_FAIL;
```

```
        // Copy the vertices into the buffer
        memcpy( pVertices, g_Vertices, sizeof(g_Vertices) );

        // Unlock the vertex buffer
        g_pVB->Unlock();

        return S_OK;
}
```

The SetupVB function requires that a variable to hold the vertex buffer is defined outside the scope of this function. The variable g_pVB refers to this variable. If the vertex buffer is created and filled successfully, the SetupVB function returns the HRESULT value of S_OK.

Drawing the Contents of the Buffer

Now that you've spent all this time creating the vertex buffer and filling it with vertices, you're probably wondering when you get to see something on the screen. Well, rendering the vertices within the vertex buffer requires three steps. The first step is setting the stream source, followed by configuring the vertex shader, and then finally drawing the vertices to the screen. These steps are explained in detail in the following sections.

Setting the Stream Source

Direct3D *streams* are arrays of component data that consist of multiple elements. The vertex buffer you created earlier is an example of such a stream. Before Direct3D can render a vertex buffer, you must associate the buffer with a data stream. This is accomplished with the function SetStreamSource, defined here:

```
HRESULT SetStreamSource(
        UINT StreamNumber,
        IDirect3DVertexBuffer9 *pStreamData,
        UINT OffsetInBytes,
        UINT Stride
);
```

SetStreamSource requires four parameters.

- **StreamNumber.** The number of the data stream. If you have created only one vertex buffer, this parameter is 0.
- **pStreamData.** The pointer to the variable that contains the vertex buffer.
- **OffsetInBytes.** The number of bytes from the start of the buffer where the vertex data is stored. This value is usually 0.
- **Stride.** The size of each vertex structure within the buffer.

An example call to SetStreamSource is shown next:

```
pd3dDevice->SetStreamSource ( 0, buffer, 0, sizeof(CUSTOMVERTEX) );
```

In this function call to SetStreamSource, the first parameter representing the stream number is set to 0. The second parameter must be a valid pointer to a properly created vertex buffer. The third parameter is set to 0, telling Direct3D to start at the beginning of the stream. The final parameter is the stride of the stream. This is set to the size in bytes of the CUSTOMVERTEX structure. The sizeof function calculates the number of bytes.

Setting the Vertex Shader

After you set the source for the stream, you must set the vertex shader. The vertex shader tells Direct3D which types of shading to apply. The SetFVF function, defined next, sets up Direct3D to use a fixed vertex function format.

```
HRESULT SetFVF(
        DWORD FVF
);
```

The SetFVF function requires only one parameter specified by the variable FVF. The FVF parameter accepts a value of type D3DFVF.

The following code sample shows how SetFVF is used.

```
HRESULT hr;
hr = pd3dDevice->SetFVF (D3DFVF_XYZRHW | D3DFVF_DIFFUSE);

// Check the return code to verify that SetFVF completed successfully
if FAILED (hr)
        return false;
```

This code sample passes the values D3DFVF_XYZRHW and D3DFVF_DIFFUSE as the parameter to SetFVF. As you'll recall, when the CUSTOMVERTEX structure was set up, it used these two values when creating the vertex buffer.

You must have already created a valid Direct3D device. It is referred to by the pd3dDevice variable.

Rendering the Vertex Buffer

Now that you have created the stream and associated it with the vertex buffer, you can render the vertices to the screen. The function needed to do this is DrawPrimitive, defined next. The DrawPrimitive function continues through the vertex buffer and renders its data to the screen.

```
HRESULT DrawPrimitive(
        D3DPRIMITIVETYPE PrimitiveType,
```

```
        UINT StartVertex,
        UINT PrimitiveCount
);
```

The DrawPrimitive function requires three parameters:

- **PrimitiveType.** The type of primitive to draw using the vertices within the stream
- **StartVertex.** The number of the first vertex in the stream
- **PrimitiveCount.** The number of primitives to render

The PrimitiveType parameter can be any of these enumerated values:

- **D3DPT_POINTLIST.** A series of individual, unconnected points
- **D3DPT_LINELIST.** Isolated lines
- **D3DPT_LINESTRIP.** A series of lines connected by a single vertex
- **D3DPT_TRIANGLELIST.** Isolated triangles consisting of three vertices
- **D3DPT_TRIANGLESTRIP.** A series of connected triangles where only one vertex is required for the definition of each additional triangle
- **D3DPT_TRIANGLEFAN.** A series of connected triangles that share a common vertex

The following code segment shows a call to DrawPrimitive using a triangle strip as the primitive type.

```
HRESULT hr;

// Call DrawPrimitive
hr = pd3dDevice->DrawPrimitive( D3DPT_TRIANGLESTRIP, 0, 1 );

// Check the return code to verify that the function was successful
if FAILED (hr)
return false;
```

The previous code sample tells Direct3D to render the vertices in the vertex buffer using a triangle strip described using the D3DPT_TRIANGLESTRIP type as the first parameter. The second parameter is set to 0, meaning that DrawPrimitive should start with the first vertex in the buffer. The last parameter is set to 1 because there were only enough vertices defined to create a single triangle.

A valid Direct3D device must exist. It is referred to by the pd3dDevice variable.

The full source for creating and rendering a vertex buffer is available in the chapter4\example1 directory on the CD-ROM.

Figure 4.8 shows the drawing of a single colored triangle.

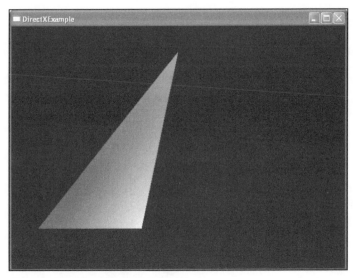

Figure 4.8 The output of Example 1.

Rendering a Scene

Before you can render 3D primitives, you must prepare Direct3D to render. The BeginScene function tells Direct3D that rendering is about to take place. Using the BeginScene function, Direct3D makes sure that the rendering surfaces are valid and ready. If the BeginScene function fails, your code should skip making rendering calls.

After rendering is done, you need to call the EndScene function. The EndScene function tells Direct3D that you are finished making rendering calls and the scene is ready to be presented to the back buffer.

The code that follows confirms the return codes from BeginScene and EndScene.

```
HRESULT hr;

if ( SUCCEEDED( pDevice->BeginScene( ) ) )
{
        // Render primitives only if the scene
        // starts successfully

        // Close the scene
        hr = pDevice->EndScene( );
        if ( FAILED ( hr ) )
                return hr;
}
```

The previous code confirms that the call to BeginScene is successful before allowing rendering to take place using the SUCCEEDED macro around the call. When rendering is complete, you call the EndScene function.

The next code sample shows what an example render function might look like.

```
/*************************************************************************
* render
*************************************************************************/
void render()
{
        // Clear the back buffer to black
        pd3dDevice->Clear( 0, NULL, D3DCLEAR_TARGET,
                                        D3DCOLOR_XRGB(0,0,0), 1.0f, 0 );

        // Tell Direct3D to begin the scene
        pd3dDevice->BeginScene();

        // Draw the contents of the vertex buffer
        // Set the data stream first
        pd3dDevice->SetStreamSource( 0, buffer, 0, sizeof(CUSTOMVERTEX) );
        // Set the Vertex format for the stream next
        pd3dDevice->SetFVF( D3DFVF_CUSTOMVERTEX );
        // Draw the vertices within the buffer using triangle strips
        pd3dDevice->DrawPrimitive( D3DPT_TRIANGLESTRIP, 0, 1 );

        // Tell Direct3D that drawing is complete
        pd3dDevice->EndScene();

        // copies the back buffer to the screen
        pd3dDevice->Present( NULL, NULL, NULL, NULL );
}
```

The render function takes all these steps and combines then into a single function. The pd3dDevice variable represents a valid Direct3D device created outside this function.

Primitive Types

Earlier, you had the option of setting the primitive type that DrawPrimitive would use to render the vertices within the vertex buffer. For the purpose of the previous example, I chose a triangle strip for its speed and ability to add additional triangles easily. This section explains in a little more detail the differences among the available primitive types.

Point List

A *point list* consists of a series of points that are not connected in any way. Figure 4.9 shows a grid containing four distinct points. Each point is defined using X, Y, and Z coordinates. For example, the top-left point would be defined as (1, 6, 0).

Line List

A *line list* consists of lines constructed by two points, one at each end. The lines within a line list are not connected. Figure 4.10 shows two lines rendered using a line list. This particular line list is constructed from four vertices. The line on the left is formed using (-6, 5, 0) for the upper coordinate and (-4, 2, 0) for the bottom coordinate.

Line Strip

A *line strip* is a series of connected lines in which each additional line is defined by a single vertex. Each vertex in the line strip is connected to the previous vertex for a line. Figure 4.11 shows how a line list is constructed and rendered. The line list in this figure is constructed using a series of six vertices, creating five lines.

Triangle List

A *triangle list* contains triangles that are not connected in any way and can appear anywhere within your world. Figure 4.12 shows two individual triangles constructed from six vertices. Each triangle requires three vertices to construct a complete triangle.

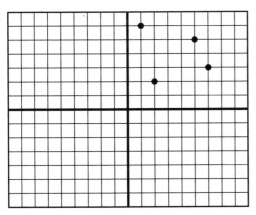

Figure 4.9 An example of rendered points using a point list.

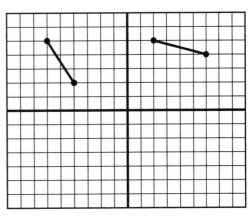

Figure 4.10 Lines rendered using a line list.

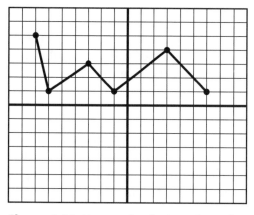

Figure 4.11 Lines rendered using a line strip.

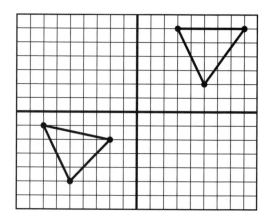

Figure 4.12 Triangles rendered using a triangle list.

Triangle Strip

A *triangle strip* is a series of triangles connected to one another in which only one vertex is required to define each additional triangle. Figure 4.13 shows four triangles created using only six vertices.

Triangle strips are constructed first by creating three vertices to define the first triangle. If an additional vertex is defined, lines are drawn between the two previously created vertices, forming another triangle. In Figure 4.13, the order of the vertices' creation is shown.

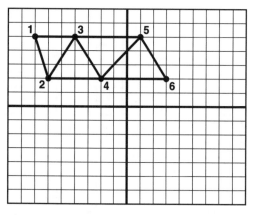

Figure 4.13 Triangles rendered using a triangle strip.

Triangle Fan

A *triangle fan* is a series of triangles that share a common vertex. After the first triangle is created, each additional vertex creates another triangle with one of its points being the first vertex defined.

Figure 4.14 shows how a triangle fan consisting of three triangles is created using only five vertices. The order of the vertices controls what the triangle fan looks like. Figure 4.14 shows the order of the vertices' creation needed to construct the displayed fan.

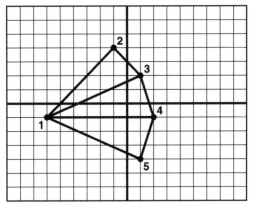

Figure 4.14 Triangles rendered using a triangle fan.

Chapter Summary

So far, you've only seen the basics of how 3D works. As the book progresses, you'll learn more advanced topics, but right now you should have a clear understanding of the virtues of vertex buffers.

Now that you have a basic understanding of how 3D space works and how to define objects within it, it's time to learn how to navigate within this world. In the next chapter, you'll learn how to rotate and move your objects.

What You Have Learned

In this chapter, you learned the following:

- The differences between 2D and 3D space
- What vertices are and how to define them
- How to create and use a vertex buffer

- How to render any number of vertices easily
- The different primitive types that Direct3D offers

Review Questions

You can find the answers to Review Questions and On Your Own exercises in Appendix A, "Answers to End-of-Chapter Exercises."

1. How is a point defined in a 3D coordinate system?
2. Which axis is commonly used to describe depth?
3. What does the SetFVF function do?
4. Which primitive type consists of a series of connected lines?
5. How many vertices are needed to create a triangle strip of five triangles?

On Your Own

1. Write a function to render a line list consisting of four lines.
2. Write a function to render multiple triangles using a triangle list.

CHAPTER 5

Matrices, Transforms, and Rotations

M ost beginners believe that matrices and 3D math are the most difficult part of learning graphics programming. This might have been true a couple of years ago, but it's not true anymore. Direct3D has advanced during that time and taken away a lot of the complexity, leaving programmers to focus more on how they want their games to work.

This chapter introduces you to matrices and shows you how easily they can be made to work for you instead of against you.

Here's what you'll learn in this chapter:

- What a 3D model is and how it's created
- How to optimize rendering by using index buffers
- What the geometry pipeline is and what its stages are
- What matrices are and how they affect your 3D world
- How D3DX can make your job easier
- What it takes to manipulate your objects within a scene
- How to create a virtual camera

Creating a 3D Model

Now that you've been introduced to drawing triangles, it's time to expand on that knowledge and create full 3D models. Almost everything in games is represented with 3D objects, from the character you play to the environment the character interacts with. A 3D object's complexity can range from a single polygon to thousands of polygons, depending on what the model represents. Full cities complete with cars, buildings, and people can be represented this way.

Although 3D objects might seem intimidating, it helps to think of them as just a series of connected triangles. By breaking down a model into its most primitive type, it becomes a little easier to grasp.

I'm going to take you through the steps you need to follow to create and render a cube. A cube isn't the most complicated object, but it does give you the basics you need to handle any 3D model.

Defining the Vertex Buffer

In Chapter 4, "3D Primer," you were introduced to vertex buffers as a clean and handy place for storing vertex information. As the complexity of the objects you're using grows, the convenience of vertex buffers will become more apparent. The vertex buffer is a great place to store object vertices, allowing you easy access and simple methods for rendering those vertices.

Your previous use of a vertex buffer needed only three vertices to create a triangle. Now that you'll be creating a more complicated object, you'll need to store more vertices.

When you're defining the vertices for a static object, consider storing them in an array. The array has a type of CUSTOMVERTEX, which, as you'll recall from Chapter 4, allows you to define the layout of your vertex data. Each element in the array holds all the information that Direct3D needs to describe a single vertex. Following is the code you need to define the vertices for a cube.

```
// a structure for your custom vertex type
struct CUSTOMVERTEX
{
    FLOAT x, y, z;    // the untransformed, 3D position for the vertex
    DWORD color;     // the color of the vertex
};

CUSTOMVERTEX g_Vertices[] =
{
    // 1
    { -64.0f,  64.0f, -64.0f, D3DCOLOR_ARGB(0,0,0,255)},
    {  64.0f,  64.0f, -64.0f, D3DCOLOR_ARGB(0,0,0,255)},
    { -64.0f, -64.0f, -64.0f, D3DCOLOR_ARGB(0,0,0,255)},
    {  64.0f, -64.0f, -64.0f, D3DCOLOR_ARGB(0,0,0,255)},

    // 2
```

```
{ -64.0f,   64.0f, 64.0f, D3DCOLOR_ARGB(0,0,0,255)},
{ -64.0f,  -64.0f, 64.0f, D3DCOLOR_ARGB(0,0,0,255)},
{  64.0f,   64.0f, 64.0f, D3DCOLOR_ARGB(0,0,0,255)},
{  64.0f,  -64.0f, 64.0f, D3DCOLOR_ARGB(0,0,0,255)},

// 3
{ -64.0f, 64.0f,  64.0f, D3DCOLOR_ARGB(0,0,0,255)},
{  64.0f, 64.0f,  64.0f, D3DCOLOR_ARGB(0,0,0,255)},
{ -64.0f, 64.0f, -64.0f, D3DCOLOR_ARGB(0,0,0,255)},
{  64.0f, 64.0f, -64.0f, D3DCOLOR_ARGB(0,0,0,255)},

// 4
{ -64.0f, -64.0f,  64.0f, D3DCOLOR_ARGB(0,0,0,255)},
{ -64.0f, -64.0f, -64.0f, D3DCOLOR_ARGB(0,0,0,255)},
{  64.0f, -64.0f,  64.0f, D3DCOLOR_ARGB(0,0,0,255)},
{  64.0f, -64.0f, -64.0f, D3DCOLOR_ARGB(0,0,0,255)},

// 5
{ 64.0f,  64.0f, -64.0f, D3DCOLOR_ARGB(0,0,0,255)},
{ 64.0f,  64.0f,  64.0f, D3DCOLOR_ARGB(0,0,0,255)},
{ 64.0f, -64.0f, -64.0f, D3DCOLOR_ARGB(0,0,0,255)},
{ 64.0f, -64.0f,  64.0f, D3DCOLOR_ARGB(0,0,0,255)},

// 6
{-64.0f,  64.0f, -64.0f, D3DCOLOR_ARGB(0,0,0,255)},
{-64.0f, -64.0f, -64.0f, D3DCOLOR_ARGB(0,0,0,255)},
{-64.0f,  64.0f,  64.0f, D3DCOLOR_ARGB(0,0,0,255)},
{-64.0f, -64.0f,  64.0f, D3DCOLOR_ARGB(0,0,0,255)},
};
```

The first thing the code does is to declare the layout of the CUSTOMVERTEX structure. This structure includes two sections: the position using the X, Y, and Z variables, and the color. After the structure is defined, the g_Vertices array is created and filled with the vertex data necessary to create a cube. The vertex data is split up into six sections, each one representing a side of the cube. Previously, you always used a value of 1.0f for the Z value in vertex declarations, which made your objects appear flat. Because the cube you are creating is a fully 3D model, the Z value is being used to define the distances of the vertices within the world.

The next step in the process is creating and filling the vertex buffer with the vertex data for the cube. The code that follows shows what is needed to do this.

```
// Create the vertex buffer
HRESULT hr;
```

```
LPDIRECT3DVERTEXBUFFER9 vertexBuffer;

// Create the vertex buffer that will store the cube's vertices
hr = pd3dDevice->CreateVertexBuffer(sizeof(g_Vertices) * sizeof(CUSTOMVERTEX),
                                    0,
                                    D3DFVF_CUSTOMVERTEX,
                                    D3DPOOL_DEFAULT,
                                    &vertexBuffer,
                                    NULL );

// Check the return code of CreateVertexBuffer call to make sure it succeeded
if FAILED (hr)
    return false;

// Prepare to copy the vertices into the vertex buffer
VOID* pVertices;

// Lock the vertex buffer
hr = vertexBuffer->Lock(0,
                        sizeof(g_Vertices),
                        (void**) &pVertices,
                        0);

// Check to make sure the vertex buffer can be locked
if FAILED (hr)
    return false;

// Copy the vertices into the buffer
memcpy ( pVertices, g_Vertices, sizeof(g_Vertices) );

// Unlock the vertex buffer
vertexBuffer->Unlock();
```

Using the call to CreateVertexBuffer creates the vertex buffer; its size and type are defined as well. Instead of specifically stating the size of the vertex buffer to create, I've used the sizeof function to calculate this at compile time. Multiply the size of the g_Vertices array by the size of the CUSTOMVERTEX structure to get the exact size that the vertex buffer needs to be to hold all the vertices.

The resulting buffer is then locked, and the vertices from the g_Vertices array are copied into it using the memcpy function.

Now that you have a filled vertex buffer, you are ready to draw your 3D object.

Rendering the Cube

Rendering the cube is just like drawing any other object from a vertex buffer, regardless of its complexity. The major difference separating a cube, a triangle, and a car is the number of vertices involved. After the object is stored in the vertex buffer, it's easy to render it.

The Render function shown here details the code needed to render the cube you defined in the g_Vertices array.

```
/***************************************************************************
* Render
***************************************************************************/
void Render(void)
{
    // Clear the back buffer to a white color
    pd3dDevice->Clear( 0,
                        NULL,
                        D3DCLEAR_TARGET,
                        D3DCOLOR_XRGB(255,255,255),
                        1.0f,
                        0 );

    pd3dDevice->BeginScene();

    // Set the vertex stream for the model
    pd3dDevice->SetStreamSource( 0, vertexBuffer, 0, sizeof(CUSTOMVERTEX) );

    // Set the vertex format
    pd3dDevice->SetFVF( D3DFVF_CUSTOMVERTEX );

    // Call DrawPrimitive to draw the cube
    pd3dDevice->DrawPrimitive( D3DPT_TRIANGLESTRIP,  0, 2 );
    pd3dDevice->DrawPrimitive( D3DPT_TRIANGLESTRIP,  4, 2 );
    pd3dDevice->DrawPrimitive( D3DPT_TRIANGLESTRIP,  8, 2 );
    pd3dDevice->DrawPrimitive( D3DPT_TRIANGLESTRIP, 12, 2 );
    pd3dDevice->DrawPrimitive( D3DPT_TRIANGLESTRIP, 16, 2 );
    pd3dDevice->DrawPrimitive( D3DPT_TRIANGLESTRIP, 20, 2 );

    pd3dDevice->EndScene();

    // Present the back buffer contents to the display
    pd3dDevice->Present( NULL, NULL, NULL, NULL );
}
```

The cube is rendered first by setting the vertex stream source and the vertex format. The biggest difference between drawing one triangle and drawing the multiple triangles required to render a 3D cube is the additional calls to DrawPrimitive. Each of the six DrawPrimitive calls renders a single side of the cube using the triangle strip primitive.

Figure 5.1 shows what the resulting cube looks like. The cube is rendered using wireframe so that you can see the triangles that go into its creation.

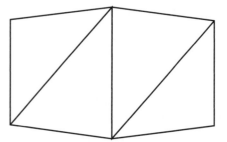

Figure 5.1 The full 3D cube.

Index Buffers

Index buffers are areas of memory that store index data. Each index in the buffer refers to a particular vertex with a vertex buffer. The indices reduce the amount of data that must be sent to the graphic card by sending only a single value for each vertex instead of the full X, Y, and Z data. The vertex data lives in the vertex buffer, and the values within the index buffer reference the vertex buffer.

You create index buffers, which are based on the IDirect3DIndexBuffer9 interface, by using the CreateIndexBuffer function, which is defined next.

```
HRESULT CreateIndexBuffer(
    UINT Length,
    DWORD Usage,
    D3DFORMAT Format,
    D3DPOOL Pool,
    IDirect3DIndexBuffer9** ppIndexBuffer,
    HANDLE* pHandle
);
```

The CreateIndexBuffer function requires six parameters:

- **Length.** The size of the index data in bytes.
- **Usage.** A value of type D3DUSAGE that details how the buffer is to be used.
- **Format.** The format of the buffer indices. You have two choices here: D3DFMT_INDEX16 or D3DFMT_INDEX32. D3DFMT_INDEX16 means the indices are 16 bits each, and D3DFMT_INDEX32 means the indices are 32 bits each.
- **Pool.** The type of memory to be used in the index buffer creation.
- **ppIndexBuffer.** An address to a pointer where the newly created index buffer will reside.
- **pHandle.** A reserved value that should be NULL.

A sample call to `CreateIndexBuffer` is shown here.

```
// Create the index buffer
hr = pd3dDevice->CreateIndexBuffer(sizeof(IndexData)*sizeof(WORD),
                                    D3DUSAGE_WRITEONLY,
                                    D3DFMT_INDEX16,
                                    D3DPOOL_DEFAULT,
                                    &iBuffer,
                                    NULL);
```

The `CreateIndexBuffer` call is similar to the `CreateVertexBuffer` function you've used before. The major difference between the two functions is the third parameter, which specifies the format of the indices that will be in the buffer. You have the option of 16- or 32-bit indices, which allows you to define your indices as either `WORD` or `DWORD` types.

Previously, I showed you how to create a cube using vertex buffers. The cube required 24 overlapping vertices to create 12 triangles. Using index buffers, you can create the same cube using only eight vertices. The next section shows you how to do this.

Generating a Cube by Using Index Buffers

The first step to creating a cube using index buffers is to define the vertices and the indices that will go into making up the model you're trying to create. As before when you were creating an object using vertex buffers, it's easiest to define the values in an array.

You define the vertices first, again using the `CUSTOMVERTEX` type you created previously. Each vertex has an `X`, `Y`, and `Z` value as well as a color component.

```
/ vertices for the vertex buffer
CUSTOMVERTEX g_Vertices[ ] = {
    // X      Y     Z     U     V
    {-1.0f,-1.0f,-1.0f, D3DCOLOR_ARGB(0,0,0,255)},    // 0
    {-1.0f, 1.0f,-1.0f, D3DCOLOR_ARGB(0,0,0,255)},    // 1
    {1.0f, 1.0f,-1.0f,  D3DCOLOR_ARGB(0,0,0,255)},    // 2
    { 1.0f,-1.0f,-1.0f, D3DCOLOR_ARGB(0,0,0,255)},    // 3
    {-1.0f,-1.0f, 1.0f, D3DCOLOR_ARGB(0,0,0,255)},    // 4
    {1.0f,-1.0f, 1.0f,  D3DCOLOR_ARGB(0,0,0,255)},    // 5
    { 1.0f, 1.0f, 1.0f, D3DCOLOR_ARGB(0,0,0,255)},    // 6
    {-1.0f, 1.0f, 1.0f, D3DCOLOR_ARGB(0,0,0,255)}     // 7
};
```

After you have the vertices defined, the next step is to generate the indices. The indices, like the vertices, are defined and stored in an array. Remember when I mentioned that the format of the indices could be 16 or 32 bits? This is where that choice comes into play.

The following code shows the array of indices that will go into creating the cube.

```
// index buffer data
WORD IndexData[ ] = {
        0,1,2,                    // triangle 1
        2,3,0,                    // triangle 2
        4,5,6,                    // triangle 3
        6,7,4,                    // triangle 4
        0,3,5,                    // triangle 5
        5,4,0,                    // triangle 6
        3,2,6,                    // triangle 7
        6,5,3,                    // triangle 8
        2,1,7,                    // triangle 9
        7,6,2,                    // triangle 10
        1,0,4,                    // triangle 11
        4,7,1                     // triangle 12
};
```

The previous IndexData array has split 36 indices into 12 groups, each consisting of 3 values that make up a triangle. Twelve triangles are needed to make a cube, using two triangles per face.

note

> Remember: If you are tight on memory and your model doesn't require a DWORD type for your indices, use a WORD type instead.

Creating and Filling the Index Buffer

Now that the values you need for the index buffer have been defined, you need to copy them into the index buffer. This process is similar to copying vertices into a vertex buffer.

First, you lock the index buffer by using the Lock function. From there, you copy the indices into the buffer by using the memcpy function and then unlock the buffer. The result is an index buffer that contains the indices you need to render the cube.

The following code shows the process of creating and filling an index buffer with data.

```
// the index buffer
LPDIRECT3DINDEXBUFFER9 iBuffer;
HRESULT hr;


// Create the index buffer
```

```
hr = pd3dDevice->CreateIndexBuffer(sizeof(IndexData)*sizeof(WORD),
                                   D3DUSAGE_WRITEONLY,
                                   D3DFMT_INDEX16,
                                   D3DPOOL_DEFAULT,
                                   &iBuffer,
                                   NULL);

// Check to make sure the index buffer was created successfully
if FAILED(hr)
    return false;

// Prepare to copy the indexes into the index buffer
VOID* IndexPtr;

// Lock the index buffer
hr = iBuffer ->Lock(0, 0, (void**)& IndexPtr, D3DLOCK_DISCARD);

// Check to make sure the index buffer can be locked
if FAILED (hr)
    return hr;

// Copy the indices into the buffer
memcpy( pVertices, IndexData, sizeof(IndexData) );

// Unlock the index buffer
iBuffer->Unlock();
```

After the index buffer is filled with data, you can use the vertex and index data together to render your object.

Rendering the Cube with Index Buffers

Before, when you were drawing using vertex buffers, you used the DrawPrimitive function. The DrawPrimitive function used the data in the vertex buffer to create primitives, such as triangle strips and triangle lists. You can draw in a similar way using index buffers and the DrawIndexedPrimitive function.

The DrawIndexedPrimitive function uses an index buffer as its data source and renders graphic primitives to draw your 3D objects. The DrawIndexedPrimitive function is defined here.

```
HRESULT DrawIndexedPrimitive(
    D3DPRIMITIVETYPE Type,
    INT BaseVertexIndex,
```

```
    UINT MinIndex,
    UINT NumVertices,
    UINT StartIndex,
    UINT PrimitiveCount
);
```

The `DrawIndexedPrimitive` function takes six parameters:

- **Type.** The primitive type to use when rendering the index data
- **BaseVertexIndex.** The starting index within the vertex buffer
- **MinIndex.** The minimum vertex index for this call
- **NumVertices.** The number of vertices that are used in this call
- **StartIndex.** The location in the vertex array to start reading vertices
- **PrimitiveCount.** The number of primitives to draw

Figure 5.2 shows a cube rendered in wireframe mode with the edge vertices highlighted. The edge vertices demonstrate the vertices referred to in the index buffers.

```
// Set the indices to use
m_pd3dDevice->SetIndices( iBuffer );
```

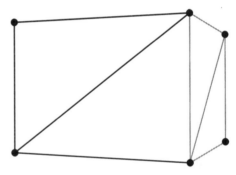

Figure 5.2 A cube with edge vertices highlighted.

```
// Call DrawIndexedPrimitive to draw the
object using the indices
m_pd3dDevice->DrawIndexedPrimitive( D3DPT_TRIANGLELIST,
                        0, // BaseVertexIndex
                        0, // MinIndex
                        numVertices, // NumVertices
                        0, // StartIndex
                        numFaces ); // primitive count
```

Right before the call to `DrawIndexedPrimitive` is the `SetIndices` function. The `SetIndices` function, defined next, tells Direct3D which index buffer is going to be used as the data source when drawing. The `SetIndices` function works in much the same way as the `SetStreamSource` function does when you're drawing with vertex buffers.

```
HRESULT SetIndices(
    IDirect3DIndexBuffer9 *pIndexData
);
```

The `SetIndices` function requires only a single parameter: a pointer to an index buffer containing valid index data.

The Geometry Pipeline

So far you've been using pretransformed coordinates to draw your objects to the screen. That means that the object's position is basically predefined in screen coordinates. This really restricts the size of the world and the movement of the objects within it.

3D models are for the most part created outside of your game code. For instance, if you're creating a racing game, you'll probably create the car models in a 3D art package. During the creation process, these models will be working off of the coordinate system provided to them in the modeler. This causes the objects to be created with a set of vertices that aren't necessarily going to place the car model exactly where and how you want it in your game environment. Because of this, you will need to move and rotate the model yourself. You can do this by using the geometry pipeline. The *geometry pipeline* is a process that allows you to transform an object from one coordinate system into another.

When a model first starts out, it is normally centered on the origin. This causes the model to be centered in the environment with a default orientation. Not every model you load needs to be at the origin, so how do you get models where they need to be? The answer to that is through transformations. Figure 5.3 shows a cube centered on the origin.

Transformations refer to the actions of translating (moving), rotating, and scaling 3D objects. By applying these actions to a model, you can make the model appear to move around. These actions are handled through the geometry pipeline.

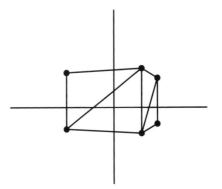

Figure 5.3 A cube centered on the origin.

Figure 5.4 shows the different stages of the geometry pipeline.

When you load a model, its vertices are in a local coordinate system called model space. *Model space* refers to the coordinate system on which the model is based that is independent of the rest of the world. For instance, upon creation, a model's vertices are in reference to the origin point around which they were created. A cube that is 2 units in size centered on the origin would have its vertices 1 unit on either side of the origin. If you then wanted to place this cube somewhere within your game, you would need to transform its vertices from the cube's local coordinate system into the system used by all the objects in your world. This world coordinate system is called *world space*, and the process of transforming vertices into this system is called *world transformation*.

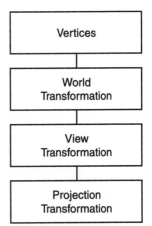

Figure 5.4 The stages of the geometry pipeline.

World Transformation

The world transformation stage of the geometry pipeline takes an existing object with its own local coordinate system and transforms that object into the world coordinate system. The world coordinate system is the system that places all objects within the 3D world in their proper locations. The world system has a single origin point that all models that are transformed into this system then become relative to. Figure 5.5 shows multiple objects within a 3D scene relative to the world origin point.

The next stage of the geometry pipeline is the view transformation. Because all objects at this point are relative to a single origin, you can only view them from this point. To allow you to view the scene from any arbitrary point, the objects must go through a view transformation.

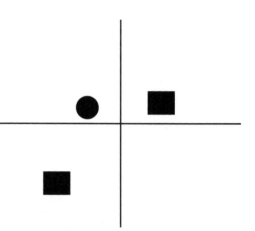

Figure 5.5 Multiple objects relative to a single world system origin point.

View Transformation

The *view transformation* transforms the coordinates from world space into camera space. *Camera space* refers to the coordinate system that is relative to the position of a virtual camera. When you choose a point of view for your virtual camera, the coordinates in world space get reoriented in respect to the camera.

note

I've been saying "virtual camera" instead of "camera" because the concept of a camera in 3D doesn't really exist. By either moving the virtual camera up along the Y axis or by moving the entire world down along that same axis, you obtain the same visual results.

At this point, you have the camera angle and view for your scene, and you're ready to display it to the screen.

Projection Transformation

The next stage in the geometry pipeline is the projection transformation. The projection transformation is the stage of the pipeline where depth is applied. When you cause objects that are closer to the camera to appear larger than those farther away, you create an illusion of depth.

Finally, the vertices are scaled to the viewport and projected into 2D space. The resulting 2D image appears on your monitor with the illusion of being a 3D scene. Table 5.1 shows the types of transformations within the geometry pipeline and the types of spaces each one affects.

Table 5.1   Coordinate System Transformations

Transformation Type	From Space	To Space
World transformation	Model space	World space
View transformation world space	View space	
Projection transformation	View space	Projection space

What Is a Matrix?

A matrix, in simplest terms, is an array of numbers that are arranged in columns and rows. Shown here is a simple 4×4 matrix containing the values 1 through 16.

1	2	3	4
5	6	7	8
9	10	11	12
13	14	15	16

Matrices are used within 3D to represent the transformations needed to move objects between coordinate spaces. The values that are contained in matrices are used to translate, rotate, and scale objects. Each row in the matrix represents the world coordinate of each axis. The first row contains the coordinate position of the X axis, the second row contains the Y axis position, and the third row contains the Z axis position.

Each position in the matrix represents a portion of a transformation.

For instance, positions 13, 14, and 15 hold the current X, Y, and Z position of a vertex. Positions 1, 6, and 11 contain the scaling values.

A matrix can be defined in code like this:

```
float matrix [4][4] = {
1.0f, 0.0f, 0.0f, 0.0f,
0.0f, 1.0f, 0.0f, 0.0f,
0.0f, 0.0f, 1.0f, 0.0f,
2.0f, 3.0f, 2.0f, 1.0f
};
```

The final row of the previous matrix places the object with an X value of 2.0f, a Y value of 3.0f, and a Z value of 2.0f.

The Identity Matrix

The identity matrix is the default matrix that centers an object about the world origin and sets the object's scaling to 1. When you place a value of 1.0f in the 1, 6, and 11 positions, an object scaling of 1.0f is generated. Positions 13, 14, and 15 hold a value of 0.0f.

Following is an identity matrix.

```
float IdentityMatrix [4][4] = {
1.0f, 0.0f, 0.0f, 0.0f,
0.0f, 1.0f, 0.0f, 0.0f,
0.0f, 0.0f, 1.0f, 0.0f,
0.0f, 0.0f, 0.0f, 1.0f
};
```

If you ever need to get an object back to the world origin, you can translate the object's vertices by the identity matrix. The object is returned to the origin with no rotation or scaling applied. You are then free to move the object anywhere within your world.

Initializing a Matrix

Initializing or updating a matrix is as simple as changing individual values within the array. For instance, if you were given the identity matrix shown earlier and wanted to apply a translation to move an object 5 units along the X axis and 3 units along the Y axis, you would update the matrix like this:

```
Matrix[0][4] = 5.0f;
Matrix[1][4] = 3.0f;
Matrix[2][4] = 0.0f;
```

The resulting updated matrix would look like this.

```
float Matrix [4][4] = {
1.0f, 0.0f, 0.0f, 0.0f,
0.0f, 1.0f, 0.0f, 0.0f,
0.0f, 0.0f, 1.0f, 0.0f,
5.0f, 3.0f, 0.0f, 1.0f
};
```

The resulting matrix then contains the needed values to transform an object by the required units.

Multiply Matrices

You're probably wondering how the matrices affect the vertices within an object. Well, each vertex in the object is multiplied individually by the matrix, resulting in a transformed vertex.

The math involved in this is fairly simple. To get the transformed X vertex, each value in the first row of the matrix is multiplied by each portion of the original vertex. The results from each of these multiplications are totaled to get the final transformed vertex. The complete method for this process is shown here.

X		A	B	C	D		AX + BY + CZ + DW		X (transformed)
Y		E	F	G	H		EX + FY + GZ + HW		Y (transformed)
Z	×	I	J	K	L	=	IX + JY + KZ + LW	=	Z (transformed)
W		M	N	O	P		MX + NY + OZ + PW		W (transformed)

The far-left column shows the matrix that the vertex will be transformed by. The next column represents the vertex being transformed. The third column demonstrates the matrix being multiplied by the vertex. The final column on the right shows the resulting transformed vertex.

As you can see, multiplying a matrix by a vector is pretty straightforward, although multiplying two matrices can get a little complicated. You can accomplish matrix multiplication by multiplying the values in each row of the first matrix by the values in each column in the second. The key to multiplying matrices is to do it one step at a time to simplify the process.

Here's a simple example to demonstrate matrix multiplication. First you define the two matrices side by side. Letters represent the values in the first matrix, whereas numbers represents the values in the second matrix. This makes it easier to describe the math involved.

A	B	C	D		1	2	3	4
E	F	G	H		5	6	7	8
I	J	K	L	×	9	10	11	12
M	N	O	P		13	14	15	16

You start by multiplying each value from the rows in the first matrix by the values in the columns of the second matrix. Through the multiplication process, you are going to end up creating a third output matrix that will contain the results of the multiplication.

The first value in the output matrix is calculated like this:

$$A \times 1 + B \times 5 + C \times 9 + D \times 13$$

You need to perform four multiplies just to gain a single value for the output matrix. You calculate the successive values for the output matrix by continuing to follow this pattern.

At this point, you're probably thinking that the math and data involved will get daunting pretty quickly. Direct3D tries to help by defining its own matrix data type.

note

Matrix multiplication is not cumulative. Multiplying Matrix A by Matrix B does not result in the same output matrix as multiplying Matrix B by Matrix A. The order in which matrices are multiplied is important.

How Direct3D Defines a Matrix

Until now, you've been defining a matrix by using a 4 × 4 array of float values. Direct3D simplifies this for you by providing the D3DMATRIX data type, defined here.

```
typedef struct _D3DMATRIX {
    union {
        struct {
        float        _11, _12, _13, _14;
        float        _21, _22, _23, _24;
        float        _31, _32, _33, _34;
        float        _41, _42, _43, _44;
        };
        float m[4][4];
    };
} D3DMATRIX;
```

By using the D3DMATRIX data type that Direct3D provides, you are given a host of common functions for performing tasks such as initializing new matrices.

D3DX Makes Matrices Easier

Previously, you were introduced to the D3DMATRIX data type that Direct3D provides. It helps to simplify the definition and maintenance of matrices but still leaves you to perform all the calculations yourself; this is where the D3DX utility library can help.

The D3DX library declares the D3DXMATRIX data type. The values within the D3DXMATRIX structure are identical to those found in a D3DMATRIX structure, but the D3DXMATRIX type gives you an added bonus. It provides some built-in functions for handling matrix calculations and comparisons.

The D3DXMATRIX type is defined here.

```
typedef struct D3DXMATRIX : public D3DMATRIX {
public:
    D3DXMATRIX() {};
```

```
        D3DXMATRIX( CONST FLOAT * );
        D3DXMATRIX( CONST D3DMATRIX& );
        D3DXMATRIX( FLOAT _11, FLOAT _12, FLOAT _13, FLOAT _14,
                    FLOAT _21, FLOAT _22, FLOAT _23, FLOAT _24,
                    FLOAT _31, FLOAT _32, FLOAT _33, FLOAT _34,
                    FLOAT _41, FLOAT _42, FLOAT _43, FLOAT _44 );

        // access grants
        FLOAT& operator () ( UINT Row, UINT Col );
        FLOAT  operator () ( UINT Row, UINT Col ) const;

        // casting operators
        operator FLOAT* ();
        operator CONST FLOAT* () const;

        // assignment operators
        D3DXMATRIX& operator *= ( CONST D3DXMATRIX& );
        D3DXMATRIX& operator += ( CONST D3DXMATRIX& );
        D3DXMATRIX& operator -= ( CONST D3DXMATRIX& );
        D3DXMATRIX& operator *= ( FLOAT );
        D3DXMATRIX& operator /= ( FLOAT );

        // unary operators
        D3DXMATRIX operator + () const;
        D3DXMATRIX operator - () const;

        // binary operators
        D3DXMATRIX operator * ( CONST D3DXMATRIX& ) const;
        D3DXMATRIX operator + ( CONST D3DXMATRIX& ) const;
        D3DXMATRIX operator - ( CONST D3DXMATRIX& ) const;
        D3DXMATRIX operator * ( FLOAT ) const;
        D3DXMATRIX operator / ( FLOAT ) const;

        friend D3DXMATRIX operator * ( FLOAT, CONST D3DXMATRIX& );

        BOOL operator == ( CONST D3DXMATRIX& ) const;
        BOOL operator != ( CONST D3DXMATRIX& ) const;
} D3DXMATRIX, *LPD3DXMATRIX;
```

The first thing you'll probably notice about the D3DXMATRIX type is that it's a structure that inherits from D3DMATRIX and includes functions that make it appear like a C++ class.

Because of the way this type is defined, you can only access it through C++, and it's treated as a full class with only public member functions.

If you look through the structure, you'll see functions that overload a lot of the assignment and comparison operators, as well as those used for calculating matrix operations. Because the D3DXMATRIX data structure is so much more useful, I'll continue to use it throughout the examples.

Manipulating 3D Objects by Using Matrices

Now that you know what matrices are, I'm going to tell you how they can be useful. You use matrices when you're manipulating objects in a scene. Whether you want to move an object around or just rotate it, you'll need matrices to do the job.

D3DX provides multiple functions that make manipulating objects easier by using matrices. I've listed a few of them here.

- **D3DXMatrixIdentity.** Resets a matrix to the origin
- **D3DXMatrixRotationX.** Rotates an object around the X axis
- **D3DXMatrixRotationY.** Rotates an object around the Y axis
- **D3DXMatrixScaling.** Scales an object by a specified amount
- **D3DXMatrixTranslation.** Moves an object along one or more axes

Moving an Object Around

To move an object around in your game world, you must translate it. *Translation* refers to the movement of an object along one or more of the coordinate system axes. If you wanted to move an object in your scene to the right, you would have to translate it along the X axis in a positive direction.

Translation of objects is handled through the D3DXMatrixTranslation function, defined next.

```
D3DXMATRIX *D3DXMatrixTranslation(
    D3DXMATRIX *pOut,
    FLOAT x,
    FLOAT y,
    FLOAT z
);
```

The D3DXMatrixTranslation function requires just four parameters.

- **pOut.** The output matrix. This parameter is a pointer to a D3DXMATRIX object.
- **x.** The amount to translate the object along the X axis. This can be a positive or a negative value.

- **y.** The amount to translate the object along the Y axis.
- **z.** The amount to translate the object along the Z axis.

The small sample of code that follows shows how to use the `D3DXMatrixTranslation` function.

```
D3DXMATRIX matTranslate;
D3DXMATRIX matFinal;

// Set the matFinal matrix to the identity
D3DXMatrixIdentity(&matFinal);

// Translate the object 64 units to the right of the origin along the X axis
// The resulting translated matrix is stored in the matTranslate variable
D3DXMatrixTranslation(&matTranslate, 64.0f, 0.0f, 0.0f);

// Multiply the translation and identity matrix together to get the final
// translated matrix stored in the finalMat variable
D3DXMatrixMultiply(&finalMat, &finalMat, & matTranslate);

// Transform the object in world space
pd3dDevice->SetTransform(D3DTS_WORLD, &finalMat);
```

The `D3DXMatrixTranslation` function is being used to translate an object 64 units to the right along the X axis. To apply the translation to the object, multiply the translation matrix by the identity matrix; then the object will be transformed into world space.

Rotating an Object

Being able to move an object along the axes is nice, but you're really limiting what your game can do. What fun would a racing game be if you couldn't drive the car around the track because the car was restricted to moving only in straight lines? That is why you need rotation. Being able to rotate the car enables it to make turns and follow the curves of the track.

Rotating 3D objects works alongside translation to give your characters freedom of movement within their environment. Rotation allows wheels on cars to spin, an arm to swing at the side of your character, or a baseball to curve right before it goes over the plate.

Rotating is the process of spinning an object around a coordinate system axis. Because rotation takes place using matrices, the D3DX library provides some helper functions to make rotating easier.

Rotation occurs along a single axis at any one time and can take place on any of the three axes. D3DX provides a specific rotation function to handle rotating around each axis. For instance, if you wanted to rotate an object around the X axis, you would use the function D3DXMatrixRotationX, defined here.

```
D3DXMATRIX *D3DXMatrixRotationX(
    D3DXMATRIX *pOut,
    FLOAT Angle
);
```

The D3DXMatrixRotationX function takes just two parameters:

- **pOut.** A pointer to a D3DXMATRIX object. This holds the resulting rotation matrix.
- **Angle.** The angle, in radians, to rotate the object.

Using the D3DXMatrixRotationX function or any of its derivatives is simple. First, define a D3DXMATRIX structure to hold the rotation matrix, and then input the angle to rotate the object. The short code that follows shows how easy this function is to use.

```
D3DXMATRIX matRotate;                       // This is the output matrix
D3DXMatrixRotationX(&matRotate, D3DXToRadian(45.0f));
```

You define the output matrix and then call the D3DXMatrixRotationX function. You'll notice that the second parameter is using a helper macro called D3DXToRadian. This macro takes an angle from 0 to 360 and converts it to radians. In the previous example, the angle of rotation is 45 degrees.

The result of this rotation is the object rotating around the X axis by 45 degrees.

Figure 5.6 shows how a cube that is rotating around the Y axis behaves.

The following code shows what you need to rotate a cube around the Y axis. The rotation is based on a timer that allows the cube to rotate continuously.

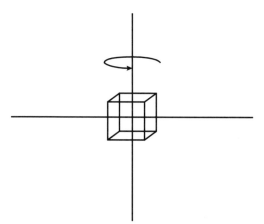

Figure 5.6 A cube rotating around the Y axis.

```
/**********************************************************************
* render
**********************************************************************/
void render(void)
{
```

```
D3DXMATRIX objMat, matRotate, finalMat;

// Clear the back buffer to a black color
pd3dDevice->Clear( 0,
                   NULL,
                   D3DCLEAR_TARGET,
                   D3DCOLOR_XRGB(255,255,255),
                   1.0f,
                   0 );

pd3dDevice->BeginScene();

// Set the vertex stream
pd3dDevice->SetStreamSource( 0, vertexBuffer, 0, sizeof(CUSTOMVERTEX) );
// Set up the vertex format for the object
pd3dDevice->SetFVF( D3DFVF_CUSTOMVERTEX );

// Set meshMat to identity
D3DXMatrixIdentity(&objMat);

// Set the rotation
D3DXMatrixRotationY(&matRotate, timeGetTime()/1000.0f);

// Multiply the scaling and rotation matrices to create the objMat matrix
D3DXMatrixMultiply(&finalMat, &objMat, &matRotate);

// Transform the object in world space
pd3dDevice->SetTransform(D3DTS_WORLD, &finalMat);

// Render the cube using triangle strips
pd3dDevice->DrawPrimitive( D3DPT_TRIANGLESTRIP,  0, 2 );
pd3dDevice->DrawPrimitive( D3DPT_TRIANGLESTRIP,  4, 2 );
pd3dDevice->DrawPrimitive( D3DPT_TRIANGLESTRIP,  8, 2 );
pd3dDevice->DrawPrimitive( D3DPT_TRIANGLESTRIP, 12, 2 );
pd3dDevice->DrawPrimitive( D3DPT_TRIANGLESTRIP, 16, 2 );
pd3dDevice->DrawPrimitive( D3DPT_TRIANGLESTRIP, 20, 2 );

pd3dDevice->EndScene();

// Present the back buffer contents to the display
pd3dDevice->Present( NULL, NULL, NULL, NULL );
}
```

Three variables are declared at the start of the render function: objMat, matRotate, and finalMat. These variables are the matrices that will store the cube's transformations. Earlier I showed you how to reset a matrix to represent the origin by setting it to the identity matrix; the objMat matrix will need to be reset each time the render function is called. This causes the rotations that you will apply to the cube to be centered on the origin. This is accomplished by using the D3DXMatrixIdentity function. The objMat matrix represents the actual position of the cube.

```
D3DXMatrixIdentity(&objMat);
```

The second matrix, matRotate, holds the rotation information for the cube. Because the cube is going to be in continuous motion, you must update the matRotate matrix each frame with the new position. The rotation takes place by using D3DXMatrixRotationY, which is one of the D3DX helper functions. The D3DX rotation functions overwrite the matrix each frame with the new rotation information, so you don't need to call the D3DXMatrixIdentity function to reset this matrix.

```
D3DXMatrixRotationY(&matRotate, timeGetTime()/1000.0f);
```

The timeGetTime function uses the current time divided by 1000.0f to allow the cube to rotate in a smooth manner.

Now that you have two matrices—one representing the position of the object and the other representing its movement—you need to multiply the two matrices to create the final matrix represented by the finalMat variable.

The resulting matrix transforms the cube into world space by using the SetTransform function shown here.

```
pd3dDevice->SetTransform(D3DTS_WORLD, &finalMat);
```

The SetTransform function results in the cube being placed in its new position and orientation in world space. The render function draws the cube by using multiple calls to the DrawPrimitive function.

You can find the full source code for rotating an object in the chapter5\example2 directory on the CD-ROM. Examples 1 and 2 make use of a set of camera functions covered later in this chapter.

Center of Rotation

The center of an object's rotation is based on the axis it is rotating around. If an object, such as the cube in Figure 5.6, were rotated, its center of rotation would cause it to spin around the origin. If an object were translated away from the origin and along one of the axes, its center of rotation would remain along the same axes and the object would be translated to a new position during the rotation.

Look at Figure 5.7, which shows a cube translated along the X and Y axis before being rotated. When the cube in this figure is rotated along the X axis, the object is translated while the rotation occurs.

To change an object's center of rotation, you must translate the object away from the origin before you apply rotation. The following code shows how to translate an object so that you can change the center of rotation.

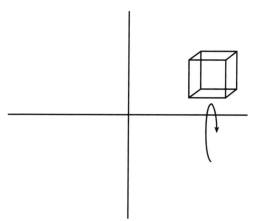

Figure 5.7 A cube being rotated around the X axis after being translated away from the origin.

```
/**************************************************************************
* render
**************************************************************************/
void render(void)
{
    // Clear the back buffer to a black color
    pd3dDevice->Clear( 0,
                       NULL,
                       D3DCLEAR_TARGET,
                       D3DCOLOR_XRGB(255,255,255),
                       1.0f,
                       0 );

    pd3dDevice->BeginScene();

    pd3dDevice->SetStreamSource( 0, vertexBuffer, 0, sizeof(CUSTOMVERTEX) );
    pd3dDevice->SetFVF( D3DFVF_CUSTOMVERTEX );

    // Translate the object away from the origin
    D3DXMatrixTranslation(&matTranslate, 64.0f, 0.0f, 0.0f);

    // Set the rotation
    D3DXMatrixRotationY(&matRotate, timeGetTime()/1000.0f);

    // Multiply the translation and rotation matrices to create the objMat matrix
    D3DXMatrixMultiply(&objMat, &matTranslate, &matRotate);
```

```
// Transform the object in world space
pd3dDevice->SetTransform(D3DTS_WORLD, &objMat);

pd3dDevice->DrawPrimitive( D3DPT_TRIANGLESTRIP,  0, 2 );
pd3dDevice->DrawPrimitive( D3DPT_TRIANGLESTRIP,  4, 2 );
pd3dDevice->DrawPrimitive( D3DPT_TRIANGLESTRIP,  8, 2 );
pd3dDevice->DrawPrimitive( D3DPT_TRIANGLESTRIP, 12, 2 );
pd3dDevice->DrawPrimitive( D3DPT_TRIANGLESTRIP, 16, 2 );
pd3dDevice->DrawPrimitive( D3DPT_TRIANGLESTRIP, 20, 2 );

pd3dDevice->EndScene();

// Present the back buffer contents to the display
pd3dDevice->Present( NULL, NULL, NULL, NULL );
}
```

The biggest change to the render function is the addition of the D3DXMatrixTranslation function. The D3DXMatrixTranslation function moves the cube 64 units away from the origin during the rotation.

In this case, the cube is being translated away from the origin along the X axis and then rotated. Two matrices are being used to move the cube: matTranslate and matRotate. The two matrices are then multiplied together to create the objMat matrix, which holds the final position of the cube. The result is the cube rotating away from the origin.

Scaling

Scaling allows you to change the size of an object by multiplying each vertex within the object by a specified amount. To perform scaling on an object, you need to create a matrix that contains the values by which to scale the object. The scaled values detail just how much to scale each vertex. Remember the matrix layout from earlier? The positions 1, 6, and 11 hold the scaling amounts for the X, Y, and Z axes, respectively. By default, these values are 1.0f and the object remains its original size. Changing any of these values affects the size of the object. If the values that are placed in these spots are greater than 1.0f, the object will be enlarged; alternatively, if the values are less than 1.0f, the object can be shrunk.

X	2	3	4
5	Y	7	8
9	10	Z	12
13	14	15	16

As I mentioned previously, scaling takes place by manipulating values within a matrix. To create a scaling matrix, simply define an identity matrix and change the values in the positions I detailed earlier. You can either change these values manually or use the D3DXMatrixScaling function, defined here.

```
D3DXMATRIX *D3DXMatrixScaling(
    D3DXMATRIX *pOut,
    FLOAT sx,
    FLOAT sy,
    FLOAT sz
);
```

The D3DXMatrixScaling function takes four parameters:

- **pOut.** A pointer to a D3DXMATRIX object that will hold the scaling matrix
- **sx.** The amount to scale the X vertices
- **sy.** The amount to scale the Y vertices
- **sz.** The amount to scale the Z vertices

The code sample that follows shows how to use the D3DXMatrixScaling function to double the size of an object.

```
D3DXMATRIX matScale;

// Set the scaling
D3DXMatrixScaling(&matScale, 2.0f, 2.0f, 2.0f);

// Multiply the object's matrix against the scaling matrix
D3DXMatrixMultiply(&objMat, & objMat, &matScaling);
```

The objMat variable in the previous code represents the object's original matrix. Multiplying the object's matrix by a scaling matrix enables you to scale the object when you draw it.

Order of Matrix Operations

The order in which matrix operations are applied is important. For instance, if you want to rotate an object around its center and then move the object somewhere in your world, you first must apply the rotation matrix operation followed by the translation matrix. If these two matrix operations were reversed, the object would first be translated into its new position in the world and then rotated around the world's origin point. This could cause your object to be in the wrong place and orientation within your world. The code that follows shows how an object should be rotated and translated correctly.

```
D3DXMATRIX objRotate;
D3DXMATRIX objTranslation;
```

```
D3DXMATRIX objFinal;

// Set the rotation
D3DXMatrixRotationY(&objRotate, D3DXToRadian(45));

// Apply the translation matrix
D3DXMatrixTranslation(&objTranslation, 1.0f, 0.0f, 0.0f);

// Multiply the rotation and translation matrices to create the final matrix
D3DXMatrixMultiply(&objFinal, &objRotate, &objTranslation);

// Transform the object in world space
pd3dDevice->SetTransform(D3DTS_WORLD, &objFinal);
```

The first step is to create the object's rotation matrix, objRatate. Using the D3DXMatrixRotationY function, the object is made to rotate 45 degrees around the Y axis.

Next, you translate the rotated object 1 unit to the right using the D3DXMatrixTranslation function.

Finally, you create the object's final transformed matrix by multiplying the rotation and translation matrices together using the D3DXMatrixMultiply function. If the rotation and translation matrices were to reverse positions in the D3DXMatrixMultiply call, the translation would take place before the rotation, dislocating the object.

Creating a Camera by Using Projections

You create a camera in Direct3D by defining a matrix for the projection transformation. This matrix defines the field of view (FOV) for the camera, the aspect ratio, and the near and far clipping planes.

After you've created the projection matrix, you apply it to your scene through the SetTransform function. You've probably noticed the SetTransform function used in the sample code earlier in this chapter. The SetTransform function, defined next, sets a matrix to a particular stage of the geometry pipeline. For instance, when you're setting the matrix for a camera, you are setting how the scene is going to be viewed during the projection stage. This stage, as the final part of the geometry pipeline, controls how the 3D scene is rendered to the 2D display.

```
HRESULT SetTransform(
    D3DTRANSFORMSTATETYPE State,
    CONST D3DMATRIX *pMatrix
);
```

The SetTransform function requires two parameters:

- **State.** The stage of the pipeline that is being modified
- **pMatrix.** A pointer to a D3DMATRIX structure that is to be applied to the pipeline

The code sample that follows shows how to create and define a matrix to be used for the projection stage.

```
D3DXMATRIX matProj;                                    // the projection matrix
/**********************************************************************
 * createCamera
 * creates a virtual camera
 **********************************************************************/
void createCamera(float nearClip, float farClip)
{
    // Here, you specify the field of view, aspect ratio,
    // and near and far clipping planes
    D3DXMatrixPerspectiveFovLH(&matProj, D3DX_PI/4, 640/480, nearClip, farClip);

    // Apply the matProj matrix to the projection stage of the pipeline
    pd3dDevice->SetTransform(D3DTS_PROJECTION, &matProj);
}
```

Instead of creating the projection matrix by hand, I used the D3DX helper function D3DXMatrixPerspectiveFovLH. This function creates an output matrix, held in the matProj variable earlier, by allowing you to specify the perspective, aspect ratio, and clipping planes in a single function call.

After you have generated the projection matrix, you apply it to the geometry pipeline by way of the SetTransform function. Because this matrix affects the projection piece of the pipeline, the value D3DTS_PROJECTION is used.

Positioning and Pointing the Camera

At this point, you can use the camera as is. The camera affects everything in the scene as the objects pass through the projection part of the geometry pipeline. There's just one problem; the camera is located at the origin, pointing off into the distance. Because a camera in the real world is a movable object, you want your virtual camera to behave the same way. The camera needs to be able to move around the scene and also be able to change the direction it's pointing. To satisfy these two criteria, you need to change the matrix that controls the view stage of the pipeline.

By default, the view matrix is set to the identity matrix, keeping your virtual camera steadfast at the origin. To change the camera's position and orientation, you need to create a new view matrix. The easiest way to create this matrix is through the D3DX helper function D3DXMatrixLookAtLH.

The D3DXMatrixLookAtLH function allows you to specify the position of the camera (defined as a D3DXVECTOR3), where the camera is looking (using a D3DXVECTOR3), and the direction that the camera should consider as up (also represented by a D3DXVECTOR3).

Following is a small code sample that will give you an idea of how to create the view matrix.

```
D3DXMATRIX matView;              // the view matrix
/***********************************************************************
* pointCamera
* points the camera at a location specified by the passed vector
***********************************************************************/
void pointCamera(D3DXVECTOR3 cameraPosition, D3DXVECTOR3 cameraLook)
{
    D3DXMatrixLookAtLH (&matView,
                        &cameraPosition,     //camera position
                        &cameraLook,         //look at position
                        &D3DXVECTOR3 (0.0f, 1.0f, 0.0f));    //up direction

    // Apply the matrix to the view stage of the pipeline
    pd3dDevice->SetTransform (D3DTS_VIEW, &matView);
}
```

The pointCamera function allows two parameters to be passed into it: the cameraLook variable and the cameraPosition variable.

The cameraPosition variable holds the camera's current position. For instance, if the camera were located 2 units away from the origin along the Z axis, the cameraPosition variable would contain the vector (0.0f, -2.0f, 0.0f).

The cameraLook variable tells the camera where it needs to point and is relative to the location of the camera. For example, assume that the camera is located 10 units up along the Y axis and 10 units back along the Z axis. Now imagine that you want the camera to point at the origin. Because the camera is currently residing above the origin, it actually needs to look down to see it. By setting the cameraLook vector to (0.0f, -10.0f; 0.0f), you are telling the camera to remain looking straight ahead but to look downward along the Y axis. The camera will then see the objects at the origin from a slightly overhead view.

The final view matrix that the D3DXMatrixLookAtLH creates is stored in the matView variable and then applied to the view stage of the pipeline. The D3DTS_VIEW value that is passed to the first parameter of SetTransform informs Direct3D that the view projection matrix will be updated.

Chapter Summary

In this chapter, you were introduced to the concepts that you'll use every time you write a 3D-based application. Whether you're creating a simple model viewer or the next first-person shooter, matrices and transforms are the foundation your games are built on.

What You Have Learned

In this chapter, you learned the following:

- How 3D objects are taken through the geometry pipeline
- What matrices are, and when and how to apply them
- How to move and rotate objects in a scene
- Why the order of matrix multiplication is important
- How to create and use a camera in your scene to view 3D objects

Review Questions

You can find the answers to Review Questions and On Your Own exercises in Appendix A, "Answers to End-of-Chapter Exercises."

1. The indices of an object can be stored in what kind of buffer?
2. What is a matrix?
3. What are the steps in the geometry pipeline?
4. What does the identity matrix do?
5. Changing a camera's aspect ratio affects which part of the pipeline?

On Your Own

1. Using the D3DXMatrixMultiply function, show the code needed to first rotate and then translate an object 5 units along the X axis.
2. Write a render function that will constantly rotate an object around the Y axis.

CHAPTER 6

VERTEX COLORS, TEXTURE MAPPING, AND 3D LIGHTING

This book previously touched on vertex colors to help give some much-needed color to your 3D scenes, but single-colored flat polygons are not all that Direct3D has to offer. Direct3D can add depth to your scene through lighting, or realism via texture mapping. Your game worlds are about to get a lot more interesting.

Here's what you'll learn in this chapter:

- How vertex colors are used
- How to change the shading that Direct3D uses
- The types of lighting that Direct3D offers
- How materials are used
- What textures are and how they can add realism to your scenes
- How to apply textures to an object

Changing the Color of an Object

In Chapter 4, "3D Primer," you used vertex colors to display a triangle filled with a rainbow of colors. In that example, each vertex was created with a different color, causing the triangle to be filled with the mixture of those colors and a gradient pattern to be created. By manipulating the color of each vertex per frame, you can create a multitude of color effects within your scene. Figure 6.1 shows the triangle that you created earlier.

Vertex coloring is also beneficial when you're running on low-end 3D hardware that doesn't support texture mapping. Vertex coloring enables polygons within your model to be colored based on the vertices that are used to create them. Also, by using colored

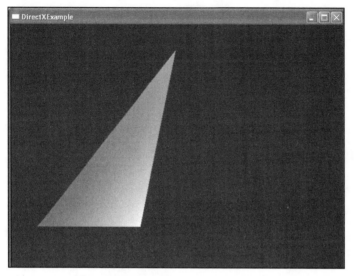

Figure 6.1 The rainbow triangle.

vertices, you don't need to enable lighting within a scene. If you were to create a nonlit scene with a triangle with no vertex colors, you would be unable to see the triangle.

Vertex Colors Revisited

As I mentioned before, vertex coloring is enabled by adding a DWORD variable in your vertex structure and adding the D3DFVF_DIFFUSE flag to your SetFVF function call. A sample CUSTOMVERTEX structure is shown here:

```
struct CUSTOMVERTEX
{
    FLOAT x, y, z, rhw;      // the untransformed, 3D position for the vertex
    DWORD color;            // the vertex color
};
```

As you'll recall, the vertex color is set when you define the properties of each vertex. The colors used for each vertex are being set next, using one of the available D3DCOLOR macros that Direct3D provides:

```
CUSTOMVERTEX g_Vertices[] =
{
    // x, y, z, rhw, color
    { 320.0f,  50.0f, 0.5f, 1.0f, D3DCOLOR_ARGB(0,255,0,0), },
    { 250.0f, 400.0f, 0.5f, 1.0f, D3DCOLOR_ARGB(0,0,255,0), },
    {  50.0f, 400.0f, 0.5f, 1.0f, D3DCOLOR_ARGB(0,0,0,255), },
};
```

Color Macros

Direct3D provides a few macros that enable easy creation of a D3DCOLOR value without resorting to describing the color in hexadecimal.

In the previous code example, the macro D3DCOLOR_ARGB is used. This macro accepts four values: an alpha or transparency setting, a red component, a green component, and a blue component. Each value passed to the D3DCOLOR_ARGB macro can be between 0 and 255, where 0 means no color and 255 represents full color. For example, a value of 0 in the blue component would have the effect of removing blue from the resulting color. A value of 255 would cause the blue component to be added fully to the overall color.

```
#define D3DCOLOR_ARGB(a,r,g,b) \
    ((D3DCOLOR)((((a)&0xff)<<24)|(((r)&0xff)<<16)|(((g)&0xff)<<8)|((b)&0xff)))
```

The next macro that Direct3D provides is the D3DCOLOR_RGBA macro. This is similar to the D3DCOLOR_ARGB macro described earlier, but it switches the order in which the values are passed. Each value that is passed to this macro must be between 0 and 255.

```
#define D3DCOLOR_RGBA(r, g, b, a) D3DCOLOR_ARGB(a, r, g, b)
```

You can use the D3DCOLOR_XRGB macro when you don't need to specifically set an alpha value. The D3DCOLOR_XRGB macro internally calls the D3DCOLOR_ARGB macro, but it automatically fills in the alpha value for you.

```
#define D3DCOLOR_XRGB(r, g, b) D3DCOLOR_ARGB (0xff, r, g, b)
```

The final macro I will describe is D3DCOLOR_COLORVALUE. This macro, shown next, accepts four components: red, green, blue, and an alpha. In the previous macros, these values were represented by a value between 0 and 255. The D3DCOLOR_COLORVALUE macro requires these values to be between 0 and 1.0. Internally, this macro calls the D3DCOLOR_RGBA macro and converts the values appropriately.

```
#define D3DCOLOR_COLORVALUE (r, g, b, a) \
    D3DCOLOR_RGBA((DWORD)((r)*255.f),
                  (DWORD)((g)*255.f),
                  (DWORD)((b)*255.f),
                  (DWORD)((a)*255.f))
```

Shading

Shading determines the look and color of each polygon in an object. Using different shading methods, you can cause your 3D models to appear smooth as the polygons are seamlessly blended, or blocky as each polygon is made distinctly visible. Direct3D supports two types of shading:

- Flat
- Gouraud

Each method of shading has its own benefits. For instance, flat shading was used predominantly before hardware acceleration became common on video cards. Because flat shading is not computationally expensive, it was relatively easy to implement in software renderers. The first *Virtua Fighter* game from Sega made extensive use of flat shading for its models.

Although Gouraud shading gives better visual results, it takes longer to calculate. As video cards have become more advanced, the restrictions on more intensive techniques have loosened, allowing for better-looking graphics.

Flat Shading

Flat shading involves treating each polygon within an object as a separate piece. The color of the polygon is determined by the color of the first vertex within it. For instance, if the color of the vertices making up a polygon is red, the whole polygon will be filled with that same red color. Figure 6.2 shows an example of a teapot rendered using flat shading. Notice how you can see each polygon that makes up the teapot.

note

By increasing the number of polygons within your model, you can create a smoother surface using flat shading. A much smoother surface appearance results from using the Gouraud technique with a low polycount model.

Figure 6.2 A teapot rendered with flat shading.

Gouraud Shading

Gouraud shading produces much better results than flat shading. Whereas flat shading determines the color of a polygon from a single vertex, Gouraud shading computes the color using multiple vertices. Assigning different colors to each vertex and then blending those colors across the face of the polygon results in a much smoother appearance. With Gouraud shading, individual polygons are more difficult to see and give a more pleasing result. Figure 6.3 shows the same teapot rendered using Gouraud shading.

Choosing the Shading Mode

Direct3D allows you to change the shading mode that it uses to render the polygons within your scene. By default, Direct3D is set to render using Gouraud shading, but you can change it to flat shading with one simple function call.

The shading type is set using the render state setting of D3DRS_SHADEMODE. By making a call to the SetRenderState function, you can choose any of the shading types shown in the D3DSHADEMODE enumeration listed here:

```
typedef enum _D3DSHADEMODE {
    D3DSHADE_FLAT = 1,
    D3DSHADE_GOURAUD = 2,
    D3DSHADE_PHONG = 3,
    D3DSHADE_FORCE_DWORD = 0x7fffffff
} D3DSHADEMODE;
```

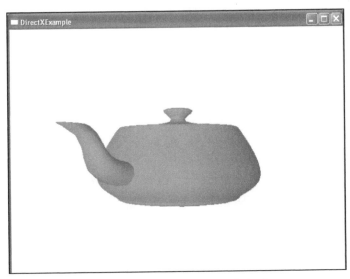

Figure 6.3 A teapot rendered with Gouraud shading.

note

Although Phong shading is mentioned within D3DSHADEMODE, it is not currently supported within Direct3D. Future implementations of Direct3D might make this type of shading available.

The small code sample that follows shows how to change the shading mode to use flat shading.

```
// Set to flat shading
HRESULT hr;

// Set the new render state
hr = pd3dDevice->SetRenderState(D3DRS_SHADEMODE,  D3DSHADE_FLAT);

// If the call to SetRenderState failed, handle the error here
if(FAILED(hr))
    return false;
```

Fill Mode

The fill mode setting tells Direct3D how you would like your polygons to be displayed. Three types of fill modes are available to you:

- **Point.** Each vertex in the model is rendered as a single point.
- **Wireframe.** The model is rendered using nonfilled polygons.
- **Solid.** Each polygon is rendered as filled using the shading mode specified.

You set the fill mode using the render state setting of D3DRS_FILLMODE. The available values for the fill mode are shown in the D3DFILLMODE enumeration that follows:

```
typedef enum _D3DFILLMODE {
    D3DFILL_POINT = 1,
    D3DFILL_WIREFRAME = 2,
    D3DFILL_SOLID = 3,
    D3DFILL_FORCE_DWORD = 0x7fffffff
} D3DFILLMODE;
```

The next code sample shows how to properly set the fill mode to use wireframe rendering. Figure 6.4 shows the teapot rendered in wireframe.

```
// Set to use wireframe fill mode
HRESULT hr;

// Set the new render state
hr = pd3dDevice->SetRenderState(D3DRS_FILLMODE, D3DFILL_WIREFRAME);
```

```
// If the call to SetRenderState failed, handle the error here
if(FAILED(hr))
    return false;
```

note

Wireframe mode is useful when you are trying to track down bugs in your rendering code. By being able to see through your models, you can confirm that they are placed in the scene correctly.

You use point rendering when you only want to display each vertex without connecting the polygons with any sort of lines. Figure 6.5 shows the teapot rendered in point fill mode.

Figure 6.4 The teapot using wireframe.

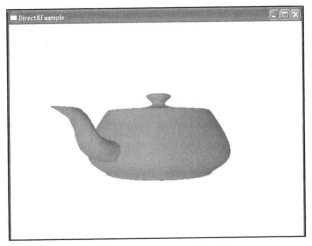

Figure 6.5 The teapot using point fill mode.

Lighting Explained

Lighting is an important element within a 3D scene. It helps to set the mood for a scene, be it with torches or simulated sunlight shining through the leaves in a forest. Dim lighting can instill fear and unease in the player, whereas bright lighting gives a happier, more comforting effect.

Because you can define a vertex format that requires a vertex color, these objects cannot be seen without a light source. Light within a scene attempts to re-create the way that light works in the real world. Because calculating lighting can be intensive, Direct3D attempts to approximate lighting conditions. The results are normally pretty close to what you would see in nature, but they are quick enough to be handled in realtime.

Lighting Types

Direct3D allows you to create and use multiple types of lights within your scene. Each type of light produces a different lighting effect. The following list presents the four types of lighting that Direct3D provides. You can use each lighting type individually or as part of a group.

- Ambient light
- Directional lights
- Point lights
- Spotlights

Each of these light types provides a different kind of lighting effect and is described in detail in the following sections.

Ambient Light

Ambient light is the most basic type of light that Direct3D provides. Ambient lighting offers constant nondirectional lighting for a scene. Because the light is not coming from any particular direction and is equal on all sides of an object, no shadows are produced. Ambient lighting can be created without the explicit creation of a Direct3D light source.

Figure 6.6 shows the teapot from earlier with a red ambient light. Notice that the teapot appears flat because of the ambient lighting.

Because ambient lighting is spread across the entire scene, only one ambient light can be active at a time.

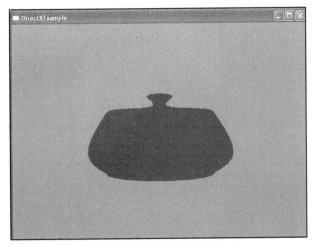

Figure 6.6 The teapot with a red ambient light.

Directional Lights

Directional lights provide you with a way of generating light from a particular direction. All light from a directional light source travels in parallel. For instance, if you wanted to create lighting in your scene that was similar to that of the sun, you would use a directional light. Directional lights have color and direction but are positionless.

Figure 6.7 shows how a directional light affects a scene.

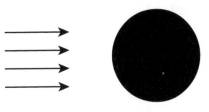

Directional Light

Figure 6.7 How a directional light affects a scene.

Direct3D allows for multiple directional lights within a scene, each one with different properties.

Point Lights

Point lights can be used to simulate a source that emits lights in all directions. A light bulb is an example of a light source that performs in this manner.

Point lights have position as well as color but are directionless. Positioning a point light in a scene causes the scene to be lit in all directions surrounding the light source.

Multiple point light sources can be present in a scene. Figure 6.8 shows how a point light to the upper left of the teapot affects how it is rendered.

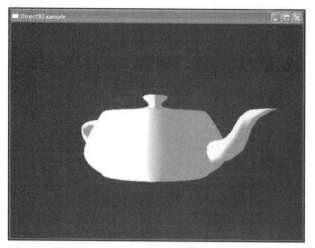

Figure 6.8 The teapot with a point light.

Spotlights

Spotlights are an example of a light source that has position, direction, and color. The main difference between spotlights and the other types of lights discussed so far is how the light is spread across an object's surface.

The light that's emitted from a spotlight is cone shaped, with the light at the center of the cone at a higher intensity than the light that's generated at the outer edges. The intensity of the light gradually decreases as it spreads from the center of the cone.

A light from a helicopter or a searchlight would be an example of a spotlight. Figure 6.9 shows how a spotlight affects how the teapot is rendered.

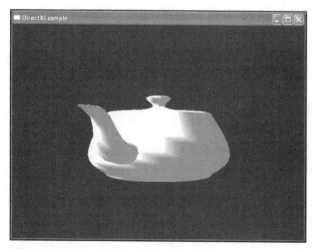

Figure 6.9 The teapot with a spotlight.

note

Spotlights are some of the more commonly used light sources, as well as the most expensive when it comes to processing time.

Light Properties

Each light you create has properties that determine how it should look after it is created.

The D3DLIGHT9 structure is defined as follows:

```
typedef struct _D3DLIGHT9 {
    D3DLIGHTTYPE Type;
    D3DCOLORVALUE Diffuse;
    D3DCOLORVALUE Specular;
    D3DCOLORVALUE Ambient;
    D3DVECTOR Position;
    D3DVECTOR Direction;
    float Range;
    float Falloff;
    float Attenuation0;
    float Attenuation1;
    float Attenuation2;
    float Theta;
    float Phi;
} D3DLIGHT9;
```

The D3DLIGHT9 structure contains 13 properties when you're creating a light:

- **Type.** The type of light you want to create. This can be any D3DLIGHTTYPE value shown here.
  - **D3DLIGHT_POINT.** Used when creating a point light.
  - **D3DLIGHT_SPOT.** Used when creating a spotlight.
  - **D3DLIGHT_DIRECTIONAL.** Used when creating a directional light.
- **Diffuse.** The diffuse color generated by this light. This will affect the color of an object based on its diffuse material property.
- **Specular.** The specular color of this light. This affects the color of any specular highlights on an object.
- **Ambient.** The ambient color of this light. An ambient light affects all objects in a scene. The color of this light determines the color that the object reflects.

- **Position.** The position of the light.
- **Direction.** The direction that the light is facing.
- **Range.** The distance from the light source where the light no longer reaches.
- **Falloff.** Used only for spotlights. Falloff is the decrease in light between the inner and outer cones of the light.
- **Attenuation0.** This value controls how the light intensity changes based on its distance from the light source. Attenuation0 provides a constant falloff based on the Range property.
- **Attenuation1.** The value that specifies how the light intensity changes as it gets farther from the light source. Attenuation1 affects the light from a light source in a linear way.
- **Attenuation2.** The value that specifies how the light intensity changes as it gets farther from the light source. Attenuation2 determines the falloff from the light based on a quadratic formula.   ✓
- **Theta.** Used only for spotlights. The angle in radians of the spotlight's inner cone.
- **Phi.** Used only for spotlights. The angle in radians of the spotlight's outer cone.

Before you can create lights, you need to tell Direct3D to enable lighting. Lighting is turned off by default. You can enable lighting through the render state property D3DRS_LIGHTING. Sending a value of TRUE to this render state enables lighting, whereas a value of FALSE turns lighting off.

The following code demonstrates how to enable lighting within Direct3D.

```
pd3dDevice->SetRenderState (D3DRS_LIGHTING, TRUE);
```

The pd3dDevice variable represents a valid Direct3D device.

Creating Lights in a Scene

Each light that you want to place in a scene requires first that you declare a D3DLIGHT9 structure. The D3DLIGHT9 structure includes properties that affect how the light will be created. For instance, the intensity or color of the light is defined within these properties.

After you have the D3DLIGHT9 structure properly filled in, you create the light with a call to the function SetLight.

The SetLight function is defined as follows:

```
HRESULT SetLight (
    DWORD Index,
    CONST D3DLIGHT9 *pLight
);
```

The SetLight function requires two parameters:

- **Index.** The zero-based index of the light to create. If a light has previously been created with an index, the properties for the light are overwritten.
- **pLight.** A pointer to a properly filled-in D3DLIGHT9 structure.

After you've made the call to SetLight for the actual light creation, you need to enable it. By default, all lights are turned off when they are created. Enabling a light requires a call to the LightEnable function that is defined next.

```
HRESULT LightEnable(
    DWORD LightIndex,
    BOOL bEnable
);
```

The LightEnable function requires two parameters:

- **LightIndex.** The index of the light that you want to enable. This will be the same index that you used during the call to SetLight.
- **bEnable.** This parameter can be either TRUE of FALSE. Passing TRUE enables the specified light, whereas passing FALSE disables it.

note

If you need to determine whether a particular light in your scene is currently enabled, you can make a call to the GetLightEnable function. If you pass this function the index of the light you want to check, the function returns a boolean value with the current state of this light.

The following sections demonstrate the code required to create a light of each type that was discussed previously.

Creating an Ambient Light

Ambient lighting does not require the specific creation of a light source; therefore, it is simple to enable this type of light.

The following code sample shows how to create an ambient light with a white color. You'll notice that the ambient light is created through a SetRenderState call and doesn't need a D3DLIGHT9 structure to be created. Because ambient light fills the entire scene, Direct3D restricts this to one light per scene. Ambient lights are created through the D3DRS_AMBIENT render state.

```
pd3dDevice->SetRenderState (D3DRS_AMBIENT, D3DCOLOR_XRGB (255, 255, 255));
```

The color of the ambient light is set using one of the D3DCOLOR macros described earlier. If you pass a D3DCOLOR of all zeros, the ambient light is effectively disabled.

You can find a full source example for the creation of ambient light in the chapter6\example3 directory on the CD-ROM.

Creating a Directional Light

The next code sample creates a directional light.

```
void createDirectionalLight ( void )
{
    // Create and turn on a directional light
    D3DLIGHT9 light;

    // Set the type of light
    vlight.Type = D3DLIGHT_DIRECTIONAL;

    // Set the direction that this light will generate light from
    vD3DXVECTOR3 vDir( 1.0f, 0.0f, 0.0f );

    // Normalize the light direction
    D3DXVec3Normalize ((D3DXVECTOR3*) &light.Direction, &vDir);

    // Set the diffuse color for this light
    light.Diffuse.r = 0.0f;
    light.Diffuse.g = 0.0f;
    light.Diffuse.b = 0.5f;

    // Set the ambient color for this light
    light.Ambient.r  = 0.0f;
    light.Ambient.g = 0.0f;
    light.Ambient.b = 0.3f;

    // Set the range of this light
    light.Range        = sqrtf (FLT_MAX);

    // Tell Direct3D to set the newly created light
    pd3dDevice->SetLight (0, &light);

    // Enable the new light
    pd3dDevice->LightEnable (0, TRUE);
}
```

The previous code first declares a variable to contain the light properties. The light variable represents the D3DLIGHT9 structure. Before you fill in the specific properties for this light, you must set the light type. In this case, the type of light is set to D3DLIGHT_DIRECTIONAL, which represents a directional light.

Now you can fill in the properties that are relevant to the light. Because a directional light is positionless, you'll notice that the position property is not set. However, the Direction property is required. In this instance, the light is created with a direction vector that points it in a positive direction along the X axis.

The color of the light is set through the Diffuse and Ambient properties. Each of these color properties requires a red, green, and blue component. A specular color property can also be set for this type of light.

After the properties are set, the light is created and enabled with the calls to SetLight and LightEnable. You can find the full source code in the chapter6\example4 directory on the CD-ROM.

Creating a Point Light

The code example that follows demonstrates how to create a point light within a scene.

```
void createPointLight (void)
{
    // Create and turn on a directional light
    D3DLIGHT9 light;

    // Set the type of light
    light.Type          = D3DLIGHT_POINT;

    // Set the position for this light
    light.Position  = D3DXVECTOR3( -2500.0f, 0.0f, 0.0f );

    // Set the red, green, and blue diffuse components for this
    // light source
    light.Diffuse.r     = 1.0f;
    light.Diffuse.g   = 0.5f;
    light.Diffuse.b   = 0.5f;

    // Set the red, green, and blue ambient components for this
    // light source
    light.Ambient.r     = 0.5f;
    light.Ambient.g   = 0.0f;
    light.Ambient.b   = 0.0f;

    light.Range     = sqrtf(FLT_MAX);
```

```
    // Tell Direct3D to create the new light
    pd3dDevice->SetLight(0, &light );

    // Enable the light
    pd3dDevice->LightEnable (0, TRUE);
}
```

This code first declares a variable to contain the light properties. The light variable represents the D3DLIGHT9 structure. Before filling in the specific properties for this light, the light type is set. In this case, the type of light is set to D3DLIGHT_POINT, which represents a point light.

Now you can fill in the properties that are relevant to the light. Because this is a point light, the Direction property is not needed, but the Position property is. In the previous code, the position is set to move the light 2,500 units to the left of origin along the X axis.

Again, the color of the light is set through the Diffuse and Ambient properties.

After the properties are set, the light is created and enabled with the calls to SetLight and LightEnable. The full source code for a point light is in the chapter6\example6 directory on the CD-ROM.

Creating a Spotlight

Creating a spotlight is similar to creating other types of lights, with the addition of a few extra parameters. Spotlights require these additional values:

- **Phi.** The angle in radians that defines the spotlight's outer cone edge. This spotlight does not light any points that fall outside this edge. Values can be between 0 and pi.
- **Theta.** The angle in radians that defines the spotlight's inner cone. This area is completely lit by the full intensity of the spotlight.
- **Falloff.** A value that determines the decrease in lighting between the inner and outer cones of a spotlight.

The following code example shows how to create a spotlight.

```
void createSpotLight(void)
{
    // Create and turn on a directional light
    D3DLIGHT9 light;

    // Set the type of light
    light.Type        = D3DLIGHT_SPOT;
```

```
// Set the position and the direction for this light
D3DXVECTOR3 vDir (1.0f, -1.0f, 0.0f);
D3DXVec3Normalize ((D3DXVECTOR3*)&light.Direction, &vDir );
light.Position     = D3DXVECTOR3 (-250.0f, 250.0f, 0.0f);

// Set the red, green, and blue diffuse color components
// for this light source
light.Diffuse.r   = 1.0f;
light.Diffuse.g  = 0.5f;
light.Diffuse.b  = 0.5f;

// Set the red, green, and blue ambient color components
// for this light source
light.Ambient.r    = 0.5f;
light.Ambient.g   = 0.0f;
light.Ambient.b   = 0.0f;

// Set the range
light.Range      = sqrtf(FLT_MAX);

// spotlight-specific parameters
light.Phi         = 1.0f;
light.Falloff     = 0.5f;
light.Theta       = 0.5f;

// Create the light
pd3dDevice->SetLight(0, &light );

// Enable the new light
pd3dDevice->LightEnable(0, TRUE );
}
```

This code first declares a variable to contain the light properties. The light variable represents the D3DLIGHT9 structure. Before you fill in the specific properties for this light, you must set the light type. In this case, the type of light is set to D3DLIGHT_SPOT, which represents a spotlight.

Now you can fill in the properties that are relevant to the light. A spotlight has both a position and a direction. In this case, the light is looking in the positive X direction and down the Y axis.

Again, the color of the light is set through the Diffuse and Ambient properties.

Spotlights also require setting three additional properties that are specific to this type of light: Phi, Theta, and Falloff.

After the properties are set, the light is created and enabled with the calls to SetLight and LightEnable. The full source code for a point light is in the chapter6\example5 directory on the CD-ROM.

Materials Explained

Materials control how an object reflects or emits light. The material properties describe to Direct3D how light in a scene is reflected by the polygons that make up an object. The following properties make up the definition of a material:

- Diffuse reflection
- Ambient reflection
- Specular reflection
- Light emission

Materials consist of these separate properties working together to describe the object. The properties are described in more detail in the next sections.

Diffuse Reflection

Diffuse lighting is directional lighting within a scene. The diffuse property of a material describes how diffuse light is reflected off an object. By changing the diffuse property, you can control the color that the object reflects.

Ambient Reflection

Because ambient lighting is nondirectional, it affects objects within a scene from all sides. A material's ambient property determines how ambient lighting is reflected off the surface of an object. Changing the ambient property changes the perceived color of the object when hit with ambient light.

Specular Reflection

Specular reflection causes highlights on objects, making them appear more realistic. The specular property of a material controls the color of this highlight, and the power property controls the sharpness of the highlight. The higher the power value, the sharper the highlight will appear. Figure 6.10 shows the teapot from earlier, rendered with a specular highlight.

Figure 6.10 The teapot rendered with a specular highlight.

Emission

The emissive material property can make an object appear to be emitting light. Other objects, however, cannot reflect the light from this property because it is not a true light within the scene. By setting the emissive property, you can control the color of the light that the object appears to give off.

How Materials Are Used

Materials are created through the use of the D3DMATERIAL9 structure. This structure contains all the properties that a material needs to control how light is reflected from an object. The D3DMATERIAL9 structure is defined here:

```
typedef struct _D3DMATERIAL9 {
    D3DCOLORVALUE Diffuse;
    D3DCOLORVALUE Ambient;
    D3DCOLORVALUE Specular;
    D3DCOLORVALUE Emissive;
    float Power;
} D3DMATERIAL9;
```

The D3DMATERIAL9 structure consists of five variables:

- **Diffuse.** The diffuse color of the material
- **Ambient.** The material's ambient color
- **Specular.** The specular color of the material
- **Emissive.** The material's emissive color
- **Power.** A value that specifies the sharpness of specular highlights

Specular Highlights

Setting just the specular property of a material does not allow an object to give off a specular highlight; you must enable the highlights first. The render state setting D3DRS_SPECULARENABLE must be set to TRUE. Setting this value to FALSE disables specular highlights.

The following code sample enables specular highlighting.

```
// Set to use specular highlights
HRESULT hr;

// Set the new render state
hr = pd3dDevice->SetRenderState (D3DRS_SPECULARENABLE, TRUE);
// If the call to SetRenderState failed, handle the error here
if(FAILED(hr))
    return false;
```

The pd3dDevice variable must contain a valid Direct3D device.

Texture Mapping

Up to this point, all the 3D objects you've created have looked pretty boring. Sure, they've been colorful, but they really haven't looked like real-world objects. They've had depth and lighting, but they lack realism. Texture mapping helps give your games the realism that everyone expects.

Texture mapping is the process of loading a picture or an image and wrapping it around your 3D objects. For instance, a green square doesn't look much like grass, but if you apply an image of grass to the square, things start looking a little more real. That's what texture mapping is all about: bringing realism to an otherwise artificial-looking world.

I'll describe the detailed steps required to add textures to your virtual worlds.

How Direct3D Uses Textures

The IDirect3DTexture9 interface represents textures within Direct3D. This interface provides you with methods for manipulating textures, such as generating mipmaps, setting the texture's level of detail, as well as the ability to lock the texture, giving you direct access to the pixel data.

Before you can use textures in your game, you need to load them and assign them to an IDirect3DTexture9 interface. Figure 6.11 shows a cube with a texture map applied to all its sides.

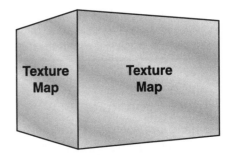

Figure 6.11 A cube with texture maps applied.

How Textures Are Applied

Textures are mapped to 3D objects using texture coordinates. The texture coordinates describe to Direct3D which portion of the texture will be applied and where.

Texture coordinates normally range in value from 0.0f to 1.0f. Because the texture images that you will apply are rectangular, the 0.0f value represents the left side and 1.0f represents the right side. The texture coordinates work in the same manner in the vertical direction, where 0.0f represents the top of the object and 1.0f represents the bottom. Figure 6.12 shows the texture coordinates of a square.

Using the texture coordinates shown in Figure 6.12, you would end up mapping the entire texture image to the square. Figure 6.13 shows what the square would look like with a texture applied to it.

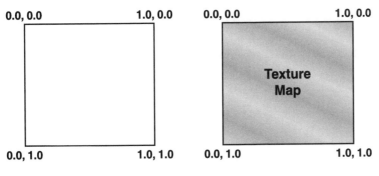

Figure 6.12 The texture coordinates of a square.

Figure 6.13 The square with a texture map applied.

Texture Coordinates

Texture coordinates are commonly represented in code by the two values u and v. To use texture mapping within Direct3D, you first need to update your vertex structure. As you can see in the new CUSTOMVERTEX structure that follows, two new float variables—u and v— have been added.

```
struct CUSTOMVERTEX
{
    FLOAT x, y, z; // the untransformed, 3D position for the vertex
    FLOAT u, v;
};
```

You also need to add the D3DFVF_TEX1 flag to your vertex format. The D3DFVF_TEX1 flag informs Direct3D that you have added texture coordinates to your vertex definition.

```
#define D3DFVF_CUSTOMVERTEX (D3DFVF_XYZ | D3DFVF_TEX1)
```

Finally, you need to add the texture coordinates to the actual vertex definitions. Previously, only the X, Y, and Z values were indicated for each vertex.

note

Direct3D allows for up to eight textures to be applied using the flags D3DFVF_TEX1 through D3DFVF_TEX8.

Shown next is an updated declaration that includes the set of texture coordinates.

```
CUSTOMVERTEX g_Vertices [] =
{
    // X      Y    Z    U     V
    {-1.0f, 1.0f,-1.0f, 0.0f, 0.0f},
    { 1.0f, 1.0f,-1.0f, 1.0f, 0.0f},
    {-1.0f,-1.0f,-1.0f, 0.0f, 1.0f},
    { 1.0f,-1.0f,-1.0f, 1.0f, 1.0f}
}
```

Texture Stages

Texture stages allow you to apply more than one texture to an object in a single rendering pass. Each rendering pass can consist of up to eight stages, with each stage letting you apply a single texture and control the type and amount of blending used.

note

Some video hardware has limits to the number of texture stages you can use. Always check the capabilities of the adapter to confirm that it can handle the number of texture stages you want to use.

The type of texture blending is controlled through the state of the texture stage.

Texture Stage States

Texture stages affect how a texture is applied to an object. The normal way for a texture to be applied is with full opacity and no blending. By setting the state for a particular texture stage, you can change whether two textures get blended together to create an effect like light mapping, or cause a texture to be applied to an object with transparency.

You change the state of a particular texture stage through the SetTextureStageState function, shown next.

```
HRESULT SetTextureStageState (
    DWORD Stage,
    D3DTEXTURESTAGESTATETYPE Type,
    DWORD Value
);
```

The SetTextureStageState function requires three parameters:

- **Stage.** The number of the stage to apply the state to.
- **Type.** The type of state that is being applied to the stage. Valid values are found in the D3DTEXTURESTAGESTATETYPE enumeration.
- **Value.** This parameter depends on the value specified in the Type parameter.

Loading a Texture

Now that you know what texture mapping is and how it works, you're probably wondering how to get textures into your game. Textures are just image files like you've used previously. Commonly, the bitmap image format is used for applications that are written for

Direct3D. They can be loaded from disk or can reside within the application executable itself as a resource. The following two sections describe the steps needed to load textures using both of these methods.

Texture Loading from a File

Loading texture images from a disk is the best way to deliver your game graphics. Because the textures are not part of the executable, you can change them easily and without rebuilding your application.

Direct3D offers the D3DXCreateTextureFromFile function from the D3DX utility library for the loading of textures. The D3DXCreateTextureFromFile function is defined next.

```
HRESULT D3DXCreateTextureFromFile(
    LPDIRECT3DDEVICE9 pDevice,
    LPCTSTR pSrcFile,
    LPDIRECT3DTEXTURE9 *ppTexture
);
```

The D3DXCreateTextureFromFile function requires three parameters:

- **pDevice.** A pointer to a valid Direct3D device
- **pSrcFile.** A string containing the path and file name of the texture image to load
- **ppTexture.** A pointer to a variable of type IDirect3DTexture9 that will hold the created texture

The code sample shown next attempts to create a Direct3D texture from the test.bmp file.

```
HRESULT hr;                              // variable to hold the return code
LPDIRECT3DTEXTURE9    g_pTexture    = NULL;  // IDirect3DTexture9 object to
                                         // hold the texture

// Call D3DXCreateTextureFromFile
hr = D3DXCreateTextureFromFile( pd3dDevice, "test.bmp", &g_pTexture );

// Check the return code to make sure you have a valid texture
if FAILED (hr)
    Return false;
```

At this point, you should have a valid Direct3D texture within the g_pTexture variable.

The D3DXCreateTextureFromFile function allows for the loading of texture image files in the following formats:

- **Bitmap.** These files have the BMP extension.
- **Windows DIB.** These files have the DIB extension.
- **Targa.** These files have the TGA extension.
- **JPEG.** These files have the JPG extension.
- **PNG.** These files have the PNG extension.
- **DDS.** These are DirectDraw surface files. They have the DDS extension.

Texture Loading from a Resource

Sometimes your application requires only one or two textures, and it doesn't make sense to ship the textures as separate files. In this instance, you can bundle the textures into the executable as an image resource. Although this method increases the size of your executable, it also gives you the benefit of not requiring outside files to function.

The D3DX utility library provides you with the D3DXCreateTextureFromResource helper function to help you load your textures from the executable. D3DXCreateTextureFromResource is shown here:

```
HRESULT D3DXCreateTextureFromResource(
    LPDIRECT3DDEVICE9 pDevice,
    HMODULE hSrcModule,
    LPCTSTR pSrcResource,
    LPDIRECT3DTEXTURE9 *ppTexture
);
```

The D3DXCreateTextureFromResource function requires four parameters:

- **pDevice.** A pointer to a valid Direct3D device.
- **hSrcModule.** A handle to the module where the resource is located. When you're loading an image from the current executable file, this parameter should be NULL.
- **pSrcResource.** A string that represents the name of the resource.
- **ppTexture.** A pointer to a variable of type IDirect3DTexture9 that will hold the newly loaded texture.

The following sample code shows how to load a texture from a resource.

```
HRESULT hr;
// IDirect3DTexture9 object to hold the texture
LPDIRECT3DTEXTURE9      g_pTexture   = NULL;
```

```
// Call D3DXCreateTextureFromResource
hr = D3DXCreateTextureFromResource( pd3dDevice,
                                    NULL,
                                    "IDB_BITMAP1",
                                    &g_pTexture );

// Check the return code to make sure you have a valid texture
if FAILED (hr)
    return false;
```

In the previous code, the texture image that is trying to load is called IDB_BITMAP1. The name of this image resource is being passed as the third parameter to the D3DXCreateTextureFromResource function call. If the call is completed successfully, the variable g_pTexture contains a valid Direct3D texture.

Applying a Texture

Textures are applied to objects through the SetTexture function. This function tells Direct3D which texture it should use to render the current set of polygons. If, after the first set of polygons are finished rendering, you want to draw a second set of polygons with another texture, you would need to make another call to SetTexture with the new texture.

note

A call to SetTexture is referred to as a *state change*. You should always strive to minimize the number of stage changes you make during a frame because they can slow down your overall frame rate.

The SetTexture function is defined next:

```
HRESULT SetTexture(
    DWORD Stage,
    IDirect3DBaseTexture9 *pTexture
);
```

The SetTexture function requires two parameters:

- **Stage.** The stage that this texture should be applied to. If you are rendering only a single texture, this value should be 0.
- **pTexture.** A pointer to the **IDirect3DTexture9** object to use.

The following code shows an example of an updated render function that applies a texture to the cube that is being drawn. Notice that the call to SetTexture is made before the calls to DrawPrimitive. After Direct3D starts drawing, it applies whichever texture is currently active. If you were to call SetTexture again halfway through the DrawPrimitive calls, all additional polygons would be rendered with the new texture applied.

```
void Render(void)
{
    // Clear the back buffer and the Z buffer
    pd3dDevice->Clear( 0,
                       NULL,
                       D3DCLEAR_TARGET | D3DCLEAR_ZBUFFER,
                       D3DCOLOR_XRGB(255,255,255),
                       1.0f,
                       0 );

    // Tell Direct3D that rendering is about to begin
    pd3dDevice->BeginScene();

    // Set the current texture to use
    pd3dDevice->SetTexture( 0, g_pTexture );

    // Set the vertex stream
    pd3dDevice->SetStreamSource( 0, buffer, 0, sizeof(CUSTOMVERTEX) );
    pd3dDevice->SetFVF( D3DFVF_CUSTOMVERTEX );

    // Draw the triangle strips that make up the cube
    pd3dDevice->DrawPrimitive( D3DPT_TRIANGLESTRIP,  0, 2 );
    pd3dDevice->DrawPrimitive( D3DPT_TRIANGLESTRIP,  4, 2 );
    pd3dDevice->DrawPrimitive( D3DPT_TRIANGLESTRIP,  8, 2 );
    pd3dDevice->DrawPrimitive( D3DPT_TRIANGLESTRIP, 12, 2 );
    pd3dDevice->DrawPrimitive( D3DPT_TRIANGLESTRIP, 16, 2 );
    pd3dDevice->DrawPrimitive( D3DPT_TRIANGLESTRIP, 20, 2 );

    // Drawing is now complete
    pd3dDevice->EndScene();

    // Flip the buffers and display this to the screen
    pd3dDevice->Present( NULL, NULL, NULL, NULL );
}
```

The previous Render function requires six calls to DrawPrimitive, each rendering a single side of the cube. You can find a full source example in the chapter6\example7 directory on the CD-ROM.

As you'll recall, the texture coordinates tell Direct3D where each part of the texture will appear on a particular polygon. So far, you've been using the standard values of 0.0f for the left side of the polygon and 1.0f for the right side. This causes the texture to be mapped onto the polygon once. Textures, though, can be repeated multiple times across a polygon if you manipulate the texture coordinates. You can increase the right-side texture coordinate past the standard 1.0f value to represent the number of times to repeat the texture.

For instance, if you want to repeat a texture twice across a polygon, you would change the right-side texture coordinate to 2.0f. The bottom texture coordinate works in the same way, allowing the texture to be repeated in the up-down direction as well.

Look at the updated vertex structure definition that follows. Notice that the texture coordinates have been changed so that the texture repeats twice in each direction.

```
CUSTOMVERTEX g_Vertices[] =
{
    // X      Y       Z      U       V
    {-1.0f, 1.0f, -1.0f, 0.0f, 0.0f},
    { 1.0f, 1.0f, -1.0f, 2.0f, 0.0f},
    {-1.0f,-1.0f, -1.0f, 0.0f, 2.0f},
    { 1.0f,-1.0f, -1.0f, 2.0f, 2.0f}
}
```

The ability to repeat textures across a surface is useful when you want to keep your polygon count low and you don't want to stretch your texture across too large of an area. Repeating a grass texture across a landscape and a brick texture across a wall are two sample applications for texture repeating. Figure 6.14 shows how texture repeating affects how the texture is applied to an object.

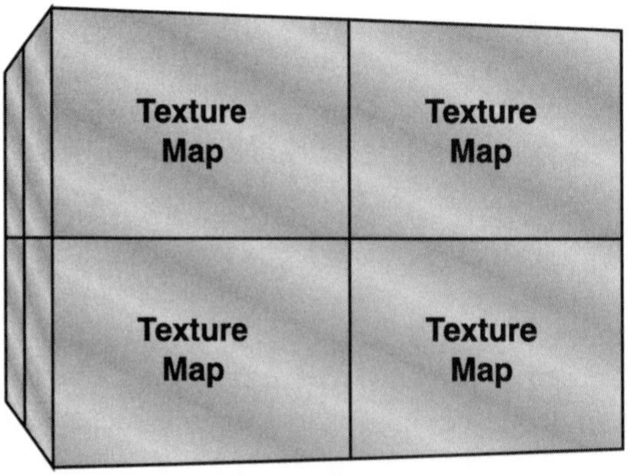

Figure 6.14 A cube with texture maps repeating twice in each direction.

A full source example is located in the chapter6\example8 directory on the CD-ROM.

Chapter Summary

Now that you know how to use textures and lighting, the 3D scenes you create will begin to get that added touch of realism. As you become more proficient with lighting, you'll learn how just the right set of lights can change the mood of a scene.

What You Have Learned

At this point, you know the following:

- How to properly use vertex colors
- What the different types of lights available to you are, and how to use each one
- How materials can affect the look of your objects
- What texture mapping is and how it can benefit your games
- How to load and map a texture to a polygon
- What texture coordinates are and how to properly use them

In the next chapter, you'll be introduced to the creation and use of 3D meshes.

Review Questions

You can find the answers to Review Questions and On Your Own exercises in Appendix A, "Answers to End-of-Chapter Exercises."

1. What does the fill mode change?
2. What are the four different types of lighting in Direct3D?
3. Which light type has a direction but not a position?
4. Which file formats are supported by the D3DX utility library for texture loading?
5. How do you change texture coordinates so that the texture repeats multiple times across a surface?

On Your Own

1. Create an example using materials that cause the teapot model to reflect only diffuse lighting.
2. Change example7 on the CD-ROM to use more than one texture on the rotating cube.

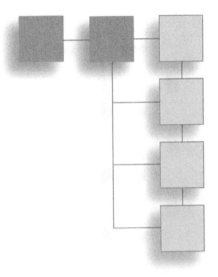

CHAPTER 7

MESHES

So far you've learned how to create 3D objects directly in your code and display them on the screen. You're probably thinking that this is a tedious process, and there's no way you would ever create all your game objects in code. Well . . . you're right. That's where 3D models come into play. They describe to your game what everything in it will look like. The models represent the items and characters in your world, and possibly even the world itself. After you have loaded a model into your game, you can represent it with a mesh object that you can move around and manipulate.

Here's what you'll learn in this chapter:

- How Direct3D handles meshes
- What is needed to properly define a 3D model
- What the X file format is
- How to create and save your own meshes
- How to load a 3D model into your game

Creating a 3D World

3D models help make up the virtual world that you create. They populate it by giving the gamer an environment to play in and enemies to destroy. So where do the models come from? If you have a 3D modeling package like 3ds max or Maya, you have the necessary tools to create everything your game will need. If these programs are a bit out of your budget, other packages like MilkShape 3D can do the job just as well.

After you've created your models, you export them into one of the many 3D file formats that are available. Just remember that you'll need to know how to load the file format within your game. For the purposes of this book, you'll be working with the file format that Microsoft created.

note

You can find MilkShape 3D at http://www.swissquake.ch/chumbalum-soft/index.html.

What Is a Mesh?

Your code handles 3D models that are loaded into your game as *meshes*. A mesh is a code container that holds everything about a 3D object, including its vertices, texture coordinates, and materials. By using the information that is contained within a mesh object, you can render your 3D models to the screen.

note

The D3DX utility library contains everything you need to use meshes within Direct3D.

How Direct3D Defines a Mesh

Most meshes within Direct3D are based on the ID3DXBaseMesh interface. This interface provides the storage container for your models and makes methods available to you for gaining access to the data within the mesh. For example, the GetVertexBuffer method, which is available through the ID3DXBaseMesh interface, gives you direct access to the vertex buffer within the mesh object.

Following are the different types of meshes:

- ID3DXMesh. This is the standard mesh interface that you will be using.
- ID3DXPMesh. This interface enables you to use progressive meshes.
- ID3DXSPMesh. Simplification mesh objects are handled through this interface.
- ID3DXPatchMesh. This interface provides Patch mesh functionality.

Each one of these mesh types can hold all the vertices of a model in a vertex buffer and give you information about the model, such as the number of faces or vertices.

Creating a Mesh

The first step to using meshes within your game is the creation of a mesh object. The mesh object is your container, holding all the information needed to describe your model to Direct3D. After you've created the mesh, you are free to copy in all the information that your model requires.

Two Direct3D functions are available for mesh creation: `D3DXCreateMesh` and `D3DXCreateMeshFVF`. Because each of these functions goes about creating the mesh in a slightly different way, I'll describe both in the following two sections.

D3DXCreateMesh

The `ID3DXMesh` interface is the simplest of the mesh interfaces and the easiest to get up and running quickly. In this section, you'll learn how to create a mesh from the `ID3DXMesh` interface by using the `D3DXCreateMesh` function.

The `D3DXCreateMesh` function is defined here:

```
HRESULT D3DXCreateMesh (
    DWORD NumFaces,
    DWORD NumVertices,
    DWORD Options,
    CONST LPD3DVERTEXELEMENT9 *pDeclaration,
    LPDIRECT3DDEVICE9 pDevice,
    LPD3DXMESH *ppMesh
);
```

The `D3DXCreateMesh` function takes six parameters:

- **NumFaces.** The number of faces that the mesh will contain.
- **NumVertices.** The number of vertices that the mesh will contain.
- **Options.** The values from the `D3DXMESH` enumeration.
- **pDeclaration.** An array of `D3DVERTEXELEMENT9` objects. These objects describe the FVF for the mesh.
- **pDevice.** A valid Direct3D device.
- **ppMesh.** A pointer to a valid `ID3DXMesh` object.

The following code shows how to create a mesh object that will contain enough vertices to hold a cube.

```
HRESULT hr;
// holds the newly created mesh
LPD3DXMESH boxMesh;

// D3DVERTEXELEMENT9 array
D3DVERTEXELEMENT9 Declaration [MAX_FVF_DECL_SIZE];

// Create the declarator needed by the D3DXCreateMesh function
D3DXDeclaratorFromFVF (D3DFVF_CUSTOMVERTEX, Declaration);
```

```
hr =D3DXCreateMesh (12,              // the number of faces for the mesh
                    8,               // the number of vertices
                    D3DXMESH_MANAGED,  // using managed memory for this mesh
                    Declaration,     // array of D3DVERTEXELEMENT9 objects
                    pd3dDevice,      // the Direct3D device
                    &boxMesh);       // variable that will hold the mesh
// Check the return code to make sure you have a valid mesh object
if FAILED (hr)
        return false;
```

As you can see, the previous code creates a mesh that contains 12 faces and 8 vertices and places it in the boxMesh variable. The third variable, D3DXMESH_MANAGED, tells Direct3D to create the mesh using managed memory for both the vertex and index buffers.

You should also notice the call to the D3DXDeclaratorFromFVF function called directly before D3DXCreateMesh. D3DXDeclaratorFromFVF creates the necessary D3DVERTEXELEMENT9 object for the fourth parameter by using the Flexible Vertex Format that your model uses.

When you use the D3DXDeclaratorFromFVF function, you aren't required to directly create the D3DVERTEXELEMENT9 objects yourself.

D3DXCreateMeshFVF

The D3DXCreateMeshFVF function differs from the D3DXCreateMesh in one way: It bases the mesh creation on a Flexible Vertex Format instead of going through a Declarator. The mesh object is identical to the one created with the D3DXCreateMesh function in the previous section.

The D3DXCreateMeshFVF function is defined next:

```
HRESULT D3DXCreateMeshFVF(
    DWORD NumFaces,
    DWORD NumVertices,
    DWORD Options,
    DWORD FVF,
    LPDIRECT3DDEVICE9 pDevice,
    LPD3DXMESH *ppMesh
);
```

The D3DXCreateMeshFVF function requires six parameters:

- **NumFaces.** The number of faces that the mesh will have
- **NumVertices.** The number of vertices that the mesh will consist of
- **Options.** The values from the D3DXMESH enumeration
- **FVF.** The Flexible Vertex Format of the vertices

- **pDevice.** A valid Direct3D device
- **ppMesh.** A pointer to an ID3DXMESH object

The following code shows a sample call to D3DXCreateMeshFVF.

```
// variable to hold the return code
HRESULT hr;

// the variable that will hold the newly created mesh
LPD3DXMESH boxMesh;

// Create the mesh with a call to D3DXCreateMeshFVF
hr = D3DXCreateMeshFVF(12,                   // NumFaces
                       8,                    // NumVertices
                       D3DXMESH_MANAGED,     // Options
                       D3DFVF_CUSTOMVERTEX,  // FVF
                       pd3dDevice,           // pDevice
                       &boxMesh);            // ppMesh

// Check the return code to make sure you have created a valid mesh
if FAILED (hr)
        return false;
```

Again, you create the mesh by using managed memory for the vertex and index buffer and specifying the D3DXMESH_MANAGED value. When this call is complete, the boxMesh variable should hold a valid mesh object.

The D3DXCreateMeshFVF function is the easiest of the two mesh creation functions to use.

Filling the Mesh

Now that you have created the mesh object, you need to fill it with data that will describe the model you want to display. At this point, you have an empty container that is the proper size to hold the data needed to create a cube.

To define the cube, you first need to lock the vertex buffer and fill it with the eight vertices that the cube needs. Next, you need to lock the index buffer and copy the indices into it.

The SetupMesh function shown here takes you through the steps to fill the mesh with the information it needs to create a cube:

```
/************************************************************************
 * SetupMesh
 * Set up the vertex buffer and index buffer of a mesh
 ***********************************************************************/
```

```
HRESULT SetupMesh()
{
        HRESULT hr;                             // variable to hold return codes

        //////////////////////////////////////////////////////////////////////
        // vertices for the vertex buffer
        CUSTOMVERTEX g_Vertices[ ] = {
                // X     Y     Z              COLOR
                {-1.0f,-1.0f,-1.0f, D3DCOLOR_ARGB(0,255,0,0)},          // 0
                {-1.0f, 1.0f,-1.0f, D3DCOLOR_ARGB(0,0,0,255)},          // 1
                {1.0f, 1.0f,-1.0f,  D3DCOLOR_ARGB(0,0,255,0)},          // 2
                { 1.0f,-1.0f,-1.0f, D3DCOLOR_ARGB(0,0,0,255)},          // 3
                {-1.0f,-1.0f, 1.0f, D3DCOLOR_ARGB(0,0,0,255)},          // 4
                {1.0f,-1.0f, 1.0f,  D3DCOLOR_ARGB(0,0,0,255)},          // 5
                { 1.0f, 1.0f, 1.0f, D3DCOLOR_ARGB(0,0,255,0)},          // 6
                {-1.0f, 1.0f, 1.0f, D3DCOLOR_ARGB(0,0,0,255)}           // 7
        };

        // Prepare to copy the vertices into the vertex buffer
        VOID* pVertices;
        // Lock the vertex buffer
        hr = boxMesh->LockVertexBuffer(D3DLOCK_DISCARD, (void**)&pVertices);

        // Check to make sure the vertex buffer can be locked
        if FAILED (hr)
                return hr;

        //////////////////////////////////////////////////////////////////////
        // index buffer data
        // The index buffer defines the faces of the cube,
        // two faces per each side of the cube
        WORD IndexData[ ] = {
                0,1,2,                   // 0
                2,3,0,                   // 1
                4,5,6,                   // 2
                6,7,4,                   // 3
                0,3,5,                   // 4
                5,4,0,                   // 5
                3,2,6,                   // 6
                6,5,3,                   // 7
                2,1,7,                   // 8
                7,6,2,                   // 9
```

```
              1,0,4,                    // 10
              4,7,1                     // 11
     };

     // Copy the vertices into the buffer
     memcpy( pVertices, g_Vertices, sizeof(g_Vertices) );

     // Unlock the vertex buffer
     boxMesh->UnlockVertexBuffer();

     // Prepare to copy the indices into the index buffer
     VOID* IndexPtr;
     // Lock the index buffer
     hr = boxMesh->LockIndexBuffer( 0, &IndexPtr );

     // Check to make sure the index buffer can be locked
     if FAILED (hr)
             return hr;

     // Copy the indices into the buffer
     memcpy( IndexPtr, IndexData, sizeof(IndexData)*sizeof(WORD) );

     // Unlock the buffer
     boxMesh->UnlockIndexBuffer();

     return S_OK;
}
```

The first thing that the SetupMesh function does is to create the g_Vertices array. This array contains the vertices and vertex colors that you need to define the cube. Next, the vertex buffer is locked, as shown in previous examples. A call to memcpy copies all the vertices into the vertex buffer and unlocks the buffer.

Next, you need to fill the index buffer. Like the vertex buffer, you must lock it before data can be copied into it. The indices that the index buffer will use are defined in the IndexData array. Notice that the IndexData array is defined as type WORD, meaning that these are 16-bit values.

After you have defined the values, lock the index buffer and copy in the indices through a call to memcpy. Then unlock the index buffer.

note

Both vertex and index buffers are required to create a valid mesh object.

Displaying a Mesh

Now that you have created the mesh and filled it with data, you are ready to render it to the screen. The drawMesh function shown next gives an example of what is needed to render a mesh. This function causes the cube to rotate on the screen.

```
/*************************************************************************
* void drawMesh (LPD3DXMESH mesh, D3DMATERIAL9 material)
* draws the mesh
*************************************************************************/
void drawMesh (LPD3DXMESH mesh, D3DMATERIAL9 *material)
{
        // Rotate the mesh
        D3DXMATRIX matRot;
        D3DXMATRIX matView;
        D3DXMATRIX matWorld;

        // Create the Rotation Matrix
        D3DXMatrixRotationY(&matRot, timeGetTime()/1000.0f);

        // Multiply the Rotation Matrix by the View Matrix
        D3DXMatrixMultiply(&matWorld, &matRot, &matView);

        // Set the world transform to the resulting World Matrix
        pd3dDevice->SetTransform( D3DTS_WORLD, &matWorld );
        // Set the material to use
        pd3dDevice->SetMaterial(material);

        // Draw the mesh
        mesh->DrawSubset(0);
}
```

The first part of the drawMesh function rotates and places the cube on the screen. Next, the material that the cube will use is set through the call to SetMaterial. The most important part of the drawMesh function is the call to DrawSubset.

The DrawSubset function tells Direct3D which portion of the mesh you want to be rendered to the screen. Because the mesh that you created previously contained only a single group, a 0 was passed to DrawSubset.

Figure 7.1 shows the resulting mesh being rendered. You can find the full source listing for creating and rendering a mesh in the chapter7\example1 directory on the CD-ROM.

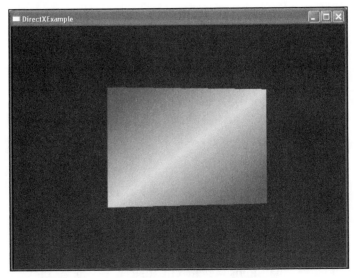

Figure 7.1 The cube being rendered as a mesh.

Optimizing a Mesh

When a mesh is created, it's not normally in the most optimized format for Direct3D to draw. For instance, your mesh might contain vertices that are duplicated and used for multiple faces, or the vertices and faces might not be in the most efficient order. By optimizing the mesh to use shared vertices and allowing the vertices and faces to be reordered, you can increase performance when rendering the mesh.

The D3DX Utility Library provides two functions for optimizing a mesh: Optimize and OptimizeInplace. Each of these functions essentially performs the same job but with one key difference: Optimize causes an output mesh to be created, whereas OptimizeInplace makes its changes to the input mesh. I'll explain how both of these functions are used with meshes.

The Optimize function, defined next, takes an input mesh, optimizes it, and generates an output mesh.

```
HRESULT Optimize(
    DWORD Flags,
    CONST DWORD *pAdjacencyIn,
    DWORD *pAdjacencyOut,
    DWORD *pFaceRemap,
    LPD3DXBUFFER *ppVertexRemap,
    LPD3DXMESH *ppOptMesh
);
```

The Optimize function requires six parameters:

- **Flags.** The flags that specify the type of optimization to perform. You can find the flags for this parameter in the D3DXMESHOPT enumeration.
- **pAdjacencyIn.** A pointer to an array that holds the current adjacency data for the input mesh.
- **pAdjacencyOut.** A pointer to an array that holds the adjacency data for the optimized output mesh.
- **pFaceRemap.** A pointer to the buffer that holds the new index order for the output mesh.
- **ppVertexRemap.** An address to a pointer of an ID3DXBuffer interface for the output mesh.
- **ppOptMesh.** An ID3DXMesh interface that holds the newly created output mesh.

The OptimizeInplace function, which makes changes to the input mesh, is defined next:

```
HRESULT OptimizeInplace(
    DWORD Flags,
    CONST DWORD *pAdjacencyIn,
    DWORD *pAdjacencyOut,
    DWORD *pFaceRemap,
    LPD3DXBUFFER *ppVertexRemap
);
```

The OptimizeInplace function requires five parameters:

- **Flags.** The flags that specify the type of optimization to perform. You can find the flags for this parameter in the D3DXMESHOPT enumeration.
- **pAdjacencyIn.** A pointer to an array that holds the current adjacency data for the mesh.
- **pAdjacencyOut.** A pointer to a buffer that holds the adjacency data for the optimized mesh. If you do not want to collect the adjacency data, you can pass a value of NULL for this parameter.

- **pFaceRemap.** A pointer to a buffer that holds the new index data for each face. If you do not want to collect this information, you can pass NULL for this parameter.
- **ppVertexRemap.** A pointer to an ID3DXBuffer interface that holds the new index for each vertex.

Table 7.1 shows the Flags parameter in more detail.

Table 7.1 D3DXMESHOPT Enumeration

Value	Description
D3DXMESHOPT_COMPACT	Reorders the faces to remove unused vertices and faces.
D3DXMESHOPT_ATTRSORT	Reorders the faces to minimize the number of material state changes.
D3DXMESHOPT_VERTEXCACHE	Reorders the faces to help with rendering cache performance.
D3DXMESHOPT_STRIPREORDER	Reorders the faces to maximize the length of the adjacent triangles.
D3DMESHOPT_IGNOREVERTS	Causes only the faces to be optimized; the vertices are ignored.
D3DMESHOPT_DONOTSPLIT	Prevents the splitting of vertices that are shared between groups.
D3DMESHOPT_DEVICEINDEPENDENT	Causes the vertex cache size to be set to a size that will work well on legacy hardware.

Getting the Mesh Details

During the process of optimizing a mesh, you might be curious as to certain details of the mesh that you are working with. For instance, you might wonder how many vertices or faces the mesh contains before optimization. The ID3DXMesh interface provides two functions that are useful for this purpose:

- **GetNumVertices.** Returns the number of vertices contained within the mesh.
- **GetNumFaces.** Returns the number of faces contained within the mesh.

The following code sample shows how to use both of these functions and display a Windows MessageBox containing the number of faces and vertices.

```
// Display the number of vertices in the mesh
std::string numVertices;
sprintf ( (char*) numVertices.c_str(),
          "numverts=%d",
          pMeshSysMem->GetNumVertices());
MessageBox (NULL, numVertices.c_str ( ), "message", MB_OK);

// Display the number of faces in the mesh
std::string numFaces;
sprintf ( (char*) numFaces.c_str(),
```

```
                          " numFaces =%d",
                          pMeshSysMem->GetNumFaces());
MessageBox (NULL, numFaces.c_str ( ), "message", MB_OK);
```

The pMeshSysMem variable must contain a valid mesh before GetNumVertices or GetNumFaces can be called.

The Attribute Table

During the mesh optimization process, you have the option of generating an attribute table. This table contains information about the attribute buffer of a mesh. The attribute buffer itself contains properties of each of the vertices within the mesh.

As I mentioned earlier, each mesh can contain multiple attribute groups. Each group contains a list of the vertices that are part of that group. Using multiple attribute groups, you can selectively split a mesh into separate pieces. For instance, a mesh of a car can be split into a group containing the body of the car and another group containing the wheels. If the group containing the body of the car were set as group 0 and the wheels as group 1, you would use the two following calls to DrawSubset to draw the entire car:

```
carMesh->DrawSubset(0);           // Draw the body group
carMesh->DrawSubset(1);           // Draw the wheels
```

Because each of these groups would require different materials as well, calls to SetMaterial would be made before each DrawSubset call.

To define separate groups within a mesh, you need to create an attribute table. You can only create an attribute table by calling one of the two optimize functions I mentioned earlier. When you call the optimize function and reorder the faces, an attribute table is generated. By default, if the mesh requires more than one material, a subset is generated for each one. In the case of the cube you created in the previous example, the entire cube contained only one material. The OptimizeMesh function that follows will take the cube contained in the boxMesh variable and split it into two separate subsets. Half of the cube will then be rendered with one material, and the second half of the cube will be rendered with an alternative material.

```
/*************************************************************************
 * OptimizeMesh
 *************************************************************************/
void OptimizeMesh (void)
{
        // Call the OptimizeInplace function to generate the attribute table
        boxMesh->OptimizeInplace(D3DXMESHOPT_ATTRSORT, 0, NULL, NULL, NULL);
```

```
    DWORD numAttr;
    D3DXATTRIBUTERANGE *attribTable = new D3DXATTRIBUTERANGE [2];

    // Get the number of items within the table
    boxMesh->GetAttributeTable(NULL, &numAttr);

    // Get the whole table into the variable attribTable
    boxMesh->GetAttributeTable(attribTable, &numAttr);

    // Set up the attributes for the first group
    attribTable[0].AttribId     = 0;
    attribTable[0].FaceStart    = 0;
    attribTable[0].FaceCount    = 6;
    attribTable[0].VertexStart = 0;
    attribTable[0].VertexCount = 8;

    // Set up the attributes for the second group
    attribTable[1].AttribId     = 1;
    attribTable[1].FaceStart    = 6;
    attribTable[1].FaceCount    = 6;
    attribTable[1].VertexStart = 0;
    attribTable[1].VertexCount = 8;

    // Write the attribute table back into the mesh
    boxMesh->SetAttributeTable(attribTable, 2);
}
```

The previous code first calls the OptimizeInplace function on the cube mesh contained in the boxMesh variable. Because I used OptimizeInplace, I continue to use the original cube mesh.

Next, because I created two separate attribute groups, I construct an array of two D3DXATTRIBUTERANGE structure variables.

```
D3DXATTRIBUTERANGE *attribTable = new D3DXATTRIBUTERANGE [2];
```

Each D3DXATTRIBUTERANGE structure contains the information that Direct3D needs to define an attribute group.

The D3DXATTRIBUTERANGE structure is shown next.

```
typedef struct _D3DXATTRIBUTERANGE {
    DWORD AttribId;
    DWORD FaceStart;
```

```
    DWORD FaceCount;
    DWORD VertexStart;
    DWORD VertexCount;
} D3DXATTRIBUTERANGE;
```

The D3DXATTRIBUTERANGE structure contains five variables:

- **AttribId**. The ID number of the current group
- **FaceStart**. The number of the face to start this group with
- **FaceCount**. The number of faces that will be included in this group
- **VertexStart**. The number of the vertex to start the group with
- **VertexCount**. The number of vertices that will be included in this group

After you create the array of D3DXATTRIBUTERANGE structures, you have to get access to the attribute table. You can access the attribute table through a call to the GetAttributeTable function. The GetAttributeTable function can be used in two different ways.

The first way allows you identify the number of items that are currently contained within the attribute table. When you pass a NULL value as the first parameter to GetAttributeTable and a pointer to a DWORD variable as the second, the mesh returns back to you the number of items currently in the table. The item count is returned in the variable passed as the second parameter. A sample call to GetAttributeTable that works in this way is shown here:

```
DWORD numAttr;       // variable that will hold the number of items in the table
// using GetAttributeTable to collect the number of items in the attribute table
boxMesh->GetAttributeTable(NULL, &numAttr);
```

As you can see in the previous call, the numAttr variable is passed as the second parameter. On completion of this function call, numAttr will contain the number of items currently in the attribute table.

Now that you have the number of items, you need to gain access to the data within the table. You can use the GetAttributeTable function in another way to gather this information. Earlier, you created an array of two D3DXATTRIBUTERANGE structures. When you pass the attribTable array as the first parameter and the numAttr variable as the second parameter, the GetAttributeTable function fills in the attribTable array with the data currently contained in the table. The call to GetAttributeTable being used in this way is shown here:

```
boxMesh->GetAttributeTable(attribTable, &numAttr);
```

At this point, you are free to manipulate and change the data with the attribTable array. If you look back at the OptimizeMesh function, you'll see that I changed the variables contained within each of the D3DXATTRIBUTERANGE structures. I changed the first structure to start at the first face in the mesh and contain only six faces; this accounts for half of the faces in the cube.

```
// Set up the attributes for the first group
attribTable[0].AttribId    = 0;      // the ID of the group
attribTable[0].FaceStart   = 0;      // the starting group face
attribTable[0].FaceCount   = 6;      //the number of faces in the group
attribTable[0].VertexStart = 0;      // the starting group vertex
attribTable[0].VertexCount = 8;      // the number of vertices
```

The second group starts at the sixth face and again continues for six faces. The only other change to this structure is the assignment of AttribId to 1.

```
// Set up the attributes for the second group
attribTable[1].AttribId    = 1;
attribTable[1].FaceStart   = 6;
attribTable[1].FaceCount   = 6;
attribTable[1].VertexStart = 0;
attribTable[1].VertexCount = 8;
```

The final step needed to split the cube into two separate attribute groups is to take the changed attribute table and update the cube mesh with it. Updating the attribute table within a mesh is accomplished through the SetAttributeTable function, defined here:

```
HRESULT SetAttributeTable (
    CONST D3DXATTRIBUTERANGE * pAttribTable,
    DWORD cAttribTableSize
);
```

The SetAttributeTable function requires only two parameters:

- **pAttribTable.** A pointer to the attribute table to update the mesh with
- **cAttribTableSize.** A value specifying the size of the attribute table

The following code shows how the SetAttributeTable function updates the table within the mesh. The attribTable variable, which represents the array of attributes, is passed as the first parameter. Because I only wanted to change the cube to include two attribute groups, I passed a value of 2 for the second parameter.

```
boxMesh->SetAttributeTable(attribTable, 2);
```

Now that the cube mesh is split into two separate groups, you must change how the cube is rendered. There must be two calls to the DrawSubset function, each one specifying the value of the group to draw. The following code shows the updated DrawSubset calls.

In addition, a call to the SetMaterial function before each DrawSubset call causes the material to change before each half of the cube is rendered.

```
// Set the material
pd3dDevice->SetMaterial (&materials[0].MatD3D);
// Draw the first subset of the mesh
mesh->DrawSubset(0);

// Set the second material
pd3dDevice->SetMaterial (&materials[1].MatD3D);
// Draw the second subset of the mesh
mesh->DrawSubset(1);
```

Figure 7.2 shows the updated cube being rendered with separate materials for each group.

Figure 7.2 The cube being rendered with two materials applied. The first material is green and the second material is red.

Predefined Meshes

Mesh creation by hand is a tedious job and should be avoided at all costs. Luckily, modeling programs usually eliminate the need for hand-modeling. There are times, however, when modeling a simple object like a cube is overkill. In such an instance, DirectX provides some functions to assist with object creation.

D3DX Object Creation

So far, all the examples I've shown involve creating the 3D model by hand. Because I've only used simple objects, like cubes, they have been easy for the demonstration. DirectX, however, provides a more hassle-free method of simple object creation through the D3DX Utility Library.

The following functions, accessed through D3DX, help you in creating simple 3D objects such as cubes, spheres, and cylinders:

- **D3DXCreateBox.** Creates a cube
- **D3DXCreateSphere.** Creates a sphere
- **D3DXCreateCylinder.** Creates a cylinder
- **D3DXCreateTeapot.** Creates a 3D model of a teapot

Creating a Box

You can use the D3DXCreateBox function, defined next, when you want to create a simple cube. The resulting cube will be a fully complete ID3DXMesh object that you can optimize or manipulate in any way.

```
HRESULT D3DXCreateBox(
    LPDIRECT3DDEVICE9 pDevice,
    FLOAT Width,
    FLOAT Height,
    FLOAT Depth,
    LPD3DXMESH *ppMesh,
    LPD3DXBUFFER *ppAdjacency
);
```

The D3DXCreateBox function takes six parameters:

- **pDevice.** A pointer to a valid Direct3D device.
- **Width.** The width in units of the cube along the X axis.
- **Height.** The height in units of the cube along the Y axis.
- **Depth.** The depth of the cube along the Z axis.
- **ppMesh.** An address to an ID3DXMesh pointer. This variable contains the mesh of the cube.
- **ppAdjacency.** The adjacency buffer. If you don't want to store this information, you can pass NULL to this parameter.

The box created with this function will look much like the box that you've been using in the previous sections. Figure 7.3 shows a cube created with the D3DXCreateBox function.

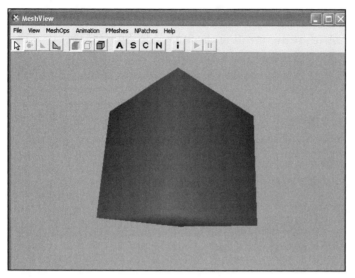

Figure 7.3 A cube created with the `D3DXCreateBox` function.

Creating a Teapot

The Utah Teapot, which has long been used as a sample model for 3D graphics, can also be created easily in Direct3D. You've already seen it rendered because I used it as a model in Chapter 6, "Vertex Colors, Texture Mapping, and 3D Lighting."

To create a 3D teapot, you need to use the `D3DXCreateTeapot` function defined here:

```
HRESULT D3DXCreateTeapot(
    LPDIRECT3DDEVICE9 pDevice,
    LPD3DXMESH *ppMesh,
    LPD3DXBUFFER *ppAdjacency
);
```

The `D3DXCreateTeapot` function requires three parameters:

- **pDevice.** A valid Direct3D object.
- **ppMesh.** An `ID3DXMesh` object in which to place the created mesh.
- **ppAdjacency.** An adjacency buffer, if you want to collect this information. You can pass `NULL` to this parameter if you do not need this.

Unfortunately, the `D3DXCreateTeapot` function doesn't let you control the size of the teapot that is created. The following single line of code creates a teapot for you:

```
D3DXCreateTeapot(pd3dDevice, &teapotMesh, NULL);
```

note

You can find a history of the Utah Teapot and how it came to be at http://sjbaker.org/teapot.

Creating a Sphere

Spheres are useful objects in 3D. Using only spheres, you can create a simulated model of the solar system. If your scene requires spheres to be generated, you can use the D3DXCreateSphere function, shown here:

```
HRESULT D3DXCreateSphere(
    LPDIRECT3DDEVICE9 pDevice,
    FLOAT Radius,
    UINT Slices,
    UINT Stacks,
    LPD3DXMESH *ppMesh,
    LPD3DXBUFFER *ppAdjacency
);
```

The D3DXCreateSphere function takes six parameters:

- **pDevice.** A valid Direct3D device.
- **Radius.** A float value that specifies the radius of the sphere.
- **Slices.** The number of vertical breaks that will be present.
- **Stacks.** The number of horizontal breaks that will be present.
- **ppMesh.** An ID3DXMesh object that will hold the created sphere.
- **ppAdjacency.** An adjacency buffer if you want to collect this information. You can pass NULL to this parameter if you don't need this.

The following snippet of code shows how to use the D3DXCreateSphere function:

```
// Create the sphere
float sphereRadius = 3.0;
int numSlices = 20;
int numStacks = 20;
D3DXCreateSphere(pd3dDevice,
                 sphereRadius,
                 numSlices,
                 numStacks,
                 &sphereMesh,
                 NULL);
```

Figure 7.4 shows a sphere created with D3DXCreateSphere. The higher the value in the Slices and Stacks, the smoother the resulting sphere will be.

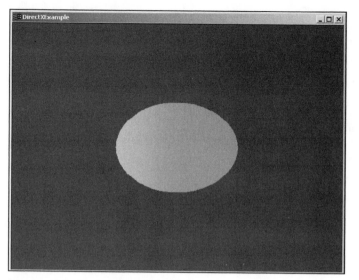

Figure 7.4 A sphere created with D3DXCreateSphere.

Creating a Cylinder

The final object that I'll demonstrate how to create is a cylinder. The D3DXCreateCylinder function, shown next, allows you to specify certain properties of the cylinder, such as its length and the radius of each end.

```
HRESULT D3DXCreateCylinder(
    LPDIRECT3DDEVICE9 pDevice,
    FLOAT Radius1,
    FLOAT Radius2,
    FLOAT Length,
    UINT Slices,
    UINT Stacks,
    LPD3DXMESH *ppMesh,
    LPD3DXBUFFER *ppAdjacency
);
```

The D3DXCreateCylinder function requires eight parameters:

- **pDevice.** A valid Direct3D device.
- **Radius1.** A float value specifying the radius of the cylinder's negative Z end.
- **Radius2.** A float value specifying the radius of the cylinder's positive Z end.
- **Length.** The length of the cylinder.
- **Slices.** The number of quads that will make up the cylinder along its length.

- **Stacks.** The number of quads that will make up the cylinder around the circumference.
- **ppMesh.** An ID3DXMesh object that will hold the created sphere.
- **ppAdjacency.** An adjacency buffer, if you want to collect this information. You can pass NULL to this parameter if you do not need it.

The following sample of code shows how to create a cylinder.

```
// Define the properties of the cylinder
float cylRadius1 = 2.0;
float cylRadius2 = 2.0;
float cylLength  = 7.0;
int cylSlices    = 10;
int cylStacks    = 10;
// Create the cylinder
D3DXCreateCylinder(pd3dDevice,
                cylRadius1,
                cylRadius2,
                cylLength,
                cylSlices,
                cylStacks,
                &cylMesh,
                NULL);
```

Figure 7.5 shows a cylinder created with the D3DXCreateCylinder function.

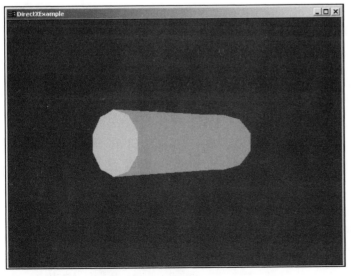

Figure 7.5 A cylinder created with the D3DXCreateCylinder function.

You can find a full source example showing how to use the D3DX functions described earlier in the chapter7\example2 directory on the CD-ROM.

The Direct3D Mesh Format: The X File

Creating meshes within your code isn't the best way to create a 3D world. Most games require models that are highly complex and detailed, which would be a pain to create by hand. As mentioned earlier, modeling tools are available that allow for the offline creation of 3D models. After you create the models, you can export them into a variety of file formats.

Microsoft has come up with its own proprietary format for 3D models called the X file. The X file format, which was introduced in DirectX 2.0, provides developers with a template-based structure for storing meshes, textures, and animations.

X files can either be text readable or in a binary format. The following code shows a small piece of an X file in text format:

```
MeshVertexColors {
    8;
    0;0.000000; 0.000000; 1.000000; 0.000000;;,
    1;0.000000; 1.000000; 1.000000; 0.000000;;,
    2;0.000000; 0.000000; 1.000000; 0.000000;;,
    3;0.000000; 1.000000; 1.000000; 0.000000;;,
    4;0.000000; 0.000000; 1.000000; 0.000000;;,
    5;0.000000; 1.000000; 1.000000; 0.000000;;,
    6;0.000000; 0.000000; 1.000000; 0.000000;;,
    7;0.000000; 1.000000; 1.000000; 0.000000;;;
}
```

A template that describes the format that the data must be in controls each section within an X file. A template of the same name, shown here, dictates the previous MeshVertexColors structure:

```
template MeshVertexColors \
{ \ <1630B821-7842-11cf-8F52-0040333594A3> \
        DWORD nVertexColors; \
        array IndexColor vertexColors[nVertexColors]; \
}
```

Each template consists of two pieces: the numerical unique identifier, enclosed in brackets, and the declaration of the data the template can contain. In this instance, the MeshVertexColors template declares two data types: a DWORD value that contains the number of vertex colors, and an array of index colors.

How X Files Are Created

X files are normally created with 3D modeling software, although this is not always the case. You can code an X file by hand, but for complex models, this would be a large chore. Typically, a graphic artist creates the model and then exports it into the X file format. Microsoft has released two programs that are capable of converting models into the proper format. The first program, conv3ds.exe, is a command-line application that takes as input a 3D model in the 3DS file format. 3DS files are typically created with 3ds max, but other modeling packages support this format as well.

The second program, XSkinExp.dle, is a plug-in for 3ds max that allows you to directly export models from within the modeling environment. Both of these applications are included with the DirectX Software Development Kit (SDK).

Saving a Mesh to an X File

Because there are already two programs for creating X files, you might be wondering why I would bother showing you how to programmatically create these files yourself. Well, not all game programming is about coding graphics engines and Artificial Intelligence (AI); you need to create tools to make your fellow programmers' lives easier. For instance, you might be asked to create an application that can read in any number of 3D file formats and export X files. Luckily, the D3DX Utility Library comes to the rescue again with functions for creating X files.

D3DXSaveMeshToX

D3DX includes a function called D3DXSaveMeshToX that you can use to generate X files. Before you can use this function, though, your data must reside in an ID3DXMesh object. As you'll recall from earlier, I took you through the process of creating and displaying a mesh. In this section, I'm going to refer back to that lesson and show you how to take the meshes you created earlier and save them as X files.

Just to refresh what you've learned about meshes so far: Meshes are created using either the D3DXCreateMesh or D3DXCreateMeshFVF function. After you create the mesh, you fill in the vertex and index buffers with the information pertaining to the model you are creating. At this point, you should have a perfectly valid ID3DXMesh object and be ready to create an X file from it.

The D3DXSaveMeshToX function, defined next, takes the mesh you created and saves it to disk in the X file format.

```
HRESULT D3DXSaveMeshToX (
        LPCTSTR pFilename,
```

```
               LPD3DXMESH pMesh,
               CONST DWORD* pAdjacency,
               CONST D3DXMATERIAL* pMaterials,
               CONST D3DXEFFECTINSTANCE* pEffectInstances,
               DWORD NumMaterials,
               DWORD Format
    );
```

The D3DXSaveMeshToX function has seven parameters:

- **pFilename.** A string variable that contains the name of the X file to save to.
- **pMesh.** A pointer to an **ID3DXMesh** variable.
- **pAdjacency.** A pointer to an array of three DWORDs per face.
- **pMaterials.** A pointer to an array of **D3DXMATERIAL** structures.
- **pEffectInstances.** A pointer to an array of effect instances.
- **NumMaterials.** The number of D3DXMATERIAL structures in the pMaterials variables.
- **Format.** The formats in which to save the X file. There are three possible format flags:
  - **DXFILEFORMAT_BINARY.** The X file will be saved in a binary format.
  - **DXFILEFORMAT_TEXT.** The X file will be saved in a text-viewable format.
  - **DXFILEFORMAT_COMPRESSED.** The X file will be saved as compressed.

The source shown next is an example of how D3DXSaveMeshToX is used:

```
LPD3DXMESH        cubeMesh;       // a pointer to an ID3DXMESH
D3DXMATERIAL      material;       // a single D3DXMATERIAL structure


HRESULT hr;
// Create the mesh that will hold the cube model
hr = D3DXCreateMeshFVF(12,
                       8,
                       D3DXMESH_MANAGED,
                       D3DFVF_CUSTOMVERTEX,
                       pd3dDevice,
                       &cubeMesh);


// Set up the vertex and index buffer
// This function is not defined here, but it fills the vertex and index
// buffers of the mesh with the required information for a cube. You can
// review the section on creating a mesh from code for the full description of
// this function.
```

```
SetupVBIB();

// Take the valid mesh object and save it to an X file
D3DXSaveMeshToX ("cube.x", // file name to save to
          cubeMesh, // the ID3DXMESH interface
            NULL, // adjacency information; none used
          &material, // array of D3DXMATERIAL structures
          NULL, // array of effect instances; none used
          1, // number of D3DXMATERIAL structures
          D3DXF_FILEFORMAT_TEXT); // saving a text version X file
```

The important portion of this code is the call to D3DXSaveMeshToX. This function details the file name to save the X file as, the mesh object to save out, and the format that X file should be saved as.

Figure 7.6 shows what the cube.x mesh looks like when viewed from the MeshView application found in the DXSDK\Bin\DXUtils directory. This application is installed when you install the DirectX SDK.

You can find a full source example showing how to use the D3DX functions described in this chapter to save X files in the chapter7\example3 directory on the CD-ROM.

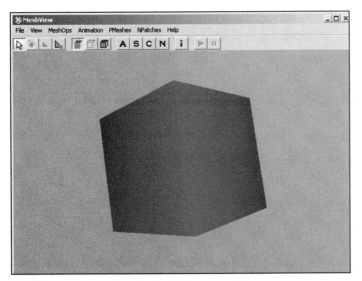

Figure 7.6 The cube.x file as shown in the MeshView application.

Loading a Mesh from an X File

Now that you know how to save an X file, the next logical question is, "How do I load one from disk?" Well, you could write a loader yourself, which would require you to learn the X file format extensively, or you can look to the D3DX library once more.

Because the X file is the file format that Microsoft is pushing for DirectX, Microsoft has also provided a function for loading these files into your application.

Using the D3DXLoadMeshFromX Function

The D3DXLoadMeshFromX function, defined here, is used to load X files from disk:

```
HRESULT D3DXLoadMeshFromX(
    LPCTSTR pFilename,
    DWORD Options,
    LPDIRECT3DDEVICE9 pDevice,
    LPD3DXBUFFER* ppAdjacency,
    LPD3DXBUFFER* ppMaterials,
    LPD3DXBUFFER* ppEffectInstances,
    DWORD* pNumMaterials,
    LPD3DXMESH* ppMesh
);
```

The D3DXLoadMeshFromX function takes eight parameters:

- **pFilename.** A string specifying the file name to save the X file to.
- **Options.** Flags that detail how the mesh will be loaded. You can find these values in the D3DXMESH enumeration.
- **pDevice.** A valid Direct3D device.
- **ppAdjacency.** The adjacency buffer.
- **ppMaterials.** A pointer to the material buffer.
- **ppEffectInstances.** A pointer to a buffer containing an array of effect instances.
- **pNumMaterials.** The number of materials that you can find in the ppMaterials variable.
- **ppMesh.** The ID3DXMesh object that will contain the mesh when this function is complete.

The following code shows how to use D3DXLoadMeshFromX to load an X file from disk.

```
// variable to hold the return code
HRESULT     hr;
// variable to hold the loaded mesh
LPD3DXMESH  pMeshSysMem;
// buffer to hold the adjacency data
```

```
LPD3DXBUFFER ppAdjacencyBuffer;
// buffer to hold materials
LPD3DXBUFFER pD3DXMtrlBuffer;

// Load the mesh from the disk
hr = D3DXLoadMeshFromX ("cube.x",
                        D3DXMESH_SYSTEMMEM,
                        pd3dDevice,
                        &ppAdjacencyBuffer,
                        &pD3DXMtrlBuffer,
                        NULL,
                        &m_dwNumMaterials,
                        &pMeshSysMem);
// Check the return code to make sure the mesh was loaded successfully
if (FAILED(hr))
        return false;
```

The previous code loads the mesh found in the cube.x file and places it into the pMeshSysMem variable. During the call to D3DXLoadMeshFromX, the m_dwNumMaterials variable was filled with the number of materials within the mesh. Using this value, you can extract the materials from the mesh and place them into a material buffer for later use. Each buffer is used when rendering the mesh to change the material associated with each subset.

Because the pD3DXMtrlBuffer variable contains all the material information for the mesh, you need to split each material into separate D3DMATERIAL9 structures. The following code gets a pointer to the material information within the mesh and extracts it into D3DMATERIAL9 structures with a for loop.

```
// Get a pointer to the material buffer within the mesh
D3DXMATERIAL* matMaterials= (D3DXMATERIAL*)pD3DXMtrlBuffer->GetBufferPointer();
// Declare an array of materials
D3DMATERIAL9* m_pMeshMaterials;

//Create two D3DMATERIAL9 structures
m_pMeshMaterials = new D3DMATERIAL9[m_dwNumMaterials];

// Loop through the materials in the mesh and create a D3DMATERIAL for each one
for(DWORD i = 0; i < m_dwNumMaterials; i++)
{
        //Copy the material
        m_pMeshMaterials[i] = matMaterials[i].MatD3D;

        //Set the ambient color for the material (D3DX does not do this)
        m_pMeshMaterials[i].Ambient = m_pMeshMaterials[i].Diffuse;
}
```

Now that the mesh is properly loaded, you are free to render the mesh to the screen. The drawMesh function that follows shows a typical way of rendering a mesh loaded from an X file.

```
/*****************************************************************************
* drawMesh
*****************************************************************************/
void dxManager::drawMesh(void)
{
        D3DXMATRIX meshMatrix, scaleMatrix, rotateMatrix;

        createCamera(1.0f, 750.0f);          // near clip plane, far clip plane
        moveCamera(D3DXVECTOR3(0.0f, 0.0f, -450.0f));
        pointCamera(D3DXVECTOR3(0.0f, 0.0f, 0.0f));

        // Set the rotation
        D3DXMatrixRotationY(&rotateMatrix, timeGetTime()/1000.0f);

        // Set the scaling
        D3DXMatrixScaling(&scaleMatrix, 0.5f, 0.5f, 0.5f);

        // Multiply the scaling and rotation matrices to create the meshMatrix
        D3DXMatrixMultiply(&meshMatrix, &scaleMatrix, &rotateMatrix);

        // Transform the object in world space
        pd3dDevice->SetTransform(D3DTS_WORLD, &meshMatrix);

        // Loop through the number of materials for this mesh
        for(DWORD i = 0; i < m_dwNumMaterials; i++)
        {
                // Set the material for this mesh subset
                pd3dDevice->SetMaterial(&m_pMeshMaterials[i]);

                // Draw the current mesh subset
                pMeshSysMem->DrawSubset(i);
        }
}
```

At this point, you should be able to see on the screen the mesh that you loaded from the X file. Figure 7.7 shows a dolphin being rendered. The dolphin X file comes with the DirectX SDK and can be found in the DXSDK\Samples\Media directory. You can find a full source code example that shows how to load an X file from disk in the chapter7\example4 directory on the CD-ROM.

Figure 7.7 A dolphin model rendered from an X file.

Chapter Summary

Now that you have the ability to load in 3D models, you'll be able to take your game's realism to the next level. You'll no longer be restricted to simple cubes or spheres but be able to include real-world objects. If you have no 3D modeling skills, you'll still be able to test your game by taking advantage of the many free 3D models available on the Internet.

What You Have Learned

In this chapter, you have learned the following:

- How to create a mesh
- How to display the mesh you've created
- What it takes to optimize the data that's contained within a mesh
- How to split a mesh into subsets to allow more than one material to be applied
- The steps needed to load a mesh into the X file format from disk
- How to create and save your own X file meshes

Review Questions

You can find the answers to Review Questions and On Your Own exercises in Appendix A, "Answers to End-of-Chapter Exercises."

1. Which two functions can you use to create a mesh?

2. The `OptimizeInplace` function is different from the `Optimize` function in what way?

3. What does the attribute table contained in a mesh do?

4. Which function returns the number of vertices within a mesh?

5. What are the three format flags you can employ when using the `D3DXSaveMeshToX` function?

On Your Own

1. Write a small sample that loads and displays more than one X file.

2. Write a function that returns an optimized version of a mesh.

CHAPTER 8

POINT SPRITES, PARTICLES, AND PYROTECHNICS

Particles are used everywhere in a game to create the effects that make the game memorable. From the rocket you see heading for your ship to the explosion it creates when it hits, particles help make virtual worlds exciting.

Here's what you'll learn in this chapter:

- What particles are and how they're used
- Which properties a particle can contain
- How to define and render particles
- What a particle emitter is and what its uses are
- How to render particles using Direct3D's point sprite capability

Particles

Particles are used within games to represent small pieces of debris, sparks from a firework, or any other small entity that requires motion.

Each particle is a single independent entity, with its movement and behavior predefined during creation. During a particle's lifetime, it updates itself using internal properties that tell it where to go and how fast to get there. Particles for a particular effect are normally created and spawned from a single point, called an *emitter*. The emitter's job is to create each particle and set its internal properties before releasing it. The emitter also controls the number of particles and the timing with which they are spawned.

Particles are made up of a textured polygon, called a *billboard*, that always faces the camera. Although a billboard has many uses, such as clouds or sometimes trees, it is used most often to create particles. Because each billboard normally contains two triangles with a single texture, you can render many billboards in quick succession, creating spectacular special effects.

Before you start tossing particles into your scene, you need to know the details of how they work.

Particle Properties

Each particle has internal properties that define its look and behavior. Listed next are a few of the basic properties that most particles have:

- **Position.** Where the particle is currently located within your scene.
- **Movement.** The property that controls where the particle is going and how quickly.
- **Color.** The color of the particle.
- **Alive Flag.** A property flag that lets your game know whether a particle is currently active. Because some particles routinely go offscreen, this flag helps to save system resources by killing off unseen particles.
- **Texture.** The texture that will be applied to the particle.

Each particle released from an emitter contains each of these properties. In the next section, I'm going to take these properties and show you to use them to create a structure that defines a particle.

The Particle Structure

The Particle structure groups together all the properties of a single particle. By creating an array of Particle structures, you can update and render more than one particle quickly.

```
typedef struct
{
    D3DXVECTOR3 m_vCurPos;      // the current position vector
    D3DXVECTOR3 m_vCurVel;      // the movement vector
    D3DCOLOR    m_vColor;       // the color of this particle
    BOOL m_bAlive;              // Is this particle currently alive?
} Particle;
```

The current position of a particle is stored in a D3DXVECTOR3 structure. This structure allows a particle to exist in three dimensions.

The movement vector holds both the direction and the velocity of a particle. The color of a particle is held in a D3DCOLOR structure. You can use any of the D3DCOLOR macros to define the color of your particles.

The final variable in the `Particle` structure is `m_bAlive`. This variable determines whether a single particle is currently active. Before a particle is launched from the emitter, this variable is `FALSE`.

How Are the Particles Created?

The particles are created by setting each variable in the `Particle` structure to an initial value. During the lifetime of each particle, the variables within its structure are updated based on the effect of the emitter. Because you'll most often need more than one particle at a time, it's best to define an array of `Particle` structures so that you can keep control over them in one place. The following code shows how to define and initialize a group of particles.

```
// Define the number of particles to create
#define MAXNUM_PARTICLES 150
// Define the structure that holds the particle properties
typedef struct
{
    // the current position of the particle
    D3DXVECTOR3 m_vCurPos;
    // the movement vector
    D3DXVECTOR3 m_vCurVel;
    // the color of the particle
    D3DCOLOR    m_vColor;
} Particle;

// Set up an array of particle structures
Particle ParticleArray[MAXNUM_PARTICLES];

// Loop through the number of particles that are to be created
// and init their values
for( int i = 0; i < MAXNUM_PARTICLES; i++ )
{
    // Set the position of each particle at the origin
    ParticleArray[i].m_vCurPos = D3DXVECTOR3(0.0f,0.0f,0.0f);

    // Generate a random value for each part of the direction/velocity vector
    float vecX = ((float)rand() / RAND_MAX);
    float vecY = ((float)rand() / RAND_MAX);
    float vecZ = ((float)rand() / RAND_MAX);
```

```
    // Using the random values generated above, set the movement vector
    // for this particle
    ParticleArray[i].m_vCurVel = D3DXVECTOR3 (vecX, vecY, vecZ);

    // Each particle is green and has full alpha
    ParticleArray[i].m_vColor = D3DCOLOR_RGBA (0, 255, 0, 255);
}
```

The previous code first defines the structure that holds the particle properties. Next, an array of particle structures is created and filled in with the information needed for each particle.

After the array is created, a for loop goes through the particles and sets up the starting position vector, a random movement vector, and the color.

How Do the Particles Move?

Particles move based on one of their internal properties called the *movement vector*. This vector describes both the direction and speed that the particle will move during one frame. The movement vector is created by using the D3DXVECTOR3 macro that specifies the X, Y, and Z values.

The code that follows shows how a single particle defines its movement vector and how the position of the particle is changed by adding together the movement and position vectors. This code uses the variables that are defined in the previous particle structure.

```
// Create the movement vector for this particle
Particle.m_vCurVel = D3DXVECTOR3 (0.0f,1.0f,0.0f);

// Change the current position of the particle by adding the
// movement vector and position vector
Particle.m_vCurPos += Particle.m_vCurVel;
```

When the movement vector is defined in the first line of code, the Y value is set to 1.0f, which, when added to the position vector, causes the particle to move up the screen one unit in the positive Y direction.

The second line of code shows how the position vector is changed when you add the movement vector to it. Calling this line of code each frame causes the particle to move around the world based on the values specified in the movement vector.

Figure 8.1 shows what a group of particles could look like after being released from an emitter.

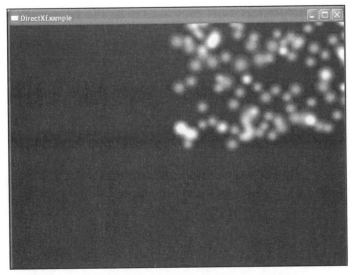

Figure 8.1 A group of particles released from an emitter.

Creating a Random Vector

Occasionally, you'll need to create a vector that has a random direction and velocity. For instance, when you're creating particles, you want each particle to follow its own random path when it's released from the emitter. One way of doing this is by using the rand function. This function returns a random value between 0 and RAND_MAX. By converting this number to a float value and dividing it by RAND_MAX, you can generate a random value between 0.0f and 1.0f.

This code shows how a random vector can be created using this method:

```
float vecX = ((float)rand() / RAND_MAX);
float vecY = ((float)rand() / RAND_MAX);
float vecZ = ((float)rand() / RAND_MAX);
D3DXVECTOR3(vecX,vecY,vecZ);
```

This method only generates positive values for the variables vecX, vecY, and vecZ.

Particle Systems

A particle system is a way of grouping particle emitters into an easy-to-use interface. When you group the emitters, rendering multiple particle effects at the same time becomes easier. During the render portion of your game, the particle system handles drawing all particle instances, while the rest of your code handles drawing the rest of your game world.

Designing a Particle System

Designing a particle system is a pretty straightforward process. The particle system controls one or more emitters in a scene, which in turn control the particles.

A particle system implementation consists of three components:

- Particle emitter objects
- The particles
- A particle system manager

The particle system manager controls the creation, movement, and use of particle emitters. The particle emitters handle the actual particles. The emitter starts and stops the particle streams and controls the streams' direction and velocity, and even the pattern that the particles create. The final pieces—the particles—are the simple textured quads that have properties dictating their behavior, such as movement, position, and color.

note

A particle effect describes the pattern or behavior of a group of particles. Examples of particle effects are fireworks, fountains, or streams.

Particle emitters are designed to be the birthplace or origin point for a batch of particles that compose an effect. Emitters initialize the internal properties of each particle to be released, such as position, starting direction, and velocity. After a particle leaves an emitter, its internal properties completely control its behavior.

Because all particles that are spawned from an emitter normally share a common texture, they're easy to render. You have to make a single texture state, and then you can render all the particles from an emitter.

Emitter Properties

Each particle emitter contains a few properties that control how the emitter behaves, as well as the behavior of the particles it releases. I've listed a few simple properties that an emitter can contain, but this is in no way an exhaustive list:

- **Position.** This is the position of the emitter. Emitters can be placed in any spot within your 3D world.
- **Movement.** Not all particle emitters stay in one place. Some emitters, such as those that generate smoke effects from missiles, are constantly on the move.
- **Texture.** The emitter normally holds a pointer to the texture that you should apply to all the particles it generates.
- **An array or vector of particles.** You need a place within the emitter to hold the particles. You can store the particles in several ways.
- **Number of particles.** It's always a good idea to keep a list of the number of particles each emitter can generate. This also makes it easy to increase or decrease the number of particles used.
- **Particle properties.** These properties are the values that set the default internal properties of each particle.
- **Gravity.** Some emitters generate gravity. For example, if the particle effect that an emitter is attempting to generate is a black hole, the gravity defines the amount of pull that the emitter has on the particles.

Emitter Structure

The Particle structure groups together all the properties of a single particle. By creating an array of Particle structures, you can update and render more than one particle quickly.

```
typedef struct
{
    // the current position vector
    D3DXVECTOR3 m_vCurPos;
    // the movement vector
    D3DXVECTOR3 m_vCurVel;
    // the texture used for particles from this emitter
    LPDIRECT3DTEXTURE9 m_texture;
    // an array to hold particle structures
    Particle m_aParticles [MAXNUM_PARTICLES];
    // the number of particles this emitter has
    Int m_NumParticles;
    // Is this emitter currently active?
    BOOL m_bAlive;
} Emitter;
```

The emitter structure contains the internal properties of an emitter.

The first variable, m_vCurPos, holds the current position of the emitter. Because emitters can actually move around in the scene, the value in this variable might change.

The second variable, m_vCurVel, is the direction and velocity of the emitter. Again, this allows the emitter to move around in the scene.

The texture that is going to be used for all the particles from an emitter is stored in the m_texture variable.

The emitter holds the particles in an array of Particle structures. The m_NumParticles variable holds the number of particles that this emitter will be able to handle.

The final variable, m_bAlive, is a boolean variable that represents whether the emitter is currently active.

You can find a code example that demonstrates a simple and generic particle implementation in the chapter8\example1 directory on the CD-ROM.

Coding a Particle System Manager

Now that you know what needs to go into creating a particle system, I'm going to detail the code you need to create a particle system manager.

The first class you need is the particle manager. This class handles the creation and placement of emitters in your scene.

The Particle Manager Class

The following code is the header file that relates to a sample particle manager.

```
#pragma once
#include <vector>
#include <string>

#include "Emitter.h"
#include "Particle.h"

// forward class declarations
class Particle;
class Emitter;

class particleManager
{
// public members and functions
public:
    particleManager(void);
    ~particleManager(void);
```

```
    // inits the particle manager
    bool init(void);

    // shuts down the particle manager
    void shutdown(void);

    // Create a new emitter in the scene
    void particleManager::createEmitter(LPDIRECT3DDEVICE9 pDevice,
                                        int numParticles,
                                        std::string textureName,
                                        D3DXVECTOR3 position,
                                        D3DCOLOR color);
    // Remove an emitter from a scene based on its index in the emitter vector
    void removeEmitter(int emitterNum);

    // Remove an emitter from a scene based on a pointer to the emitter
    void removeEmitter(Emitter *which);

    // updates the position of the emitter and the particles it contains
    void update(void);

    // renders the particles within an emitter
    void render(LPDIRECT3DDEVICE9 pDevice);

// private members and functions
private:
    // the vector of emitter objects
    std::vector <Emitter*> emitters;
};
```

Because the number of emitters in your scene can vary, I decided to store them in a vector. A vector can dynamically resize itself based on the number of emitters you are creating; it doesn't limit you to a fixed number like an array does.

Here are the important functions within the particle manager class:

- **createEmitter.** This function actually creates another emitter in your scene. Its parameters allow you to specify the location, movement, color, and texture to use for an emitter.
- **removeEmitter.** This function lets you remove an emitter from your scene.

- **update.** The update function causes the emitter's update function to be called. When update is called, the positions of the particles and possibly the emitter are changed, allowing for motion.

- **render.** This function calls the render function of the emitter, which in turn actually draws all the particles within an emitter.

Following is the full code for the createEmitter function:

```
/*****************************************************************************
* createEmitter
*****************************************************************************/
void particleManager::createEmitter(LPDIRECT3DDEVICE9 pDevice,
                                    int numParticles,
                                    std::string textureName,
                                    D3DXVECTOR3 position,
                                    D3DCOLOR color)
{
    // Create a new emitter
    Emitter *tempEmitter = new Emitter(pDevice);

    // Load the texture
    tempEmitter->addTexture(textureName);
    // Set the number of particles
    tempEmitter->setNumParticles(numParticles);

    tempEmitter->initParticles(position, color);

    // Add this emitter to the vector
    emitters.push_back(tempEmitter);
}
```

The createEmitter function first creates a pointer to an Emitter object called tempEmitter. Next, the function passes the name of the texture from the textureName parameter into the new Emitter object, along with the numParticles parameters.

Afterward, the initParticles function is called with the position of the emitter and the default color of the particles. In the background, the Emitter class creates and initializes the particles.

Finally, the newly created emitter is added to the back of the emitters vector.

Now that an emitter has been created successfully and particles have been initialized, the next question is this: How do the particles get updated? Well, the particle manager calls the emitter's update function. The update function, shown next, loops through the emitter's vector, checking for active emitters and calling their update functions.

```
/*************************************************************************
* update
*************************************************************************/
void particleManager::update(void)
{
    // Loop through the emitters
    for (unsigned int i=0; i<emitters.size(); i++)
    {
        // Check whether this emitter is active
        if (emitters[i]->getAlive())
            // If so, then update it
            emitters[i]->update();
    }
}
```

Instead of constantly storing the number of emitters currently in the vector, I'm using the size built-in vector function. As emitters are added or removed, the size of the vector changes. Using the size function, I'm not required to keep track of this.

The update function loops through all the emitters in the vector, calling their update functions.

After the particles are updated, you need to get them on the screen. You can do this through the render function, shown here:

```
/*************************************************************************
* render
*************************************************************************/
void particleManager::render(LPDIRECT3DDEVICE9 pDevice)
{
    // Loop through the emitters
    for (unsigned int i=0; i<emitters.size(); i++)
    {
        // Check whether this emitter is active
        if (emitters[i]->getAlive())
            // If so, render this emitter
            emitters[i]->render();
    }
}
```

Again, I'm looping through the vector of emitters, checking for active emitters. When an active emitter is found, its render function is called. This results in all the particles within an emitter being rendered to the screen.

Creating an Emitter Class

The emitter class encapsulates all the functionality needed for an emitter into a single object. Besides holding the standard emitter properties, the emitter class handles the loading and storing of the texture for the particles. Each emitter stores one texture to apply to all the particles it generates.

The header file that follows shows how the emitter class is constructed.

```
#pragma once
#include <string>
#include <vector>

// Include the needed DirectX headers
#include <d3d9.h>
#include <d3dx9tex.h>

#include the Particle class header and a forward class declaration
#include "Particle.h"
class Particle;

class Emitter
{
    // Set up the vertex structure for the particles
    struct CUSTOMVERTEX
    {
        D3DXVECTOR3 psPosition;
        D3DCOLOR color;
    };

    #define D3DFVF_CUSTOMVERTEX (D3DFVF_XYZ|D3DFVF_DIFFUSE)

public:
    Emitter(void);
    Emitter(LPDIRECT3DDEVICE9 pDevice);
    ~Emitter(void);

    // Add a texture to this emitter
    void addTexture(std::string textureName);
```

```cpp
    // Set the number of particles and size the vector
    void setNumParticles(int nParticles);

    // Init the particles and set the position of the emitter
    void initParticles(D3DXVECTOR3 position, D3DCOLOR color);

    // Update all the particles in this emitter
    void update(void);
    // Render the particles in this emitter
    void render();

    // inline functions
    inline bool getAlive(void) { return m_bAlive; }
    // inline function that converts a float to a DWORD value
    inline DWORD FLOAT_TO_DWORD( FLOAT f ) { return *((DWORD*)&f); }

private:
    // Store a copy of the Direct3D device so that it doesn't have to be passed
    // around all the time
    LPDIRECT3DDEVICE9 emitterDevice;

    // the current position of this particle
    D3DXVECTOR3 m_vCurPos;
    // the direction and velocity of this particle
    D3DXVECTOR3 m_vCurVel;

    // vertex buffer to hold the point sprites
    LPDIRECT3DVERTEXBUFFER9 pVertexBuffer;
    // the texture that will be applied to each particle
    LPDIRECT3DTEXTURE9      pTexture;
    // a pointer of type Particle; will be used to create an array of particles
    Particle *m_particles;
    // the number of particles in this emitter
    int numParticles;
    // value to hold whether this emitter is active
    bool m_bAlive;

    // Private functions create the vertex buffer to hold the particles
    LPDIRECT3DVERTEXBUFFER9 createVertexBuffer(unsigned int size,
                                               DWORD usage,
                                               DWORD fvf);
};
```

The Emitter class defines a few needed functions:

- **addTexture.** This function loads the texture for the particles and stores it in the pTexture variable.

- **setNumParticles.** The particle array is sized in this function to the number of particles needed for the emitter.

- **initParticles.** The vertex buffer is created and all the internal properties of the particles are set in this function.

- **createVertexBuffer.** This private member function generates the vertex buffer that holds all particle vertices.

- **Update.** This function handles moving around the particles within the scene.

- **Render.** This function handles the rendering of the particles to the screen.

The three most important functions are initParticles, update, and render. I'll explain each of these functions in more detail next:

```
/****************************************************************************
* initParticles
****************************************************************************/
void Emitter::initParticles(D3DXVECTOR3 position, D3DCOLOR color)
{
    // Create the vertex buffer for this emitter and store it in the
    // pVertexBuffer variable
    pVertexBuffer = createVertexBuffer(numParticles * sizeof(CUSTOMVERTEX),
        D3DUSAGE_DYNAMIC | D3DUSAGE_WRITEONLY | D3DUSAGE_POINTS,
        D3DFVF_CUSTOMVERTEX);

    // Loop through the number of particles for this emitter and set their
    // initial properties
    for (int i=0; i<numParticles; i++)
    {
        // This particle is alive
        m_particles[i].m_bAlive = true;
        // setting the color to the value passed from the particle manager
        m_particles[i].m_vColor = color;
        // setting the position to the value passed from the particle manager
        m_particles[i].m_vCurPos = position;

        // Create a random value for each part of the direction/velocity vector
        float vecX = ((float)rand() / RAND_MAX);
        float vecY = ((float)rand() / RAND_MAX);
```

```
        float vecZ = ((float)rand() / RAND_MAX);
        m_particles[i].m_vCurVel = D3DXVECTOR3(vecX,vecY,vecZ);
    }
}
```

The first line in initParticles calls for the creation of the emitter's vertex buffer. Because the vertex buffer is going to be updated each frame with new information, the buffer is created with the D3DUSAGE_DYNAMIC | D3DUSAGE_WRITEONLY flags.

Next, a for loop goes through each of the particles for the emitter and sets the alive flag, defines the color, and sets the starting position. Normally, particles from an emitter start off at a single location.

The direction and velocity of the particle are set using random values. This allows each particle to go off in a different direction when rendered.

The update function, shown here, updates the position of each particle every frame:

```
/**************************************************************************
* update
**************************************************************************/
void Emitter::update(void)
{
    // Loop through and update the positions of the particles
    for (int i=0; i<numParticles; i++)
    {
        // Add the current direction and velocity to the current position
        m_particles[i].m_vCurPos += m_particles[i].m_vCurVel;
    }
}
```

Each particle's position is updated by adding the movement vector—which determines the particle's direction and velocity—to the particle's current position. Because this value is updated every frame, the particles appear to move around the screen.

The final function is render, shown here:

```
/**************************************************************************
* render
**************************************************************************/
void Emitter::render()
{
    CUSTOMVERTEX *pPointVertices;

    // Lock the vertex buffer and update the particles within it
```

```
pVertexBuffer->Lock( 0,
                     numParticles * sizeof(CUSTOMVERTEX),
                     (void**)&pPointVertices,
                     D3DLOCK_DISCARD );

// Loop through the particles
for( int i = 0; i < numParticles; ++i )
{
    pPointVertices->psPosition = m_particles[i].m_vCurPos;
    pPointVertices->color = m_particles[i].m_vColor;
    pPointVertices++;
}

// Unlock the vertex buffer
pVertexBuffer->Unlock();

// Set the texture for the particles
emitterDevice->SetTexture( 0, pTexture );
// Set the vertex stream
emitterDevice->SetStreamSource( 0, pVertexBuffer, 0, sizeof(CUSTOMVERTEX) );
// Set the vertex format
emitterDevice->SetFVF( D3DFVF_CUSTOMVERTEX );
// Call DrawPrimitive to render the particles to the screen
emitterDevice->DrawPrimitive( D3DPT_POINTLIST, 0, numParticles );
}
```

The render function first locks the vertex buffer and loops through the array of particles for the emitter, copying each particle into the buffer. Then the render function unlocks the vertex buffer and sets the texture for the particle with Direct3D through the SetTexture function. After that, the function sets the stream source and vertex format before calling DrawPrimitive. You'll notice that DrawPrimitive uses a primitive type of D3DPT_POINTLIST, which causes all the particles to be rendered as a series of unconnected points.

Creating a Particle Class

The final class needed for a particle system is the Particle class. Because the emitter class handles most of the particle manipulation, this class is really just used to store the internal properties. The header file for this class is shown here:

```
#pragma once

#include <d3d9.h>
```

```
#include <d3dx9tex.h>

class Particle
{
public:
    Particle(void);
    ~Particle(void);

    // the current position of this particle
    D3DXVECTOR3 m_vCurPos;
    // the direction and velocity of this particle
    D3DXVECTOR3 m_vCurVel;
    // the color of this particle
    D3DCOLOR    m_vColor;
    // Is this particle alive?
    bool m_bAlive;
};
```

I've also made all the properties of the Particle class public so that they can be accessed directly from within the emitter. Because the number of particles can be in the thousands, keeping them public helps to reduce the overhead of getter and setter functions.

Point Sprites: Making Particles Easy

The particles I've explained so far are based on billboards, which are camera-facing quads with a texture applied. Each of the particles created in this manner requires two triangles if you use the methods described so far. To minimize the drawing that needs to be done for each particle, DirectX has introduced point sprites. A point sprite is plotted like a generic point, using a single X, Y, and Z coordinate. Unlike normal points, point sprites have a texture applied and can vary in size.

Point sprites have an advantage over particles that are created using billboards. Whereas billboards require constant transformation to face the camera, point sprites are camera facing by default.

Using Point Sprites in Direct3D

The biggest difference between using billboards for particles and using point sprites is the primitive type used to render them. Billboard particles normally require two triangles rendered in a triangle strip, causing four vertices to be used. Point sprites are rendered as a series of point primitives, minimizing the amount of data that needs to be sent for rendering.

The code that follows shows how the call to DrawPrimitive changes to support point sprites.

emitterDevice->DrawPrimitive(D3DPT_POINTLIST, 0, 100);

The DrawPrimitive call shown here uses the D3DPT_POINTLIST primitive type to render the 100 particles that are being used.

How to Use Point Sprites

Point sprites require only minor changes to what you've learned so far. To give you an idea of what is needed to use point sprites, I've detailed the steps here:

1. Load the texture that the point sprites will use. You can do this by using the D3DXCreateTextureFromFile function.

2. Create a dynamic vertex buffer. By specifying the D3DUSAGE_DYNAMIC, D3DUSAGE_WRITEONLY, and D3DUSAGE_POINTS flags, you create a vertex buffer that you can change and update each frame. Notice that the D3DUSAGE_POINTS flag was also specified. This flag tells Direct3D that the vertex buffer is being used to draw points.

3. Define the CUSTOMVERTEX structure that you will use, along with the vertex format. The following code shows a sample structure and format.

```
struct CUSTOMVERTEX
{
        D3DXVECTOR3 psPosition;
        D3DCOLOR color;
};
#define D3DFVF_CUSTOMVERTEX (D3DFVF_XYZ|D3DFVF_DIFFUSE)
```

4. At this point, you are ready to render the point sprites during your main game loop. You start off drawing by locking the vertex buffer you created earlier and copying the data from the particle structure into it. After this data is in the vertex buffer, unlock the buffer.

5. Change the render states to allow for point sprite rendering.

6. Call DrawPrimitive with the D3DPT_POINTLIST primitive type.

Following are the render states that pertain to point sprites:

■ **D3DRS_ALPHABLENDENABLE.** Alpha blending is turned on through this render state. This allows the point sprites to be arbitrary shapes based on the texture map that's applied to them.

■ **D3DRS_ZWRITEENABLE.** This enables the application to write values to the depth buffer.

■ **D3DRS_POINTSPRITEENABLE.** This render state enables the full texture to be applied to the point sprite.

- **D3DRS_POINTSCALEENABLE.** If this render state if set to TRUE, the point is scaled based on its distance from the camera.
- **D3DRS_POINTSIZE.** This is the size of the point sprite.
- **D3DRS_POINTSIZE_MIN.** This is the minimum size of a point sprite.

Now that you know what you need to work with point sprites, I'll show you the updated render function that includes everything discussed so far.

```
/****************************************************************************
* render
* uses point sprites to render the particles
****************************************************************************/
void Emitter::render()
{
    emitterDevice->SetRenderState( D3DRS_ZWRITEENABLE, FALSE );

    emitterDevice->SetRenderState( D3DRS_ALPHABLENDENABLE, TRUE );
    emitterDevice->SetRenderState( D3DRS_DESTBLEND, D3DBLEND_ONE );

    // Enable point sprite render states
    // Turn on point sprites
    emitterDevice->SetRenderState( D3DRS_POINTSPRITEENABLE, TRUE );

    // Enable scaling
    emitterDevice->SetRenderState( D3DRS_POINTSCALEENABLE,   TRUE );

    // the point size to use when the vertex does not include this information
    emitterDevice->SetRenderState( D3DRS_POINTSIZE,      FLOAT_TO_DWORD(1.0f) );

    // the minimum size of the points
    emitterDevice->SetRenderState( D3DRS_POINTSIZE_MIN, FLOAT_TO_DWORD(1.0f) );

    // These three render states control the scaling of the point sprite
    emitterDevice->SetRenderState( D3DRS_POINTSCALE_A,  FLOAT_TO_DWORD(0.0f) );
    emitterDevice->SetRenderState( D3DRS_POINTSCALE_B,  FLOAT_TO_DWORD(0.0f) );
    emitterDevice->SetRenderState( D3DRS_POINTSCALE_C,  FLOAT_TO_DWORD(1.0f) );

    // Lock the vertex buffer and set up our point sprites in accordance with
    // your particles that you're keeping track of in your application
    CUSTOMVERTEX *pPointVertices;
```

```
// Lock the vertex buffer each frame to allow the point sprites to move
pVertexBuffer->Lock( 0,
                     numParticles * sizeof(CUSTOMVERTEX),
                     (void**)&pPointVertices,
                     D3DLOCK_DISCARD );

// Loop through the particle structures, setting the values in the
// vertex buffer
for( int i = 0; i < numParticles; ++i )
{
    pPointVertices->psPosition = m_particles[i].m_vCurPos;
    pPointVertices->color = m_particles[i].m_vColor;
    pPointVertices++;
}

// Unlock the vertex buffer
pVertexBuffer->Unlock();

// Draw the point sprites
// Set the texture for these point sprites
emitterDevice->SetTexture( 0, pTexture );
// Set the vertex stream
emitterDevice->SetStreamSource( 0,
                                pVertexBuffer,
                                0,
                                sizeof(CUSTOMVERTEX) );
// Set the vertex format
emitterDevice->SetFVF( D3DFVF_CUSTOMVERTEX );
// Draw the point sprites using the D3DPT_POINTLIST primitive
emitterDevice->DrawPrimitive( D3DPT_POINTLIST, 0, numParticles );

// Set the render states back
emitterDevice->SetRenderState( D3DRS_ZWRITEENABLE, TRUE );
emitterDevice->SetRenderState( D3DRS_ALPHABLENDENABLE, FALSE );
emitterDevice->SetRenderState( D3DRS_POINTSPRITEENABLE, FALSE );
emitterDevice->SetRenderState( D3DRS_POINTSCALEENABLE,  FALSE );
}
```

The first thing that the previous render function does is set the render states that will be needed when drawing the point sprites. Next, render enables alpha blending and turns on point sprites. It then sets the minimal point size and values needed for scaling.

After setting the proper render states, render updates the vertex buffer. The buffer is locked and the particle structures are looped through, causing new values to be written to the vertex buffer.

After unlocking the vertex buffer, the point sprites are rendered to the screen. Finally, the render function resets the render states back to their defaults to allow other 3D objects within the scene to be rendered properly.

You can find a full source code example detailing everything needed to use point sprites in the chapter8\example2 directory on the CD-ROM.

note

Certain render states, such as D3DRS_POINTSIZE and D3DRS_POINTSCALE_A, require a DWORD value to be passed in. By defining the following inline function, you easily can convert float values into the proper format:

```
inline DWORD FLOAT_TO_DWORD( FLOAT f ) { return *((DWORD*)&f); }
```

Chapter Summary

At this point, you should have the basics you need to create your own particle system. By slightly changing the values you use to create each particle, you can create many of your own amazing particle effects.

What You Have Learned

In this chapter, you learned the following:

- What particles are used for
- How particle systems are used
- How to design and implement particle emitters
- How point sprites make it easier to create particles
- How to render point sprites within your scene

Review Questions

You can find the answers to Review Questions and On Your Own exercises in Appendix A, "Answers to End-of-Chapter Exercises."

1. Which properties do you need to define a single particle?
2. Which two values are normally combined to make a particle move around a scene?
3. Which object initializes the internal properties of a particle?

4. Which primitive type is needed in the call to DrawPrimitive to enable point sprite rendering?

5. What are the advantages of point sprites over billboards?

On Your Own

1. Design an update function that makes a particle expire after 300 frames.

2. Code a particle emitter that continually releases particles.

PART III

ADDITIONAL NEEDS

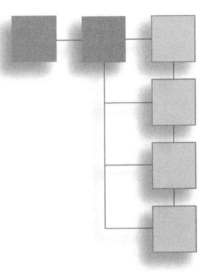

CHAPTER 9

USING DIRECTINPUT

eing able to interact with your virtual world is critical in any game, whether it's through the keyboard, mouse, or any number of other devices. In this chapter, I'll explain the benefits of DirectInput and how to use it.

Here's what you'll learn in this chapter:

- How DirectInput can make your life easier
- The types of devices that DirectInput can support
- How to detect the input devices that are currently installed
- How to use keyboards, mice, and joysticks
- How to use analog or digital controls
- How to support more than one input device
- How to use force feedback

I Need Input

Every game needs to be able to interact with its user. Your game requires a way of getting direction from the player. An input device can be used to drive a car around a track, move your character around his world, or anything else that you can imagine.

Back in the days of DOS, programmers had little choice but to poll hardware interrupts if they wanted to get keystrokes from the keyboard. Standard C functions of the time, such as getchar, were too slow and not useful enough for games. They needed a better way. Enter the Basic Input Output System (BIOS), which is the lowest level of software in a computer.

Stored normally in a flash ROM on the motherboard, the BIOS tells the system how to initialize and prepares the hardware for the operating system. Under DOS, programmers had direct access to the BIOS through assembly language. Because the BIOS knew everything that the hardware was doing, developers could ask it for certain information. One of the important bits of the system that the BIOS was always watching was the keyboard. Every stroke of a key triggered a hardware interrupt, informing the system that a key had been pressed. Because this happened almost instantaneously, a quick and efficient method for getting keystrokes from the keyboard was available.

Windows NT eliminated the ability to read the keyboard directly from the hardware. Windows became an absolute boundary between applications and the hardware. Any information needed about the system had to be gained from the operating system because applications were no longer allowed direct access to the hardware. Windows had its own way of getting user input, and that was through the message queue. You saw the message queue earlier in the book:

```
MSG msg;
ZeroMemory( &msg, sizeof(msg) );
while( msg.message!=WM_QUIT )
{
    // Check for messages
    if( PeekMessage( &msg, NULL, OU, OU, PM_REMOVE ) )
    {
        TranslateMessage( &msg );
        DispatchMessage( &msg );
    }
}
```

The message queue collected events such as mouse movement and keyboard input from the system. Although this method was normally sufficient for Windows applications, it wasn't fast enough for games. Most developers turned to another Windows function— GetAsyncKeyState—to get the information they needed.

GetAsyncKeyState allowed for quick checking of the keys on the keyboard, and even allowed for checking of multiple keys and the state of the mouse buttons. This method of collecting user input became common among game developers, but it had one major problem: It didn't allow for input to be collected from other devices, such as gamepads and joysticks. Game makers were stuck specifically supporting only certain devices because each device had a different way of collecting and transmitting the input data to the system.

A standard way of getting fast input from the user was needed, regardless of the method or the device used. DirectInput provided the common layer needed to solve this problem.

DirectInput allows your game to support a myriad of input devices without forcing you to know the exact details of each device. A small sample of the devices supported by DirectInput follows:

- Keyboard
- Mouse
- Gamepads
- Joysticks
- Steering wheels

Using DirectInput

DirectInput is initialized in a similar manner to other DirectX components.

The DirectInput object provides the interface needed to access DirectInput devices. Through this interface, you can create devices, enumerate the devices on a system, or check the status of a particular device.

After you've created the DirectInput object, you must create the device. The DirectInput device that you'll create will enable you to gain specific access to an input device, be it a keyboard, joystick, or other gaming device.

After creating the device, you need to gain access to its input. This is done through a process called "acquiring a device." When you acquire a device, you can initialize the device, get a list of its capabilities, or read its input.

It might seem like a lot of trouble to go through just to get a couple of keystrokes from a keyboard or gamepad, but having direct access to your input device will make your life a lot more simple later on.

Now that you have access to the device, you can read input from it for each frame. For example, if you are using a gamepad as your input device, you can check to see if the user has pressed the direction buttons or one of the predefined action buttons. If so, you can act on this information.

At this point, you should have a clear understanding of getting DirectInput up and running and getting data from an input device. I'm now going to step you through the code needed to do just that.

Creating the DirectInput Object

As I mentioned before, the first step to using DirectInput is the creation of the DirectInput object. The function `DirectInput8Create` creates the DirectInput object.

The `DirectInput8Create` function is defined as follows:

```
HRESULT WINAPI DirectInput8Create(
    HINSTANCE hinst,
    DWORD dwVersion,
    REFIID riidltf,
    LPVOID *ppvOut,
    LPUNKNOWN punkOuter
);
```

Five parameters must be passed to the `DirectInput8Create` function:

- **hInst.** The instance of the application that is creating the DirectInput object.
- **dwVersion.** The version number of DirectInput that this application requires. The standard value for this parameter is `DIRECTINPUT_VERSION`.
- **riidltf.** The identifier of the required interface. Using the default value of `IID_IDirectInput8` is acceptable for this parameter.
- **ppvOut.** The pointer to the variable that will hold the created DirectInput object.
- **punkOuter.** This parameter is normally set to `NULL`.

Following is a small snippet of code that creates a DirectInput object:

```
HRESULT         hr;           // variable used to hold return codes
LPDIRECTINPUT8  DI_Object;    // the DirectInput object

// Create the DirectInput object
hr = DirectInput8Create( hInst,
                         DIRECTINPUT_VERSION,
                         IID_IDirectInput8,
                         (void** )&DI_Object,
                         NULL );

// Check the return code for DirectInput8Create
if FAILED( hr )
return false;
```

note

As a reminder, make sure to check the return value when you're creating DirectX objects. This informs you when an object creation has failed and helps you track down bugs in your code.

The previous creates two variables: hr and DI_object. hr is defined as a standard HRESULT. It checks the return code of a function call. The second variable, DI_object, holds the soon-to-be-created DirectInput object.

The code then continues by making the call to DirectInput8Create. A quick check of the return code in the hr variable is done to make sure that the function has returned successfully.

Creating the DirectInput Device

Now that you have a valid DirectInput object, you are free to create the device by using the function CreateDevice.

```
HRESULT CreateDevice(
    REFGUID rguid,
    LPDIRECTINPUTDEVICE *lplpDirectInputDevice,
    LPUNKNOWN pUnkOuter
);
```

The CreateDevice function requires three parameters:

- **rguid.** The variable holds a reference to the GUID of the desired input device. This value can be either a GUID returned from the function EnumDevices or one of the two default values:
  - GUID_SysKeyboard
  - GUID_SysMouse
- **lplpDirectInputDevice.** The variable that will hold the returned DirectInput device upon its creation.
- **pUnkOuter.** The address of the controlling object's interface. This value will normally be NULL.

The following code assumes that you want to create a DirectInput device for an installed system keyboard.

```
HRESULT          hr;        // variable used to hold function return codes
LPDIRECTINPUTDEVICE8       DI_Device;    // the DirectInput device

// Retrieve a pointer to an IDirectInputDevice8 interface
hr = DI_object ->CreateDevice( GUID_SysKeyboard, &DI_Device, NULL );

// Check the return code from CreateDevice
if FAILED( hr )
    return false;
```

This code creates the variable DI_Device first. This variable of type LPDIRECTINPUTDEVICE8 holds the created DirectInput device.

The call to CreateDevice, which is a method available to you through the DirectInput object, is made by passing in the value GUID_SysKeyboard as the first parameter. This tells CreateDevice that you want to create a device based on the system keyboard. The second parameter is the DI_Device variable that was created earlier, and the third parameter is NULL.

After this function call is complete, the DI_Device variable holds a valid DirectInput device. Be sure to check the return code for this function to confirm that the device is valid.

Setting the Data Format

After you've created a valid DirectInput device, you need to set up the data format that DirectInput will use to read input from the device. The SetDataFormat function defined next requires a DIDATAFORMAT structure as its only parameter.

```
HRESULT SetDataFormat (
    LPCDIDATAFORMAT lpdf
);
```

The DIDATAFORMAT structure describes various elements of the device for DirectInput. The DIDATAFORMAT structure is defined here:

```
typedef struct DIDATAFORMAT {
    DWORD dwSize;
    DWORD dwObjSize;
    DWORD dwFlags;
    DWORD dwDataSize;
    DWORD dwNumObjs;
    LPDIOBJECTDATAFORMAT rgodf;
} DIDATAFORMAT, *LPDIDATAFORMAT;
```

The DIDATAFORMAT structure is described in Table 9.1.

Table 9.1 DIDATAFORMAT Structure

Member	Description
dwSize	The size of this structure in bytes.
dwObjSize	The size of the DIOBJECTDATAFORMAT in bytes.
dwFlags	A DWORD value that specifies attributes of this data format. Valid values are DIDF_ABSAXIS, which means that the axes are absolute values, or DIDF_RELAXIS, which means that the axes of this device are relative.
dwDataSize	This value holds the size of the data packet returned from the input device in bytes.
dwNumObjs	The number of objects with the rgodf array.
rgodf	An address to an array of DIOBJECTDATAFORMAT structures.

You need to create and use your own DIDATAFORMAT structure if the input device you want to use is not a standard device. Following are the predefined DIDATAFORMAT structures for common input devices:

- **c_dfDIKeyboard.** This is the data format structure that represents a system keyboard object.
- **c_dfDIMouse.** You use this data format structure when the input device being used is a mouse with up to four buttons.
- **c_dfDIMouse2.** You use this data format structure when the input device being used is a mouse or similar device with up to eight available buttons.
- **c_dfDIJoystick.** This is the data format structure for a joystick.
- **c_dfDIJoystick2.** This is the data format structure for a joystick with extended capabilities.

If the input device you want to use is not included as one of the predefined types, you need to specifically create a DIDATAFORMAT structure. Most of the common input devices don't require this.

The code sample that follows calls the SetDataFormat function using the predefined DIDATAFORMAT structure for a keyboard device.

```
// variable to hold the return code
HRESULT hr;

// Set the data format for the device
// Call the SetDataFormat function
hr = DI_Device->SetDataFormat(&c_dfDIKeyboard);

// Check the SetDataFormat return code
if FAILED( hr )
    return false;
```

Setting the Cooperative Level

The cooperative level tells the system how the input device that you are creating works with the system. You can set input devices to use either exclusive or nonexclusive access. Exclusive access means that only your application can use a particular device and does not need to share it with other applications that Windows might be running. This is most useful when your game is a full-screen application. When a game is exclusively using a device, such as a mouse or keyboard, any attempt for another application to use this device fails.

If your game doesn't mind sharing the device, this is called *nonexclusive access*. When a game creates the device with nonexclusive access, other applications that are running can utilize that same device. This is most helpful when your game is running in windowed mode on the Windows desktop. Using the mouse as a nonexclusive input device does not restrict its use in other application windows.

For each game that you want to use with a DirectInput device, you must set the cooperative level for its use. You do this through the SetCooperativeLevel function, defined next.

```
HRESULT SetCooperativeLevel(
    HWND hwnd,
    DWORD dwFlags
);
```

The SetCooperativeLevel function requires two parameters:

- **hwnd.** A handle to the window that is requesting access to the device.
- **dwFlags.** A series of flags that describe the type of access you are requesting. The available flags are as follows:
  - **DISCL_BACKGROUND.** The application requires background access to the device. This means that you can use the input device even when the game window is not the currently active window.
  - **DISCL_EXCLUSIVE.** The game requests total and complete control over the input device, restricting other applications from using it.
  - **DISCL_FOREGROUND.** The game requires input only when the window is the current active window on the desktop. If the game window loses focus, input to this window is halted.
  - **DISCL_NONEXCLUSIVE.** Exclusive access is not needed for this application. Defining this flag allows other running applications to continue using the device.
  - **DISCL_NOWINKEY.** This tells DirectInput to disable the Windows key on the keyboard. When this key is pressed, the Start button on the desktop is activated and focus is removed from the currently active window. When this flag is set, the Windows key is deactivated, allowing your game to retain focus.

note

Each application must specify whether it needs foreground or background access to the device by setting either the DISCL_BACKGROUND or DISCL_FOREGROUND flag. The application is also required to set either the DISCL_EXCLUSIVE or DISCL_NONEXCLUSIVE flag. The DISCL_NOWINKEY flag is optional.

The following code sample sets the device to use nonexclusive access and be active only when the application window has focus.

```
// Set the cooperative level
hr = DI_Device->SetCooperativeLevel( wndHandle,
                            DISCL_FOREGROUND | DISCL_NONEXCLUSIVE );
```

```
// Check the return code for SetCooperativeLevel
if FAILED( hr )
    return false;
```

The SetCooperativeLevel function is a method that's callable through the DirectInput device interface. The DI_Device variable in the previous code represents the current Direct-Input device created by the call to CreateDevice.

The parameters that are being passed in the sample SetCooperativeLevel function consist of wndHandle, which represents the handle to the window requesting access to the input device, and the flags DISCL_FOREGROUND and DISCL_NONEXCLUSIVE, telling DirectInput the access you are requesting for the device.

Acquiring Access

The final step required before you can read input from a particular device is called "acquiring the device." When you acquire access to an input device, you are telling the system that you are ready to use and read from this device. This function, which is another method of the DirectInput device, performs this action. This function, defined next, takes no parameters and returns only whether it was successful.

```
HRESULT Acquire(VOID);
// The small code example that follows shows how the Acquire function is called.
// Get access to the input device.
hr = DI_Device->Acquire();
if FAILED( hr )
    return false;
```

The return code for this function is checked to make sure it has completed successfully. Because this is the last step needed before reading input from a device, it's best to check the return code to make sure the device is ready and available.

Getting Input

Now that you've completed the required steps to initialize an input device through Direct-Input, it's time to actually utilize it. All devices use the function GetDeviceState when reading input. Whether the input device is a keyboard, mouse, or gamepad, the GetDeviceState function is used.

```
HRESULT GetDeviceState(
    DWORD cbData,
    LPVOID lpvData
);
```

The first parameter required is a DWORD value that holds the size of the buffer being passed as the second parameter. The second parameter is a pointer to the buffer that will hold the data that's read from the device. As a reminder, the format of the data from the input device was defined earlier using the SetDataFormat function.

The next few sections show how to enumerate the input devices available to your application through DirectInput.

Enumerating Input Devices

Most games that are available for the PC allow for the use of input devices other than a keyboard or a mouse, such as a gamepad or joystick. Many computers do not have these nonstandard devices by default, so DirectInput cannot just assume their presence. Also, because Windows allows for multiple gamepads or joysticks to be installed simultaneously, DirectInput needs a way of determining how many and of what type these devices are. The method that DirectInput uses to get the needed information on the input devices is called *enumeration*.

Just as Direct3D can enumerate through the video adapters installed in a system and get their capabilities, DirectInput can do the same for input devices.

Using functions available through the DirectInput object, DirectInput can retrieve the number of input devices available in a system, as well as each one's type and functionality. For instance, if your game requires the use of a gamepad with an analog control stick, you can enumerate the installed devices and see if any of them meet your criteria.

The process of enumerating the installed devices on a system requires gathering a list of the devices that meet your input needs and then gathering the specific capabilities of those devices.

DirectInput uses the EnumDevices function to gather the list of installed input devices. Because there might be different types of devices installed on a machine and you probably wouldn't be interested in getting a list of all of them, EnumDevices allows you to specify the type of devices you are searching for. For instance, if you're not interested in the mouse and keyboard devices and are searching specifically for joystick devices, EnumDevices provides a way of eliminating the unwanted devices from the list.

First, I'm going to explain how EnumDevices is used. The function EnumDevices is defined as follows:

```
HRESULT EnumDevices(
    DWORD dwDevType,
    LPDIENUMDEVICESCALLBACK lpCallback,
    LPVOID pvRef,
```

```
    DWORD dwFlags
);
```

This function requires four parameters:

- **dwDevType.** This parameter sets the filter for the device search. As I mentioned earlier, you can tell EnumDevices to only search the system for a particular type of device. This parameter can use any of the following values:
    - **DI8DEVCLASS_ALL.** This value causes EnumDevices to return a list of all input devices that are installed in a system.
    - **DI8DEVCLASS_DEVICE.** This value causes a search for devices that do not fall into another class of device, such as keyboards, mice, or game controllers.
    - **DI8DEVCLASS_GAMECTRL.** This causes EnumDevices to search for all game controller device types, such as gamepads or joysticks.
    - **DI8DEVCLASS_KEYBOARD.** EnumDevices searches the system for all keyboard devices.
    - **DI8DEVCLASS_POINTER.** This value tells EnumDevices to search for pointer devices such as mice.
- **lpCallback.** EnumDevices utilizes a callback mechanism when searching the system for input devices. This parameter is the address of the function you define to work as the callback.
- **pvRef.** This parameter passes data to the callback function that is defined in the lpCallback parameter. You can use any 32-bit value here. If you don't need to send information to the callback function, you can pass NULL.
- **dwFlags.** The final parameter is a DWORD value consisting of a set of flags letting EnumDevices know the scope of the enumeration. For instance, if you want EnumDevices to search the system only for installed devices or those that have force feedback, you need to specify one of the following values:
    - **DIEDFL_ALLDEVICES.** This is the default value. All devices in the system are enumerated.
    - **DIEDFL_ATTACHEDONLY.** Only devices that are currently attached to the system are returned.
    - **DIEDFL_FORCEFEEDBACK.** Only the devices that support force feedback are returned.
    - **DIEDFL_INCLUDEALIASES.** Windows allows aliases to be created for devices. These aliases appear to the system as input devices, but they represent another device in the system.
    - **DIEDFL_INCLUDEHIDDEN.** This causes EnumDevices to return hidden devices.
    - **DIEDFL_INCLUDEPHANTOMS.** Some hardware devices have more than one input device, such as a keyboard that also includes a built-in mouse. This value causes DirectInput to return multiple devices.

The following code sample utilizes the EnumDevices function call to gather a list of game controllers that are currently attached to the system.

```
HRESULT    hr;         // variable used to hold the return code

// Call the EnumDevices function
hr = DI_Object->EnumDevices( DI8DEVCLASS_GAMECTRL,
                             EnumJoysticksCallback,
                             NULL,
                             DIEDFL_ATTACHEDONLY ) ;

// Check the return value of the EnumDevices function
If FAILED( hr )
    return false;
```

The previous call to EnumDevices used the value DI8DEVCLASS_GAMECTRL to search for game controllers. The value DIEDFL_ATTACHEDONLY only looked for those devices that were attached to the system.

The second parameter value of EnumJoysticksCallback represents the name of the callback function to receive the devices found.

The third parameter is NULL because no additional information needs to be sent to the callback function.

The callback function provided to EnumDevices is called every time a device that matches the search criteria is found. For instance, if you are searching the system for gamepads and there are currently four of them plugged in, the callback function is called four times.

The purpose of the callback function is to give your application the chance to create a DirectInput device for each piece of hardware, allowing you to then scan the device for its capabilities.

The callback function must be defined in your code utilizing a specific format: DIEnumDevicesCallback.

```
BOOL CALLBACK DIEnumDevicesCallback(
    LPCDIDEVICEINSTANCE lpddi,
    LPVOID pvRef
);
```

The DIEnumDevicesCallback function requires two parameters: a pointer to a DIDEVICEINSTANCE structure, and the value passed to the pvRef parameter of EnumDevices.

The DIDEVICEINSTANCE structure, defined next, holds the details concerning an input device, such as its GUID and its product name. The information within this structure is useful when displaying a choice of devices to the user because it enables him to recognize a device based on its name.

```
typedef struct DIDEVICEINSTANCE {
    DWORD dwSize;
    GUID  guidInstance;
    GUID  guidProduct;
    DWORD dwDevType;
    TCHAR tszInstanceName[MAX_PATH];
    TCHAR tszProductName[MAX_PATH];
    GUID  guidFFDriver;
    WORD  wUsagePage;
    WORD  wUsage;
} DIDEVICEINSTANCE, *LPDIDEVICEINSTANCE;
```

Table 9.2 describes the DIDEVICEINSTANCE structure in more detail.

Table 9.2 DIDEVICEINSTANCE Structure

Member Name	Description
dwSize	The size of this structure in bytes.
guidInstance	The GUID for the specific device. This value can be saved and used later with CreateDevice to gain access to the device.
guidProduct	The unique identifier for the input device. This is basically the device's product ID.
dwDevType	This value is the device type specifier. This can be any value specified in the DirectX documentation for this structure.
tszInstanceName	The friendly name for the device, such as Joystick 1 or AxisPad.
tszProductName	This is the full product name for this device.
guidFFDriver	If this device supports force feedback, this value represents the GUID of the driver being used.
wUsagePage	This value holds the Human Interface Device (HID) usage page code.
wUsage	This is the usage code for an HID.

The DIEnumDevicesCallback function requires a boolean value to be returned. DirectInput has defined two values that should be used instead of the standard TRUE or FALSE:

- **DIENUM_CONTINUE.** This value tells the enumeration to continue.
- **DIENUM_STOP.** This value forces the device enumeration to stop.

These values control the device enumeration process. If you are searching the system for only one joystick device, it's useless to enumerate through all the installed joysticks. Returning DIENUM_STOP after finding the first suitable device is all that's needed.

Commonly, you will want to collect a list of all the suitable devices so that the user can select which specific device he wants to use. Using the callback mechanism, you can create DirectInput devices for each piece of hardware and place them in a list. The user can then select the device he wants to use.

The code example that follows shows the callback function that will return upon finding the first joystick device that meets the EnumDevices criteria:

```
BOOL CALLBACK DeviceEnumCallback( const DIDEVICEINSTANCE* pdidInstance,
                                  VOID* pContext )
{
    // variable to hold the return code
    HRESULT hr;

    // Use create device
    hr = DI_Object->CreateDevice( pdidInstance->guidInstance,
                                  &g_pJoystick,
                                  NULL );

    // The call to CreateDevice failed; keep looking for another
    if( FAILED(hr) )
        return DIENUM_CONTINUE;

    // The device was found and is valid; stop the enumeration
    return DIENUM_STOP;
}
```

The previous code first attempts to use the CreateDevice function to gain access to the device passed into the callback function. If the call to CreateDevice fails, the callback function returns DIENUM_CONTINUE, which tells the enumeration of input devices to continue. In contrast, if the call to CreateDevice succeeds, the callback returns the value DIENUM_STOP.

You can find an example demonstrating how to enumerate the devices in your system and display their device names in the chapter9\example3 directory on the CD-ROM. Figure 9.1 shows the dialog box created from this example.

Figure 9.1 Listing of installed input devices.

Getting the Device Capabilities

After you have a valid device returned from EnumDevices, you might need to check for specific functionality. For instance, you might need to find the type of force feedback that the device can support.

Enumerating the capabilities of a device is similar to enumerating the devices. To get the specific details for a device, you must call the EnumObjects function. Like the call to EnumDevices, this function works along with a callback method.

```
HRESULT EnumObjects(
    LPDIENUMDEVICEOBJECTSCALLBACK lpCallback,
    LPVOID pvRef,
    DWORD dwFlags
);
```

The EnumObjects function requires three parameters:

- **lpCallback.** This is the name of the callback function.
- **pvRef.** This is extra data that will be sent to the callback function when it is called.
- **dwFlags.** The flags are a DWORD value that specifies the types of objects on the input device that you are interested in enumerating.

Table 9.3 describes the dwFlags parameter in more detail.

Table 9.3 EnumObjects Flags

Flag Name	Description
DIDFT_ABSAXIS	Uses an absolute axis
DIDFT_ALIAS	Looks for controls identified by an HID usage alias
DIDFT_ALL	Looks for all types of objects on the device
DIDFT_AXIS	Looks for an axis: relative or absolute
DIDFT_BUTTON	Checks for push or toggle buttons
DIDFT_COLLECTION	Lists the HID link collections
DIDFT_ENUMCOLLECTION	Belongs to a link collection
DIDFT_FFACTUATOR	Contains a force feedback actuator
DIDFT_FFEFFECTTRIGGER	Contains a force feedback trigger
DIDFT_NOCOLLECTION	Looks for objects that do not belong to a link collection
DIDFT_NODATA	Does not generate data
DIDFT_OUTPUT	Supports output
DIDFT_POV	Looks for a POV controller
DIDFT_PSHBUTTON	Looks for a push button
DIDFT_RELAXIS	Uses a relative axis
DIDFT_TGLBUTTON	Looks for a toggle button
DIDFT_VENDORDEFINED	Returns an object of a type defined by the manufacturer

The purpose of the `EnumObjects` callback function is to gather information regarding a particular input device. The information collected for each device is passed to the callback as a `DIDEVICEOBJECTINSTANCE` structure.

The callback function defined in the call to `EnumObjects` must follow the function signature of `DIEnumDeviceObjectsCallback`.

```
BOOL CALLBACK DIEnumDeviceObjectsCallback (
    LPCDIDEVICEOBJECTINSTANCE lpddoi,
    LPVOID pvRef
);
```

The `DIEnumDeviceObjectsCallback` function takes two parameters. The first parameter is the structure of type `DIDEVICEOBJECTINSTANCE` that holds the returned information regarding the device. The second parameter is any value that was passed into the `EnumObjects` function in its `pvRef` parameter.

The `DIDEVICEOBJECTINSTANCE` structure contains a wealth of valuable information about the device. It's useful for setting the limits for force feedback, as well as helping to determine the specific types and number of controls on the device.

You can find a full explanation of the `DIDEVICEOBJECTINSTANCE` structure in the DirectInput documentation.

Getting Input from a Keyboard

Getting input from the keyboard is rather simple because it is a default device. The keyboard requires a buffer consisting of a 256-element character array.

```
char     buffer[256];
```

The character array holds the state of each key on the keyboard. The state of one or multiple keys can be held in this array each time the keyboard device is read from. Most games require that the input device be read from each frame from within the main game loop.

Before you can read from the keyboard, you need an easy way of determining which key on the keyboard was pressed. The macro `KEYDOWN`, provided next, returns `TRUE` or `FALSE` based on whether the key you are checking for was pressed.

```
#define KEYDOWN(name, key) (name[key] & 0x80)
```

Following is an example of reading from the keyboard:

```
// Define the macro needed to check the state of the keys on the keyboard
#define KEYDOWN(name, key) (name[key] & 0x80)
```

```
// This is the required keyboard buffer
char    buffer[256];

// This is the main game loop, read from the input device each frame
while ( 1 )
{
    // Check the keyboard and see if any keys are currently
    // being pressed
    g_lpDIDevice->GetDeviceState( sizeof( buffer ),
                                  (LPVOID )&buffer );

    // Do something with the input

    // Here the KEYDOWN macro checks whether the left arrow key was pressed
    if (KEYDOWN(buffer, DIK_LEFT))
    {
        // Do something with the left arrow
    }
    // KEYDOWN is used again to check whether the up arrow key was pressed
    if (KEYDOWN(buffer, DIK_UP))
    {
        // Do something with the up arrow
    }
}
```

As you can see, the main game loop calls the GetDeviceState each frame and places the current state of the keyboard into the input buffer. The KEYDOWN macro then checks for the state of certain keys.

Figure 9.2 shows a small demonstration of using keyboard input to display which directional arrow was pressed.

You can find a full source listing for this example in the chapter9\example1 directory on the CD-ROM.

Getting Input from a Mouse

Reading input from a mouse is similar to reading it from the keyboard. The main differences are the GUID that's passed to the CreateDevice function and the DIDATAFORMAT structure that holds the input for this device.

Figure 9.2 Keyboard demonstration sample.

In the previous example, the call to CreateDevice used GUID_SysKeyboard as the first parameter. When you're using the mouse, you must set the GUID for CreateDevice to GUID_SysMouse.

note

Setting the cooperative level to exclusive mode for mouse input keeps the Windows cursor from being displayed. In exclusive mode, you are responsible for drawing the mouse cursor.

The following code shows how to use the CreateDevice function.

```
// Call the CreateDevice function using the GUID_SysMouse parameter
hr = g_lpDI->CreateDevice(GUID_SysMouse, &g_lpDIDevice, NULL);

// Check the return code for the CreateDevice function
if FAILED(hr)
    return FALSE;
```

The call to SetDataFormat used the predefined data format c_dfDIKeyboard. You must change this value to c_dfDIMouse when you're using the mouse as the input device.

```
// Set the data format for the mouse
hr = g_lpDIDevice->SetDataFormat( &c_dfDIMouse );

// Check the return code for the SetDataFormat function
if FAILED( hr )
    return FALSE;
```

The final change that needs to be made before you can read from the mouse is the buffer that's defined by DIDATAFORMAT. The keyboard needs a character buffer consisting of 256 elements, whereas the mouse needs a buffer of type DIMOUSESTATE.

The DIMOUSESTATE structure consists of three variables for holding the X, Y, and Z position of the mouse, as well as a BYTE array of four elements for holding the state of the mouse buttons. The DIMOUSESTATE structure is defined as follows:

```
typedef struct DIMOUSESTATE {
LONG lX;            // holds the distance the mouse has traveled in the X direction
LONG lY;            // holds the distance the mouse has traveled in the Y direction
LONG lZ;            // holds the distance the mouse has traveled in the Z direction
BYTE rgbButtons[4]; // the current state of the mouse buttons
} DIMOUSESTATE, *LPDIMOUSESTATE;
```

Previously, a macro helped determine whether specific keys on the keyboard had been pressed. You can use a similar macro to check the state of the mouse buttons.

```
#define BUTTONDOWN( name, key ) ( name.rgbButtons[ key ] & 0x80 )
```

This macro returns TRUE or FALSE for each button on the mouse.

note

The X, Y, and Z values in the DIMOUSESTATE structure do not hold the current position of the mouse; rather, they hold the position relative to where the mouse was previously. For example, if you moved the mouse slightly to the left about 5 units, the X value would be equal to −5. If you moved the mouse down 10 units, the Y value would be equal to 10.

When you're reading from a mouse, you must keep track of the values read from the mouse on the previous frame so that you can correctly interpret the mouse movement.

The following code fragment demonstrates the code needed to read from the mouse device. This code handles checking both the movement of the mouse and the state of the mouse buttons.

```
// Define the macro needed to check the state of the keys on the keyboard
#define BUTTONDOWN (name, key) (name.rgbButtons[key] & 0x80)

// This is required to hold the state of the mouse
// This variable holds the current state of the mouse device
DIMOUSESTATE    mouseState;
// This variable holds the current X position of the sprite
LONG    currentXpos;
// This variable holds the current Y position of the sprite
LONG    currentYpos;
```

```
// Set the default position for the sprite
currentXpos = 320;
currentYpos = 240;

// This is the main game loop, read from the input device each frame
while ( 1 )
{
    // Check the mouse and get the current state of the device
    // being pressed
    g_lpDIDevice->GetDeviceState (sizeof ( mouseState ),
                                  LPVOID) &mouseState);

    // Do something with the input

    // Here the BUTTONDOWN macro checks if the first mouse button is pressed
    if (BUTTONDOWN( mouseState, 0 ) )
    {
        // Do something with the first mouse button
    }

    // BUTTONDOWN is used again to check if the second mouse button is pressed
    if ( BUTTONDOWN( mouseState, 1 ) )
    {
        // Do something with the up arrow
    }
    // Next, check the movement of the mouse

    // See how far in the X direction the mouse has been moved
    currentXpos += mouseState.lX;
    // See how far in the Y direction the mouse has been moved
    currentYpos += mouseState.lY;

    // Do something with the mouse movement
}
```

You can find a full code example in the chapter9\example2 directory on the CD-ROM. This sample demonstrates the movement of the mouse using a 2D sprite, as well as the pressing of the left and right mouse buttons by displaying directional arrows on the screen. Figure 9.3 shows this sample in action.

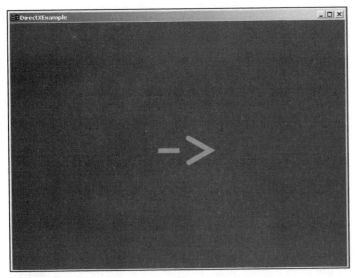

Figure 9.3 Showing mouse movement with a sprite.

n o t e

The structure `DIMOUSESTATE2` provides variables to hold the current state of up to eight mouse buttons.

Using a Gamepad or Joystick

Gamepads and joysticks have been common game input devices for a while now. Whereas most joystick controllers used to be plugged into the game port on sound cards, most devices sold now utilize a Universal Serial Bus (USB) connection. The USB connection gives devices an advantage over the previous devices. USB devices are easily detectable by the system and are handled through the common HID interface. Because of this, reading from gamepads and joysticks has become easier.

The main difference between using a joystick and using a gamepad is the absolute need to enumerate the input devices. Because multiple joysticks can be plugged into a system, DirectInput does not have a `GUID` predefined for these devices. Before you can call `CreateDevice` to prepare a joystick for use, you must enumerate the input devices that are installed on the system.

Joystick Enumeration

Enumerating the devices causes DirectInput to query each device against the search criteria you have set. For instance, if you called `EnumDevices` like this

```
hr = g_lpDI ->EnumDevices( DI8DEVCLASS_GAMECTRL,
                           EnumDevicesCallback,
                           NULL,
                           DIEDFL_ATTACHEDONLY ) ;
```

then the devices returned to the `EnumDevicesCallback` function would only be of type `DI8DEVCLASS_GAMECTRL`, which is exactly what you need when searching for joysticks.

Polling a Joystick

Keyboards and mice generate hardware interrupts informing the system that there is new input data available. Most joysticks require that they be "polled" occasionally. The term *polling* refers to the checking of the device for new input. After a device has been polled, you can retrieve the new valid input from it.

note

Joysticks and gamepads use the predefined `DIDATAFORMAT` structures `DIJOYSTATE` and `DIJOYSTATE2`.

Joysticks are not completely digital devices; they consist of an analog piece as well. Commonly, joysticks utilize digital input for buttons, meaning that they are either up or down, and they use analog input for the stick itself. Analog input allows you detect the distance that the joystick was moved.

A slight movement of the joystick toward the right sends a small value to the controlling program, whereas pulling the joystick completely to the right sends a much higher value. The amount of this value is determined by the range property of the device.

The range property is normally set for the analog portions of a joystick and consists of the maximum and minimum value that the device will generate. For instance, setting the minimum portion of the range to –1000 and the maximum range to 1000 provides your game only with values that fall into this range. Moving the joystick all the way to the left sends the value of –1000, whereas moving it to the right sends up to a value of 1000. You can set the range of the device to any values that will make sense to your application.

Setting the Range of a Joystick

To set the range property for the analog portion of the joystick, you must use the `EnumObjects` function. As you will recall from earlier, the `EnumObjects` function works similarly to EnumDevices but instead sends its callback function details on the different pieces of the device. A sample callback function is shown next.

```
/********************************************************************
* EnumObjCallback
********************************************************************/
BOOL CALLBACK EnumObjCallback( const DIDEVICEOBJECTINSTANCE* pdidoi,
                               VOID* pContext )
{
    // If this object is an axis type object, attempt to set its range
    if( pdidoi->dwType & DIDFT_AXIS )
    {
        // Create a DIPROPRANGE structure
        DIPROPRANGE diprg;

        // Each structure requires that a DIPROPHEADER structure
        // be initialized
        diprg.diph.dwSize       = sizeof(DIPROPRANGE);
        diprg.diph.dwHeaderSize = sizeof(DIPROPHEADER);
        diprg.diph.dwHow        = DIPH_BYID;
        diprg.diph.dwObj        = pdidoi->dwType; // Specify the enumerated axis

        // The minimum and maximum portions of the range are being set here
        diprg.lMin              = -100;
        diprg.lMax              = 100;

        HRESULT hr;

        // Set the range for the axis
        hr = g_joystickDevice->SetProperty( DIPROP_RANGE, &diprg.diph ) ;
        // Check to see if setting the range property was successful
        if FAILED ( hr )
            return DIENUM_STOP;
    }
    // Tell EnumObjects to continue to the next object in this device
    return DIENUM_CONTINUE;
}
```

This example first checks to see if the object being passed to the callback is an axis type. An *axis object* is a type representing the analog stick portions of a joystick controller. If a valid axis device is used, the code attempts to set its range.

First, a DIPROPRANGE structure is created, which holds the information regarding the range. A DIPROPRANGE structure is defined like this:

```
typedef struct DIPROPRANGE {
    DIPROPHEADER diph;
    LONG         lMin;
    LONG         lMax;
} DIPROPRANGE, *LPDIPROPRANGE;
```

The second and third variables within this structure—lMin and lMax—actually represent the minimum and maximum range values. You can set these two values to anything that your game requires, as long as the lMin variable is less than the value stored in lMax.

The first variable within the DIPROPRANGE structure is actually another structure: DIPROPHEADER. The DIPROPHEADER structure is required for all property structures.

```
typedef struct DIPROPHEADER {
    DWORD     dwSize;
    DWORD     dwHeaderSize;
    DWORD     dwObj;
    DWORD     dwHow;
} DIPROPHEADER, *LPDIPROPHEADER;
```

The DIPROPHEADER structure requires only four variables to be set. The first variable, dwSize, represents the size of the enclosing structure in bytes. In this instance, it's the DIPROPRANGE structure.

The second variable, dwHeaderSize, is the size of the DIPROPHEADER structure.

The third and fourth variables work together. The contents of the dwHow variable describe the type of data within the dwObj variable. dwHow can be any of the following values:

- **DIPH_DEVICE.** dwObj must be set to 0.
- **DIPH_BYOFFSET.** dwObj is the offset into the current data format.
- **DIPH_BYUSAGE.** dwObj must be set to the HID usage page and usage values.
- **DIPH_BYID.** dwObj is set to the object identifier. You can find this in the DIDEVICEOBJECTINSTANCE structure that's passed to the callback function.

Finally, after these structures are filled in, you can call the SetProperty function. This function accepts the GUID of the property to be set as its first parameter and an address to the structure containing the new property information.

note

Some devices do not allow the range to be changed. The range property is read-only.

You can change other properties of a device via the same method by which the range property was changed. Properties exist for other settings. For example, DIPROP_DEADZONE is a range value that specifies which portion of the joystick movement to ignore. DIPROP_FFGAIN sets the gain for force feedback, and DIPROP_AUTOCENTER tells the device whether it should auto-center itself when the user releases the device.

Reading from a Joystick

Joysticks, like other input devices, require the use of the GetDeviceState function. In the instance of joysticks and gamepads, though, the buffer that must hold the input data is either of type DIJOYSTATE or DIJOYSTATE2. The main difference between the two structures is the number of objects on a joystick device that can be read. The DIJOYSTATE structure allows for just two analog devices, whereas the DIJOYSTATE2 structure can handle more.

Because the input from the joystick is not an absolute position, you must keep track of any previous movement by your game. For instance, if you're using joystick input to control the movement of a sprite around the screen, you need to keep in separate variables the sprite's current X and Y positions. When new input is read from the joystick, the new input is added to the current X and Y positions. The code sample that followsdemonstrates this.

```
// These two variables will hold the current position of the sprite
LONG curX;
LONG curY;

// Here, the default sprite positions are set
curX = 320;
curY = 240;
while (1)
{
    // Use the DIJOYSTATE2 structure to hold the data from the joystick
    DIJOYSTATE2 js;

    // First, poll the joystick
    g_joystickDevice->Poll();

    // Get the current input from the device
    g_joystickDevice->GetDeviceState( sizeof(DIJOYSTATE2), &js ) );

    // Add the new values to the current X and Y positions
    curX += js.lX;
    curY += js.lY;

    // Draw the sprite in its updated position
}
```

This small bit of code first polls the joystick device for new input. Then the new input is placed into the DIJOYSTATE2 structure. Finally, the lX and lY values are added to the current X and Y position of the sprite. The lX and lY variables represent the returned input from the first analog stick.

You can find a full source example of reading from the joystick in the chapter9\example4 directory on the CD-ROM.

Supporting Multiple Input Devices

Most console games allow more than one player. PCs are no different. With the ability to plug in many USB gamepads or joysticks, games on the PC are limited only by what you can think of. In this section, I'm going to explain the process needed to support multiple devices.

As you'll recall from earlier, each input device requires its own DirectInput device. Because of this, your code needs to be able to hold multiple DirectInput devices. Creating either an array or a vector of IDirectInputDevice8 objects enables you to do this.

The next step is the enumeration of the installed devices. For instance, if your game needs to support four gamepads, you must call EnumDevices and gather the information returned through its callback function for each gamepad device. After you have stored the data for each device, you can call CreateDevice. You need to use the CreateDevice function for each device that your callback has saved. After you have created all the devices, you will have access to do whatever you want with them.

The code that follows shows an elementary example of this process.

```
#define NUM_DEVICES 4
// The four DirectInput devices
LPDIRECTINPUTDEVICE8  devices[ NUM_DEVICES ];
// The DirectInput object
LPDIRECTINPUT8        g_lpDI  =  NULL;

Int curCount = 0;       // holds the number of devices you currently have
int APIENTRY WinMain( HINSTANCE hInst, HINSTANCE, LPSTR, int )
{
    // variable to hold the return code
    HRESULT    hr;

    // Create the DirectInput object
hr = DirectInput8Create(hInstance,
                        DIRECTINPUT_VERSION,
```

```
                        IID_IDirectInput8,
                        ( void** ) &g_lpDI,
                        NULL );

 // Call the EnumDevices function
hr = g_lpDI ->EnumDevices( DI8DEVCLASS_GAMECTRL,
                            EnumDevicesCallback,
                            NULL,
                            DIEDFL_ATTACHEDONLY ) ;

// Check the return value of the EnumDevices function
if FAILED( hr )
    return false;

    // Do something interesting with the devices here
}


/************************************************************************
* EnumDevicesCallback
************************************************************************/
BOOL CALLBACK EnumDevicesCallback( const DIDEVICEINSTANCE* pdidInstance,
                                    VOID* pContext )
{
    // variable to hold the return code
    HRESULT hr;

    // Call CreateDevice for this returned device
    hr = g_lpDI->CreateDevice( pdidInstance->guidInstance,
                                &devices[curCount]
                                NULL );

    // If the call to CreateDevice fails, stop enumerating more devices
    if( FAILED(hr) )
    {
        return DIENUM_CONTINUE;
    }
    // else, increase the curCount variable by one and grab another device
    else
    {
        curCount++;
        if (curCount >= NUM_DEVICES)
```

```
                return DIENUM_STOP;
    }
    // Continue the enumeration
    return DIENUM_CONTINUE;
}
```

This callback function doesn't do much. It attempts to call CreateDevice on each input device that is passed to it. If a device can be created, it increments the counter variable and keeps looking for more. The code currently supports up to four devices. If more than four gamepads are needed, the size of the array holding the DirectInput devices must change. If you don't know how many devices you might have or you want to keep things dynamic, use a vector of IDIRECTINPUTDEVICE8 objects.

Reacquiring an Input Device

Sometimes during the course of a game, the input device is lost. If your game has set the cooperative level for the device to nonexclusive, another application might start and restrict your access to the device. In this case, you would need to reacquire the device before you could continue to read from it and use its input.

When access to a device has been lost, the return code from the GetDeviceState function is equal to DIERR_INPUTLOST. When this happens, you need to call the Acquire function in a loop until access to the device is restored.

The following sample code demonstrates how to reacquire a device once access to it has been lost.

```
HRESULT    hr;    // variable to hold return codes

// This is the main game loop; read from the input device each frame
while ( 1 )
{
    // Call the GetDeviceState function and save the return code
    hr = DI_Device->GetDeviceState( sizeof( DIMOUSESTATE ),
                                    ( LPVOID )&mouseState );

    // Check the return state to see whether the device is still accessible
    if ( FAILED ( hr ) )
    {
        // Try to reacquire the input device
        hr = DI_Device->Acquire( );

        // Do a continuous loop until the device is reacquired
```

```
        while( hr == DIERR_INPUTLOST )
            hr = DI_Device->Acquire( );

        // Just return and do nothing this frame
        continue;
    }

    // Check the input and do something with it
}
```

Cleaning Up DirectInput

DirectInput, like Direct3D, requires that you release the objects you've created upon completion of your application. In addition to the DirectInput objects, you must also unacquire any devices that you have gained control over. If you forget to unacquire the input devices you've been using, when your game ends, those devices might still be locked by the system so you can't use them. Although a locked joystick or gamepad wouldn't be too big of a deal, forgetting to release the mouse or keyboard could make you have to restart your machine to get them back.

The Unacquire function releases a device that had been acquired previously through DirectInput.

```
HRESULT Unacquire( VOID );
```

Unacquire is a method that the DirectInput device interface provides.

The following sample code correctly unacquires the input devices and releases both the DirectInput device and the object.

```
// Check whether you have a valid DirectInput object
if ( DI_Object )
{
    // Check to see whether you have a valid DirectInput device
    if ( DI_Device )
    {
        // Unacquire the input device
        DI_Device->Unacquire( );
```

```
        // Release the DirectInput device
        DI_Device->Release( );

        // Set the DirectInput device variable to NULL
        DI_Device = NULL;
    }

    // Release the DirectInput object
    DI_Object->Release( );

    // Set the DirectInput object variable to NULL
    DI_Object = NULL;
}
```

At this point, you should have a clear understanding of initializing and reading from standard input devices through DirectInput. In the next section, you will learn how to use force feedback to help immerse the player in your world.

Force Feedback

Since the release of the current generation of video game consoles onto the market, gamers have become familiar with the concept of force feedback. *Force feedback* is the ability to send different levels of vibration to an input device. Gamepads for console systems commonly support force feedback, whereas feedback in PC input devices is still rare.

Force Feedback Effects

Force feedback devices perform their vibrations based on effects. A force feedback effect is made up of one or more forces acting on the controller. Forces within DirectInput are the push or resistance felt on a controller during the playing of an effect. Effects come in a few different flavors:

- **Constant Force.** A steady continual force in a single direction
- **Ramp Force.** A force that increases or decreases in intensity steadily over time
- **Periodic Effect.** A pulsating force
- **Conditional.** An effect that is triggered as a reaction to a particular motion

Each force has a *magnitude*, or intensity, and a *duration*, or length of time. Changing the magnitude allows you to increase or decrease the amount of vibration or resistance the user feels while playing your game.

tip

Overusing force feedback or using it at the wrong times within your game might annoy the player. Use force feedback sparingly.

To use a force feedback device—such as a gamepad—with your game, you need to do the following:

1. Create the DirectInput object.
2. Enumerate the installed game controller devices that support force feedback.
3. Create a device based on the gamepad.
4. Create the force feedback effect you want to use.
5. Start the effect.

Enumerating the Input Devices for Force Feedback

Because force feedback is still not widespread in game controllers, you need to specifically look for this feature when enumerating the input devices. Previously, the only flag that you sent to EnumDevices was DIEDL_ATTACHEDONLY, which specified that this function should only return installed and attached devices to the callback. If this is left as the only flag, the callback will receive both force feedback and nonfeedback devices. Because you know from the start that you want to look only for force feedback devices, you should add the flag DIEDFL_FORCEFEEDBACK to the EnumDevices call. This informs EnumDevices to only report back with force feedback-enabled devices.

The example code that follows shows the updated call to EnumDevices.

```
// the variable used to hold the input device
LPDIRECTINPUTDEVICE8 FFDevice    = NULL;

// Enumerate through the installed devices looking for a game controller
// or joystick that supports force feedback
HRESULT hr;
hr = g_pDI->EnumDevices( DI8DEVCLASS_GAMECTRL,
                         FFDeviceCallback,
                         NULL,
                         DIEDFL_ATTACHEDONLY | DIEDFL_FORCEFEEDBACK ) );
```

The previous EnumDevices function call has been updated with the DIEDFL_FORCEFEEDBACK flag.

The code that follows shows the callback function needed to find the force feedback device.

```
/****************************************************************************
 * FFDeviceCallback
 ****************************************************************************/
BOOL CALLBACK FFDeviceCallback ( const DIDEVICEINSTANCE* pInst,
                                 VOID* pContext )
{
    HRESULT              hr;

    // Create the device
    hr = g_pDI->CreateDevice( pInst->guidInstance, & FFDevice, NULL );

    // This device could not be created, so keep looking for another one
    if( FAILED(hr) )
        return DIENUM_CONTINUE;

    // We found a device; stop the enumeration
    return DIENUM_STOP;
}
```

At this point, only valid force feedback devices are being reported to the callback function. The callback attempts to create a device based on the first one it comes across. If the callback succeeds in creating the device, it stops the enumeration; otherwise, the enumeration continues to look for a suitable device.

Creating a Force Feedback Effect

After you've found the controller you're going to use and you've created a DirectInput device for it, you need to create an effect object. DirectInput force feedback effect objects are based on the IDirectInputEffect interface. Each IDirectInputEffect object details the effect to the system.

The effect is created first by filling in a DIEFFECT structure. This structure describes the different aspects of the effect, such as the duration, which axes are affected, and its force.

The DIEFFECT structure is then passed as a parameter to the CreateEffect function. The CreateEffect function registers the effect with DirectInput and downloads the effect to the device. After the effect has been downloaded to the force feedback device, it's ready to be played.

note

For an effect to be downloaded to a force feedback device, the device must be set to a cooperative level of exclusive. Force feedback devices cannot share their feedback functionality among different applications.

I'm going to take you through a quick rundown of the DIEFFECT structure and using CreateEffect so that you can see the process in more detail.

You must declare the DIEFFECT structure for each effect object that you want to create. The DIEFFECT structure is defined here:

```
typedef struct DIEFFECT {
    DWORD       dwSize;
    DWORD       dwFlags;
    DWORD       dwDuration;
    DWORD       dwSamplePeriod;
    DWORD       dwGain;
    DWORD       dwTriggerButton;
    DWORD       dwTriggerRepeatInterval;
    DWORD       cAxes;
    LPDWORD     rgdwAxes;
    LPLONG      rglDirection;
    LPDIENVELOPE lpEnvelope;
    DWORD       cbTypeSpecificParams;
    LPVOID      lpvTypeSpecificParams;
    DWORD       dwStartDelay;
} DIEFFECT, *LPDIEFFECT;
```

The DIEFFECT structure consists of the following variables:

- **dwSize.** The size of the DIEFFECT structure in bytes.
- **dwFlags.** The flags that describe how some of the variables are to be used.
    - **DIEFF_CARTESIAN.** The values within the rglDirection variable are considered to be Cartesian coordinates.
    - **DIEFF_OBJECTIDS.** The values within the dwTriggerButton and rgdwAxes variables are object identifiers.
    - **DIEFF_OBJECTOFFSETS.** The values within the dwTriggerButton and rgdwAxes variables are data format offsets.
    - **DIEFF_POLAR.** The values within the rglDirection variable are considered to be Polar coordinates.
    - **DIEFF_SPHERICAL.** The values within the rglDirection variable are considered to be Spherical coordinates.

- **dwDuration.** The duration of the effect in microseconds. If the duration of the effect should be continuous, use the value of INFINITE.

- **dwSamplePeriod.** The sample rate of the effect playback. 0 indicates that the default sample rate is to be used.

- **dwGain.** The gain of the effect.

- **dwTriggerButton.** The identifier of the button to be used to trigger the effect. This variable depends on the value within the dwFlags variable.

- **dwTriggerRepeatInterval.** The delay time between repeating the effect. This value is in microseconds.

- **cAxes.** The number of axes that the effect uses.

- **rgdwAxes.** A pointer to a DWORD array that contains the IDs or offsets to the axes that the effect will use.

- **rglDirection.** An array of coordinates corresponding to the types of coordinates selected in the dwFlags variable.

- **lpEnvelope.** An optional pointer to a DIENVELOPE structure. This structure defines the envelope to be applied to this effect. Because no effects require this, you can use NULL.

- **cbTypeSpecificParams.** The number of bytes of additional parameters for the type of effect.

- **lpvTypeSpecificParams.** This variable holds the parameters discussed in the previous variable. This variable can hold any of the following defined structures:
  - **DIEFT_CUSTOMFORCE.** A structure of type DICUSTOMFORCE is passed.
  - **DIEFT_PERIODIC.** A structure of type DIPERIODIC is used.
  - **DIEFT_CONSTANTFORCE.** A constant force structure, DICONSTANTFORCE, is used.
  - **DIEFT_RAMPFORCE.** A ramp force structure of DIRAMPFORCE is used.
  - **DIEFT_CONDITION.** A structure of type DICONDITION must be passed.

- **dwStartDelay.** The time in microseconds that the device should wait before playing an effect.

The complete DIEFFECT structure is then passed to the CreateEffect function. The CreateEffect function requires four parameters and is defined like this:

```
HRESULT CreateEffect(
    REFGUID rguid,
    LPCDIEFFECT lpeff,
    LPDIRECTINPUTEFFECT *ppdeff,
    LPUNKNOWN punkOuter
);
```

The first parameter refers to the GUID of the type of force to be created. For instance, if you are trying to create a constant force effect, use the predefined GUID of GUID_ConstantForce. The second parameter is the passed-in DIEFFECT structure defined earlier. The third parameter is the address of the variable that will hold the newly created effect. This variable must be of type IDirectInputEffect. The final parameter to CreateEffect is normally NULL.

After you have your effect created and ready to go, the next step is playing it.

Starting an Effect

Before the user can feel your effect in action, it has to be played. The playback of a force feedback effect is handled through the Start function, which is a member function of IDirectInputEffect.

The Start function requires two parameters. The first is the number of times the effect should be played. The second parameter is a set of flags that relate to how the effect should be played on the device.

There are only two valid flags for the second parameter. Both can be applied. If no flags are required, you can set this parameter to 0.

- DIES_SOLO. Any other effects that are currently playing stop when this effect is played.
- DIES_NODOWNLOAD. The effect is not automatically downloaded to the device.

note

If an effect is currently playing and the Start function is called, this effect is started over from the beginning.

This sample call to the Start function tells DirectInput to play the effect once and specifies that no flags should be applied.

```
g_pEffect->Start( 1, 0 );
```

After calling the Start function, the effect begins to play on the device. If the effect has a duration, the effect ends when the duration is reached. If the duration of the effect is infinite, you must stop the effect.

Stopping an Effect

As mentioned previously, if an effect has a duration, it ends when the duration is reached. But what about an effect whose duration is infinite, or what if the user has hit the pause button? Both of these instances require that an effect be stopped manually.

This is accomplished through the Stop function. This function requires no parameters and returns only whether the call was successful. The Stop function is declared here:

```
HRESULT Stop(VOID);
```

A return code of DI_OK means that the call to the Stop function was successful.

Chapter Summary

Input is such an integral part of any game that you should pay special attention to it during the development cycle. When games are reviewed, the performance of the input can make or break it. Paying proper attention to the input system during development enhances the gamer's experience.

What You Have Learned

In this chapter, you learned how to use input devices. You should now understand the following points:

- How to use the mouse and keyboard devices
- The difference between analog and digital controls
- How to support more than one input device
- How to create and play force feedback effects through a game controller
- The proper way to release and shut down DirectInput

In the next chapter, you'll be introduced to DirectSound and how to use music and sound to enhance your game.

Review Questions

You can find the answers to Review Questions and On Your Own exercises in Appendix A, "Answers to End-of-Chapter Exercises."

1. DirectInput allows for what type of input devices?
2. Which function creates the IDirectInput8 interface?
3. What is the detection of input devices on a system called?
4. Reading from the keyboard requires what kind of buffer?
5. What is the data format type for mouse input?

On Your Own

1. Change the mouse input example to remove the Windows cursor.
2. Modify the gamepad example to read from the controller buttons.

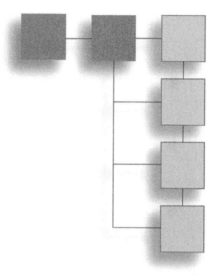

CHAPTER 10

DirectSound

irectSound helps your game come to life. When you take advantage of background music and sound effects, the world you create takes on a whole new depth. In this chapter, you'll learn how you can use sound effectively in your game.

Here's what you'll learn in this chapter:

- What DirectSound is
- How to use DirectSound
- What sound buffers are
- How to play a sound file
- How to cause a sound file to loop
- How to set and change a sound's volume

Sound

Sound is important in every game. It's used to set the mood, building tension or celebration at the end of a level. Sound helps create your environment, from the sound of cars racing around a track to the gunfire you hear as it zooms over your head. Without sound, games would lose their ability to bring you into their world. DirectX provides you with DirectSound, allowing you to easily add an audio element to your game.

DirectSound

DirectSound provides a single Application Programming Interface (API) for the playback of sounds and music. Previously, developers had to make do with support for only certain sound cards because they were tasked with writing software for each one. With the birth of DirectX and its Hardware Abstraction Layer (HAL), developers only need to write to one common set of functions, which can support a wide array of sound cards.

How Does DirectSound Work?

DirectSound manages the sound data through the use of *buffers*. Buffers are areas of memory that hold sound data. When you're using DirectSound, you can have multiple buffers that hold any sound data you want to load. You can then manipulate or play the data within these buffers. DirectSound mixes these sounds into a single buffer. This single buffer contains the final sound that the user hears.

The sound buffers can reside either on sound card memory or in system memory.

note

You can access buffers that are contained in memory on the sound card more quickly than those buffers in system memory. You should use the latter type of buffers sparingly because they are limited by the amount of memory on the sound card.

Sound buffers are the areas that hold the sound data. For example, if you were loading a WAV file to be played, the sound data within that file would be placed into a sound buffer. You could then change, manipulate, or play the data within that buffer.

Following are the types of buffers that DirectSound uses:

- **Primary buffer.** All sounds played are mixed into the primary buffer. The sound card uses the resulting mixed sound in the primary buffer to create the actual sound that you hear.
- **Secondary buffer.** These are the buffers that hold all the sound data that your game needs. DirectSound lets you play multiple sounds by accessing more than one secondary buffer simultaneously.
- **Static buffer.** When sound data is of limited size, you can create a static or fixed-size buffer. This buffer allows for the complete loading of a particular sound into memory.
- **Streaming buffer.** Sometimes, sounds that you want to play might be too large to fit into memory at one time. In this instance, you need a streaming buffer. The streaming buffer allows for only a portion of a sound to be loaded into it before

being sent off to be played. As the sound within the streaming buffer is played, new sound data is loaded into it.

Using DirectSound

Before you can use DirectSound, you need to know the steps involved. Like other DirectX components, DirectSound must be initialized before you can use it. The first step to using DirectSound is creating the DirectSound device. This device is represented by the IDirectSound8 interface, which provides methods for creating sound buffers, getting sound hardware capabilities, and setting the cooperative level of the sound card.

The DirectSound Device

The DirectSound device represents an interface to a specific piece of sound hardware within your machine. For DirectSound to work, you must select a sound card and create a DirectSound device to represent it. Because most machines contain only a single sound card, DirectSound allows you to create a DirectSound device based on a default sound card. If a machine has more than one sound card, you might need to enumerate through them to find the one that best meets your application's needs.

You create the DirectSound device by using the DirectSoundCreate8 function, defined next:

```
HRESULT WINAPI DirectSoundCreate8(
  LPCGUID  lpcGuidDevice,
  LPDIRECTSOUND8 * ppDS8,
  LPUNKNOWN  pUnkOuter
);
```

The DirectSoundCreate8 function requires three parameters:

- **lpcGuidDevice.** The GUID that represents the sound device to use. This can be either DSDEVID_DefaultPlayback or NULL. Use NULL if you want to use the default sound device.
- **ppDS8.** The address to the variable that will hold the newly created DirectSound device.
- **pUnkOuter.** The controlling object's IUnknown interface. This value should be NULL.

A standard call to DirectSoundCreate8 that uses the default sound device is shown next:

```
// variable that will hold the return code
HRESULT hr;
// variable that will hold the created DirectSound device
LPDIRECTSOUND8 m_pDS;
```

```
// Attempt to create the DirectSound device
hr = DirectSoundCreate8( NULL, &m_pDS, NULL ) ;

// Check the return value to confirm that a valid device was created
if FAILED ( hr )
    return false;
```

If the previous code fails to create a valid DirectSound device, the function returns FALSE.

Enumerating the Sound Devices

Occasionally, you might want to enumerate the sound hardware within a system. If, for instance, the default sound device does not have all the functions that your game might need, you can search for another device in the system.

If you're not going to use the default sound device, you need to enumerate through the available devices before calling the DirectSoundCreate8 function. When your enumeration is complete, you will have the needed GUID for the device, which you will then pass to DirectSoundCreate8 instead of NULL.

The process of enumeration is handled through the function DirectSoundEnumerate. Like previous components within DirectX, enumerating the devices requires a callback function. The DirectSoundEnumerate function calls the callback every time a new sound device is detected. Within the callback function, you can determine the capabilities of the device and choose whether you want to use it.

The DirectSoundEnumerate function is defined as follows:

```
HRESULT WINAPI DirectSoundEnumerate(
    LPDSENUMCALLBACK  lpDSEnumCallback,
    LPVOID  lpContext
);
```

The DirectSoundEnumerate function requires just two parameters:

- **lpDSEnumCallback.** The address of the callback function
- **lpContext.** Any data that you want to be sent to the callback function

The following code shows a sample DirectSoundEnumerate function call:

```
// variable to hold the return code
HRESULT     hr;

// Call DirectSoundEnumerate
hr = DirectSoundEnumerate( (LPDSENUMCALLBACK)DSoundEnumCallback, 0);
```

```
// Check the return code to make sure that the call was successful
if FAILED ( hr)
    return false;
```

The previous code creates a callback function called DSoundEnumCallback. The second parameter is 0 because no information needs to be sent to the callback function.

The DirectSoundEnumerate Callback Function

The callback function provided to DirectSoundEnumerate is called every time the enumeration finds a new sound device. If multiple sound devices are installed in the system, the callback function is called once for each of them.

The main purpose of the callback function is to give your code a chance to create a Direct-Sound device and to use it to gather information about the device. If you were searching for a sound device that allowed for sound capture, you would check the capabilities of each device passed to the callback function to see if this functionality existed.

The DirectSoundEnumerate function requires the callback function to be in the DSEnumCallback format.

```
BOOL CALLBACK DSEnumCallback(
    LPGUID   lpGuid,
    LPCSTR   lpcstrDescription,
    LPCSTR   lpcstrModule,
    LPVOID   lpContext
);
```

You must declare the callback function using the signature shown next. The callback function requires four parameters:

- **lpGuid.** The address to the GUID that identifies the current sound device. If this value is NULL, then the current device being enumerated is the primary device.

- **lpcstrDescription.** A NULL-terminated string that provides a text description of the current device.

- **lpcstrModule.** A NULL-terminated string that provides the module name of the DirectSound driver for this device.

- **lpContext.** The extra data that was passed to the callback function through the lpContext variable in DirectSoundEnumerate.

The DSEnumCallback function returns a boolean value. If the return value is TRUE, the DirectSoundEnumerate function continues to enumerate additional devices. If the return value is FALSE, the enumeration of additional devices stops.

The primary device is always enumerated twice: once with a value of NULL being passed to the lpGuid parameter, and a second time with its proper GUID.

The sample callback function that follows creates a message box that displays the name of the current sound device and its driver.

```
/******************************************************************************
* DirectSoundEnumerate callback function
******************************************************************************/
BOOL CALLBACK DSCallback( GUID* pGUID,
                          LPSTR strDesc,
                          LPSTR strDrvName,
                          VOID* pContext )
{
    // temporary variable to hold the information about the device
    string tempString;

    // Build the string using the information provided to the callback function
    tempString = "Device name = ";
    tempString += strDesc;
    tempString += "\nDriver name = ";
    tempString += strDrvName;

    // Pop up the message box and display the results
    MessageBox (NULL, tempString.c_str(), "message", MB_OK );

    // Continue to enumerate additional devices; return TRUE
    return true;
}
```

A temporary string variable is created to hold the informa-tion. The function returns a value of TRUE, so it will enu-merate all the sound devices in the system. The full source listing for this example is located in the chapter10\exam-ple1 directory on the CD-ROM. Figure 10.1 shows what the message box will look like when displaying the sound device information.

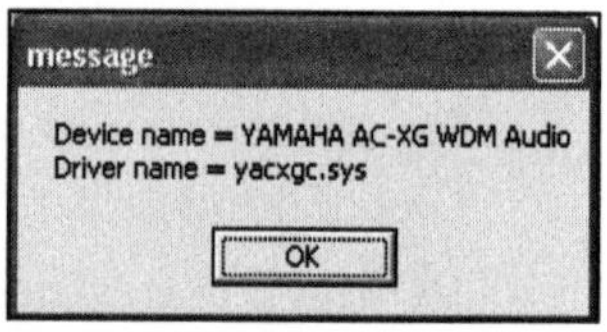

Figure 10.1 Message box showing the sound device's name and driver.

Setting the Cooperative Level

Because DirectSound gives you access to a hardware device, it needs to have a cooperative level set. Similar to DirectInput, DirectSound attempts to gain primary access to a device. In DirectInput, you can gain exclusive access to an input device, restricting its use to only your application. In DirectSound, you cannot gain exclusive access to the sound device, but you can let the operating system know that you want your application to have the highest priority when it comes to using the sound hardware. Because you cannot gain exclusive access to the sound card, other applications—including the operating system—can still trigger sounds to be played.

The three DirectSound cooperative levels are shown next:

- DSSCL_NORMAL. This level works best with other applications that still allow other events. Because your application must share the device, though, you cannot change the format of the primary buffer.
- DSSCL_PRIORITY. If you want more control over the primary buffer and your sounds, you should use this cooperative level. Most games should use this level.
- DSSCL_WRITEPRIMARY. This level gives your application write access to the primary buffer.

The cooperative level is set using the SetCooperativeLevel function. The IDirectSound8 interface provides this function. The SetCooperativeLevel function is defined as follows:

```
HRESULT SetCooperativeLevel(
    HWND hwnd,
    DWORD dwLevel
);
```

The previous function requires two parameters:

- hwnd. The handle of the application window requesting the change in cooperative level
- dwLevel. One of the three cooperative levels shown earlier

Here is a sample call to SetCooperativeLevel:

```
// variable to hold the return code
HRESULT hr;
// variable that contains a valid DirectSound device
LPDIRECTSOUND8 g_pDS = NULL;
```

```
hr = DirectSoundCreate8( NULL, & g_pDS, NULL ) ;

// Set DirectSound cooperative level
hr = g_pDS->SetCooperativeLevel( hwnd, DSSCL_PRIORITY );

// Check the return code
if FAILED ( hr )
    return false;
```

In the previous code sample, the cooperative level is being set to the value of DSSCL_PRIORITY. Before you can call the SetCooperativeLevel function, you must have a valid pointer to a DirectSound device.

Now that the cooperative level is set, you can create buffers and load sound data.

Sound Files

You must load sound data within DirectSound into secondary buffers before using it. You can load background music or sound effects into either a static buffer or a streaming buffer.

A *static buffer* is a fixed-length buffer that has full sound loaded into it. A *streaming buffer* is needed when the sound being loaded is larger than what the buffer can accommodate. In this case, a small buffer is used, and parts of the sound data are continuously loaded in and played. The next section discusses how buffers are used in DirectSound.

The Secondary Buffer

DirectSound uses buffers to store the audio data that it needs. Before you can play a sound, you must create a secondary buffer where the sound can reside. After the buffer is created, the sound is loaded into it fully (or partially for a streaming sound) and then played. DirectSound allows for any number of secondary buffers to be played simultaneously, all being mixed into the primary buffer.

Before you can create a secondary buffer, you need to know the format of the sound that will reside in it. DirectSound requires that the buffers you create are of the same format as the sound within them. For example, if you are loading a 16-bit WAV file that needs two channels of sound, the secondary buffer you create must be of this format.

Most of the time, all the sounds you use for your game will share a common format, allowing you to know beforehand which format your buffers require. If you are tasked with writing a generic audio player, though, you cannot be guaranteed that all the sound files you load will be the same format.

The formats of the buffers in DirectSound are described using the WAVEFORMATEX structure. The WAVEFORMATEX structure is defined next:

```
typedef struct {
  WORD  wFormatTag;
  WORD  nChannels;
  DWORD nSamplesPerSec;
  DWORD nAvgBytesPerSec;
  WORD  nBlockAlign;
  WORD  wBitsPerSample;
  WORD  cbSize;
} WAVEFORMATEX;
```

This structure consists of seven variables.

- **wFormatTag.** The type of waveform audio. For one- or two-channel PCM data, this value should be WAVE_FORMAT_PCM.
- **nChannels.** The number of channels needed.
- **nSamplesPerSec.** The sample rate.
- **nAvgBytesPerSec.** The average data-transfer rate in bytes per second.
- **nBlockAlign.** The alignment in bytes. You determine the value needed here by multiplying the number of channels by the bits per sample and then dividing by 8.
- **wBitsPerSample.** The number of bits per sample. This value will be either 8 or 16.
- **cbSize.** The extra number of bytes to append to this structure.

You can create a standard WAVEFORMATEX structure if you know the format of the WAV file data that you will be using. If you aren't sure, you can create this structure and fill it in after opening the audio file.

The WAVEFORMATEX structure is only part of the information you need when creating a secondary buffer. Besides specifying the format of the buffer, you need to know additional information, such as the size of the audio data that the buffer needs to hold.

You need a second structure to finish describing the secondary buffer to DirectSound: DSBUFFERDESC. The DSBUFFERDESC structure is defined here:

```
typedef struct {
  DWORD         dwSize;
  DWORD         dwFlags;
  DWORD         dwBufferBytes;
  DWORD         dwReserved;
  LPWAVEFORMATEX lpwfxFormat;
  GUID          guid3DAlgorithm;
} DSBUFFERDESC, *LPDSBUFFERDESC;
```

The DSBUFFERDESC structure contains six variable components:

- **dwSize.** The size of the DSBUFFERDESC structure in bytes.
- **dwFlags.** A DWORD set of flags that specify the capabilities of the buffer.
- **dwBufferBytes.** The size of the new buffer. This is the number of bytes of sound data that this buffer can hold.
- **dwReserved.** A reserved value that must be 0.
- **lpwfxFormat.** An address to a WAVEFORMATEX structure.
- **guid3DAlgorithm.** A GUID identifier to the two-speaker virtualization algorithm to use.

The dwFlags parameter is described in detail in Table 10.1.

Buffers, besides having a format associated with them, also have controls. The controls of a buffer allow you to manipulate the volume, frequency, and movement. You must specify the types of controls you want in the DSBUFFERDESC structure, shown earlier.

Table 10.1 DSBUFFERDESC Flags

Value	Description
DSBCAPS_CTRL3D	The buffer has 3D control.
DSBCAPS_CTRLFREQUENCY	The buffer can control the frequency of the sound.
DSBCAPS_CTRLFX	The buffer supports effects processing.
DSBCAPS_CTRLPAN	The buffer can pan the sound.
DSBCAPS_CTRLPOSITIONNOTIFY	This is the position notification buffer.
DSBCAPS_CTRLVOLUME	You can control the volume of this buffer.
DSBCAPS_GLOBALFOCUS	If this flag is set and the user switches focus to another application, the sounds in the current application continue to play.
DSBCAPS_LOCDEFER	You can place the buffer in software or hardware memory at runtime.
DSBCAPS_LOCHARDWARE	The buffer is to use hardware mixing. If this flag is specified and not enough memory is available, the call to create the buffer fails.
DSBCAPS_LOCSOFTWARE	The buffer is to be placed in software memory, and software mixing is to be used.
DSBCAPS_MUTE3DATMAXDISTANCE	The sound in this buffer is reduced as its virtual position gets farther away.
DSBCAPS_PRIMARYBUFFER	This is the primary buffer.
DSBCAPS_STATIC	The buffer is to be placed in on-board hardware memory.
DSBCAPS_STICKYFOCUS	When you're switching focus to another application, you can still hear buffers with sticky focus. Normal buffers are muted when this occurs.

Creating a Secondary Buffer

Now that you've created the DSBUFFERDESC structure, you are ready to create the actual secondary buffer. The secondary buffer is created with a call to CreateSoundBuffer, defined here:

```
HRESULT CreateSoundBuffer(
  LPCDSBUFFERDESC pcDSBufferDesc,
  LPDIRECTSOUNDBUFFER * ppDSBuffer,
  LPUNKNOWN pUnkOuter
);
```

The CreateSoundBuffer function requires only three parameters:

- **pcDSBufferDesc**. Address to an already-defined DSBUFFERDESC structure.

- **ppDSBuffer**. Address to the variable that will hold the newly created buffer.

- **pUnkOuter**. Address to the controlling object's IUnKnown interface. This value should be NULL.

A sample call to CreateSoundBuffer is shown here:

```
// Define a WAVEFORMATEX structure
WAVEFORMATEX wfx;
// Clear the structure to all zeros
ZeroMemory( &wfx, sizeof(WAVEFORMATEX) );

// Set the format to WAVE_FORMAT_PCM
wfx.wFormatTag    = (WORD) WAVE_FORMAT_PCM;
// Set the number of channels to 2
wfx.nChannels      = 2;
// Set the samples per second to 22050
wfx.nSamplesPerSec = 22050;
// Compute the nBlockAlign value
wfx.wBitsPerSample = 16;
wfx.nBlockAlign    = (WORD) (wfx.wBitsPerSample / 8 * wfx.nChannels);
// Compute the nAvgBytesPerSec value
wfx.nAvgBytesPerSec = (DWORD) (wfx.nSamplesPerSec * wfx.nBlockAlign);

// Define a DSBUFFERDESC structure
DSBUFFERDESC dsbd;
// Clear the structure to all zeros
ZeroMemory( &dsbd, sizeof(DSBUFFERDESC) );
```

```
// Set the size of the structure
dsbd.dwSize           = sizeof(DSBUFFERDESC);
// Set the flags
dsbd.dwFlags          = 0;
// the size of the buffer
 dsbd.dwBufferBytes    = 64000;
// the GUID of the algorithm
 dsbd.guid3DAlgorithm = GUID_NULL;
// the address of the WAVEFORMATEX structure
 dsbd.lpwfxFormat      = &wfx;


// Define the variable to hold the newly created buffer
LPDIRECTSOUNDBUFFER DSBuffer = NULL;
// Create the sound buffer
hr = g_pDS->CreateSoundBuffer( &dsbd, &DSBuffer, NULL );
// Check the return code to make sure the call to CreateSoundBuffer succeeded
if FAILED (hr)
    return NULL;
```

If the call to CreateSoundBuffer was successful, the variable DSBuffer will be a valid DirectSoundBuffer. In the previous example, the format of the WAVEFORMATEX structure was hard-coded, forcing any sound files that were loaded into this buffer to be of the specified format and up to 64000 bytes long.

Loading a Sound File into a Buffer

Now that you've created the sound buffer, you need to load the sound data into it. Loading sound data into a buffer requires you to first open the file containing the sound data and then copy its contents into the buffer you created. With a static buffer, all the sound data is copied into the buffer.

Because a sound buffer is an area of memory controlled by DirectSound, you must lock it before you can write to it. Locking the buffer prepares the memory to be written to. After a buffer is locked, your application can begin loading sound data into it. When you are finished loading the sound data, you must remember to unlock the buffer. Unlocking the buffer allows DirectSound to manipulate the buffer's contents again.

Locking the Sound Buffer

Locking the sound buffer gives your code a chance to manipulate and change the sound data within a buffer. Locking the buffer requires the Lock function, defined here:

```
HRESULT Lock(
  DWORD dwOffset,
```

```
    DWORD dwBytes,
    LPVOID * ppvAudioPtr1,
    LPDWORD pdwAudioBytes1,
    LPVOID * ppvAudioPtr2,
    LPDWORD pdwAudioBytes2,
    DWORD dwFlags
);
```

The Lock function requires seven parameters.

- **dwOffset.** This variable specifies where in the buffer the lock should begin.
- **dwBytes.** This is the number of bytes within the buffer to lock.
- **ppvAudioPtr1.** This variable receives a pointer to the first part of the locked buffer.
- **pdwAudioBytes1.** This variable receives the number of bytes in the block pointer by ppvAudioPtr1.
- **ppvAudioPtr2.** This variable receives a pointer to the second part of the locked buffer. If you are filling the whole buffer with sound data, this variable should be NULL.
- **pdwAudioBytes2.** This variable receives the number of bytes in the block pointer by ppvAudioPtr2. This variable should be NULL if you are filling the whole buffer with sound data.
- **dwFlags.** These are the flags that specify how the lock should occur:
  - DSBLOCK_FROMWRITECURSOR. Start the lock from the write cursor.
  - DSBLOCK_ENTIREBUFFER. Lock the entire buffer. If this flag is set, the dwBytes variable is ignored.

Unlocking the Sound Buffer

At this point, you are free to read in the sound data and load it into the buffer. After that is complete, you can unlock the buffer using the Unlock function, shown next:

```
HRESULT Unlock(
    LPVOID pvAudioPtr1,
    DWORD dwAudioBytes1,
    LPVOID pvAudioPtr2,
    DWORD dwAudioBytes2
);
```

The `Unlock` function requires four parameters:

- **pvAudioPtr1.** The address of the value from the `ppvAudioPtr1` parameter used in `Lock`.
- **dwAudioBytes1.** The number of bytes written to `pvAudioPtr1`.
- **pvAudioPtr2.** The address of the value from the `ppvAudioPtr2` parameter used in `Lock`.
- **dwAudioBytes2.** The number of bytes written to `pvAudioPtr2`.

Reading the Sound Data into the Buffer

Reading the sound data into the secondary buffer can be complex. To make the explanation easier to understand, I'll detail this process using the `CWaveFile` class found in the DirectSound framework classes. The DirectSound framework provides a simple way to load in sound data using the WAV file format. WAV files are the default Windows sound format; they have a file extension of WAV.

note

> The DirectSound framework classes declared within the dsutil.cpp and dsutil.h files provide common functions that pertain to DirectSound. You can find them in the Samples\C++\Common\Src and Samples\C++\Common\Inc directories in the folder where you installed the DirectX Software Development Kit (SDK).

The first step in loading a WAV file in a DirectSound buffer is to create a `CWaveFile` object. This object provides you with methods for opening, closing, and reading WAV files. The line of code that follows shows you how to create a `CWaveFile` object.

```
CWaveFile wavFileObj = new CWaveFile( );
```

Next, using the `Open` method provided by `CWaveFile`, you can gain access to the WAV file you want to use. The code that follows uses the `Open` function and checks to see if the WAV file contains data.

```
// Open the WAV file test.wav
wavFile->Open("test.wav", NULL, WAVEFILE_READ );
// Check to make sure that the size of the data within the wave file is valid
if( wavFile->GetSize( ) == 0 )
    return false;
```

The previous code opens a file called `test.wav` for reading. It then checks the size of the data within this file. If the file does not contain data, the code stops reading it.

The next step is the creation of the secondary sound buffer to hold the WAV data. This process was shown earlier. After you create the sound buffer, you need to lock it before you can write the WAV data to it. The following code demonstrates use of the Lock function in preparing a buffer for reading an entire WAV file.

```
HRESULT hr;
VOID*    pDSLockedBuffer       = NULL;      // pointer to locked buffer memory
DWORD    dwDSLockedBufferSize  = 0;  // size of the locked DirectSound buffer

// Start the beginning of the buffer
hr = DSBuffer->Lock( 0,
                    // This assumes a buffer of 64000 bytes
                    64000,
                    // The variable holds a pointer to the start of the buffer
                    &pDSLockedBuffer,
                    // holds the size of the locked buffer
                    &dwDSLockedBufferSize,
                    NULL,// No secondary is needed
                    NULL, // No secondary is needed
                    // Lock the entire buffer
                    DSBLOCK_ENTIREBUFFER);
// Check the return code to make sure the lock was successful
if FAILED (hr)
    return NULL;
```

The previous code locks a buffer using the DSBLOCK_ENTIREBUFFER flag. This causes the buffer to be locked from beginning to end. The DSBuffer variable must be a valid DirectSoundBuffer.

Now that the buffer is properly locked, you can write the WAV data into it. Again, I'll be using methods provided through the CWaveFile class. Before you read the WAV data into the buffer, you need to reset the WAV data to the beginning. You accomplish this by using the ResetFile method. Next, you use the Read method to place the WAV data into the buffer. The following code sample resets the WAV file for reading and then places the data into the buffer.

```
HRESULT hr;    // variable to hold the return code
DWORD   dwWavDataRead   = 0;   // amount of data read from the WAV file

wavFile->ResetFile( );    // Reset the WAV file to the beginning

// Read the WAV file
```

```
hr = wavFile->Read( ( BYTE* ) pDSLockedBuffer,
                      dwDSLockedBufferSize,
                      &dwWavDataRead );

// Check to make sure that this was successful
if FAILED (hr)
    return NULL;
```

The wavFile variable must contain a valid CWaveFile object before its use. First, the ResetFile function is called, followed by a call to the Read function. The Read function requires three parameters. The first parameter is a pointer to the area of buffer memory to copy the WAV data into. The second parameter is the size of the locked buffer. The last parameter receives the amount of data read from the WAV file, in bytes.

After the call to the Read function, the buffer is filled with the data from the WAV file. You can now safely unlock the buffer.

Playing Sound in a Buffer

Now that you have valid sound data in your DirectSoundBuffer, you can play the sound that it contains. After all the work it's taken to create the buffer and fill it with sound data, playing it is easy. A simple function called Play accomplishes this. The Play function is a method provided to you through the DirectSoundBuffer object. It's defined like this:

```
HRESULT Play(
   DWORD dwReserved1,
   DWORD dwPriority,
   DWORD dwFlags
);
```

The Play function requires three parameters:

- **dwReserved1.** A reserved value that must be set to 0.
- **dwPriority.** The priority level to play the sound. This can be any value between 0 and 0xFFFFFFFF. You must set the priority level to 0 if the DSBCAPS_LOCDEFER flag was not set when the buffer was created.
- **dwFlags.** The flags that specify how the sound should be played. The only flag that I'll explain here is DSBPLAY_LOOPING. This flag causes the sound to loop when the end of the buffer is reached. If this sound should only be played once, a value of 0 should be passed in the dwFlags parameter.

The following code causes a sound buffer to play its contents.

```
DSBuffer->Play( 0, 0, DSBPLAY_LOOPING);
```

The DSBuffer variable must contain a valid DirectSoundBuffer object filled with sound data. In this instance, the DSBPLAY_LOOPING flag is being passed, which causes this sound to loop after it finishes playing.

Stopping a Sound

Normally, after you start playing a sound, you don't need to worry about it unless you have told the sound to loop. In this case, you would need to specifically cause the sound to stop playing. You do this through the Stop method provided by the DirectSoundBuffer object, defined next.

```
HRESULT Stop( );
```

The Stop function does not require parameters. It passes back only a return code that informs you whether the call was successful.

You can find a full source example that shows how to load a sound file and play it in the chapter10\example2 directory on the CD-ROM.

Using the Buffer Controls

As I mentioned earlier, DirectSound buffers can control certain aspects of the sound within them. For instance, through a buffer, you can change the volume, change the frequency, or pan a sound. In this section, you're going to learn how to use these controls.

Changing the Volume

You can adjust the volume of a sound through the buffer in which it resides. You are able to adjust the volume between the values of DSBVOLUME_MIN and DSBVOLUME_MAX. The DSBVOLUME_MIN value represents silence, and the DSBVOLUME_MAX value represents the original volume of the sound.

note

DirectSound does not support amplifying sounds, so you can never increase the volume.

You can adjust the volume of a sound through the SetVolume function defined here:

```
HRESULT SetVolume (
  LONG lVolume
);
```

The SetVolume function requires only one parameter: lVolume. You can set the lVolume value to any value between 0 (DSBVOLUME_MAX) and -10000 (DSBVOLUME_MIN).

You can get the current volume at which a sound is playing by using the GetVolume function. This function is defined next:

```
HRESULT GetVolume (
  LPLONG plVolume
);
```

The GetVolume function requires only one parameter: a pointer to a variable that will receive the current volume.

note

Before you can use the SetVolume and GetVolume functions, you must set the buffer to use these controls. You need to set the flag DSBCAPS_CTRLVOLUME in the DSBUFFERDESC structure when you create the secondary buffer.

Panning the Sound

DirectSound buffers allow a sound to be panned between the left and right speakers. *Panning* is lowering the volume of a sound in one speaker and increasing it in the opposite speaker. Sounds seem to move around.

Panning uses a similar concept to the SetVolume function. The left and right speakers can be made to raise and lower their volumes independently using two values: DSBPAN_LEFT and DSBPAN_RIGHT.

The DSBPAN_LEFT value, which is equivalent to –10000, increases the volume of sound in the left speaker to full while silencing the sound in the right speaker. The DSBPAN_RIGHT value, which is defined as 10000, does the opposite, increasing the volume in the right speaker while silencing the sound in the left. By using values between DSBPAN_LEFT and DSBPAN_RIGHT, sounds can be made to pan from one speaker to the other.

A third value, DSBPAN_CENTER, defined as 0, resets both the left and right sides to full volume.

The amount of panning that the sound in the buffer uses is set using the function SetPan, defined next:

```
HRESULT SetPan(
  LONG lPan
);
```

The SetPan function requires only one parameter, lPan, which takes any value between DSBPAN_LEFT and DSBPAN_RIGHT.

If you want to get the current pan value, use the function GetPan, shown here:

```
HRESULT GetPan(
  LPLONG plPan
);
```

The GetPan function needs one parameter: plPan. The plPan variable is a pointer to a LONG that will receive the current value of panning.

note

Before you can use the SetPan and GetPan functions, you must set the buffer to use these controls. You need to set the DSBCAPS_CTRLPAN flag in the DSBUFFERDESC structure when you create the secondary buffer.

Chapter Summary

Using what you've learned in this chapter, you should be able to play background music or simple sound effects within your game. You can extend the lessons in this chapter to playing multiple sounds simultaneously, creating dynamic music that can be changed and manipulated within your game.

In the next chapter, you'll put together everything you've learned to create a simple game that utilizes each of the areas covered in this book.

What You Have Learned

In this chapter, you learned the following:

- How DirectSound is used
- Which different types of sound buffers are available
- How to enumerate sound devices installed on the system
- How to load and play a WAV file
- How to control the playback of a sound file

Review Questions

You can find the answers to Review Questions and On Your Own exercises in Appendix A, "Answers to End-of-Chapter Exercises."

1. When must you use the DirectSoundEnumerate function?
2. Which three important pieces of data are passed to the enumeration callback function?

3. Does the format of a buffer need to match the format of its contents?

4. What is the purpose of the primary buffer?

5. What value is passed to `DirectSoundCreate8` to specify that the default sound device is used?

On Your Own

1. Write a small sample that allows you to adjust the volume of a sound while it's playing.

2. Write a small sample to allow the sound to be panned using the arrow keys.

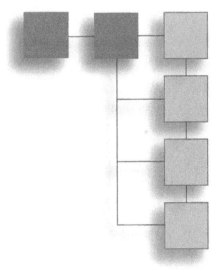

CHAPTER 11

THE FINAL PROJECT

Y ou've made it to the final chapter! Congratulations! You've seen DirectX take a simple empty window and fill it with a virtual world. Now it's your turn to create a working 3D demo using the components of DirectX.

After the demo is completed, I'll explain how you can release your game creation to the world.

Here's what you'll learn in this chapter:

- How to create a DirectX Manager to simplify DirectX creation
- How to design and code a simple game framework
- Why it's best to use inheritance when creating game objects
- How to encompass rendering of all your in-game objects
- How to allow your 3D objects to move in relative directions
- How to bundle and release your game to the world

Welcome to the Final Project

The final project takes a lot of what you've learned throughout this book and applies it to a single application. I'm going to show you how to encapsulate the functionality of the DirectX components to keep your game code neat and easy to maintain. Even though this is the final project, I'm still going to explain each step in detail, reducing the amount of time you'll need to spend rereading other chapters.

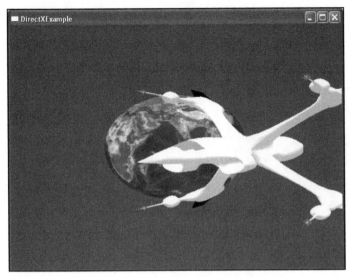

Figure 11.1 This is what the final project will look like.

The final project gives you the chance to take flight in a spaceship as you circle an Earth-like planet. The spaceship, which can fly in multiple directions, will be yours to control. Figure 11.1 shows what the final outcome of this project will be.

Now that you know where you're going, let's get started.

Creating the Application Window

The application window is the container in which your game world will live; it's the first thing you need to create. You can start out by loading the winmain.cpp file from the chapter11\part1 directory on the CD-ROM and following along, or just look at the code listings in this chapter.

I've chosen to encapsulate all the main interface and window creation code in a single place. The WinMain function is the entry point for any Windows application, and this is where you'll start.

WinMain

The WinMain function serves two main purposes. First, it's where you initialize your application; second, it provides your application with a message loop. The message loop, which is required by every windowed application, handles the collecting and processing of messages that the system sends to the application.

The WinMain function that I've provided in the following code has only the absolute minimum code you need to start the application.

```
/***************************************************************************
 * WinMain
 ***************************************************************************/
int WINAPI WinMain(HINSTANCE hInstance,
                   HINSTANCE hPrevInstance,
                   LPTSTR lpCmdLine,
                   int nCmdShow)
{
        // Call the function to init and create the window
        if (!initWindow (hInstance))
        {
                MessageBox (NULL, "Unable to create window", "ERROR", MB_OK);
                return false;
        }

        // main message loop
        // Enter the message loop
        MSG msg;
        ZeroMemory (&msg, sizeof (msg));
        while ( msg.message!=WM_QUIT )
        {
                // Check for messages
                if (PeekMessage ( &msg, NULL, 0U, 0U, PM_REMOVE ) )
                {
                        TranslateMessage (&msg);
                        DispatchMessage (&msg);
                }
        }

        return (int) msg.wParam;
}
```

Because the code needed to create the application window can be cumbersome, I've separated it into the initWindow function.

initWindow

The initWindow function handles the actual window creation. As you might recall, each application window that is created needs to have a window class registered with the system. The window class, defined in the WNDCLASSEX structure, contains a collection of properties that the system uses to define the window. After the window class is defined in the WNDCLASSEX structure, it is passed to the RegisterClassEx function to notify the system of its existence.

After the window class is registered, you can create your window. You create the application by using the CreateWindow function. This function pulls together the properties from the window class and its own parameters to define and create the application window. The size of the window and its name are passed as parameters to the CreateWindow function.

```
/**************************************************************************
* initWindow
**************************************************************************/
bool initWindow (HINSTANCE hInstance)
{
        WNDCLASSEX wcex;

        // Register the window class for this application
        wcex.cbSize                     = sizeof (WNDCLASSEX);
        wcex.style                      = CS_HREDRAW | CS_VREDRAW;
        wcex.lpfnWndProc                = (WNDPROC) WndProc;
        wcex.cbClsExtra                 = 0;
        wcex.cbWndExtra                 = 0;
        wcex.hInstance                  = hInstance;
        wcex.hIcon                      = 0;
        wcex.hCursor                    = LoadCursor (NULL, IDC_ARROW);
        wcex.hbrBackground              = (HBRUSH) (COLOR_WINDOW+1);
        wcex.lpszMenuName               = NULL;
        wcex.lpszClassName              = "DirectXExample";
        wcex.hIconSm                    = 0;
        RegisterClassEx (&wcex);

        // Create the application window
        wndHandle = CreateWindow("DirectXExample",
                        "DirectXExample",
                        WS_OVERLAPPEDWINDOW,
                        CW_USEDEFAULT,
                        CW_USEDEFAULT,
                        640,
                        480,
                        NULL,
                        NULL,
                        hInstance,
```

```
                    NULL);
    // Make sure that the window handle is valid
    if (!wndHandle)
            return false;

    // Show and update the newly created window
    ShowWindow (wndHandle, SW_SHOW);
    UpdateWindow (wndHandle);

    return true;
}
```

At this point, the system considers you to have a valid and usable window that you can display using the ShowWindow and UpdateWindow functions. Although you might have a window, without a window procedure, you won't be able to process messages that come to your application. The final step needed in window creation is the addition of the window procedure.

WndProc

The window procedure is where the messages for your application from the user and the system are sent. Using a simple switch statement, you determine the messages that your application needs to handle.

For this example, only one message needs to be handled: WM_DESTROY. This message is sent to an application when the user clicks on the X button of the window.

```
/**************************************************************************
* WndProc
**************************************************************************/
LRESULT CALLBACK WndProc(HWND hWnd, UINT message, WPARAM wParam, LPARAM lParam)
{
        switch (message)
        {
                case WM_DESTROY:
                        PostQuitMessage(0);
                        break;
        }
        return DefWindowProc(hWnd, message, wParam, lParam);
}
```

You can find everything that I've explained so far in the chapter11\part1 directory on the CD-ROM. If you load the project in that directory and compile it, you'll see the blank window shown in Figure 11.2.

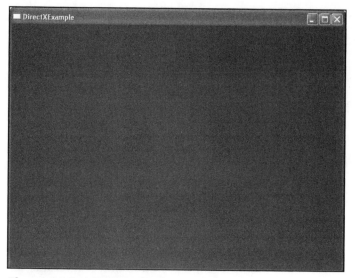

Figure 11.2 A blank application window.

Initializing DirectX

Getting DirectX up and running is the next step in the project. You'll be using multiple components from DirectX to provide your application with 3D object rendering, as well as input. To make setting up DirectX easy, I've packed all the functions you need into the DirectX Manager class.

The DirectX Manager

The DirectX Manager is responsible for setting up your application and giving it a place to render game objects. Because it's easiest to keep all the needed DirectX functions together, I've placed them into a class called dxManager.

The dxManager class contains functions for creating the Direct3D object, setting the default rendering states, and preparing your scene for rendering. The following list presents dxManager functions:

- **init.** Initializes the dxManager and creates the Direct3D object.
- **shutdown.** Cleans up and releases the Direct3D object.
- **beginRender.** Prepares DirectX for rendering. This function is called before you draw anything to the screen.
- **endRender.** Ends drawing and presents the objects to the screen.
- **getSurfaceFromBitmap.** Loads a bitmap from disk and applies it to an offscreen surface.

- **getBackBuffer.** Returns a pointer to the current back buffer.
- **blitToSurface.** Copies a rectangular portion of an offscreen surface to the back buffer.
- **createVertexBuffer.** Simplifies the creation of a vertex buffer.

The following code defines the structure of the dxManager class.

```
/****************************************************************************
* dxManager class
****************************************************************************/
class dxManager
{
public:
        ~dxManager(void);

        // The dxManager is treated as a single object using the
        // singleton design pattern
        static dxManager& getInstance()
        {
                static dxManager pInstance;
                return pInstance;
        }

        // Initialize the dxManager
        bool init(HWND hwnd);

        // Shut down the dxManager
        void shutdown(void);

        // called before any rendering
        void beginRender(void);

        // follows any rendering
        void endRender(void);

        // loads a bitmap into a Direct3D surface
        IDirect3DSurface9* getSurfaceFromBitmap(std::string filename);

        // returns a pointer to the back buffer
        IDirect3DSurface9* getBackBuffer(void);

        // an inline function used to return the current Direct3D device
        inline LPDIRECT3DDEVICE9 getD3DDevice(void) { return pd3dDevice; }
```

```
        // Copy an offscreen surface to the back buffer
        void blitToSurface(IDirect3DSurface9* srcSurface,
                                  const RECT *srcRect,
                                  const RECT *destRect);

        // used to easily create a vertex buffer
        LPDIRECT3DVERTEXBUFFER9 createVertexBuffer(int size, DWORD usage);

private:
        dxManager(void);

        // the Direct3D object
        LPDIRECT3D9            pD3D;
        // the Direct3D device
        LPDIRECT3DDEVICE9       pd3dDevice;
        // screen details
        int screen_width;
        int screen_height;
};
```

If you are interested in the implementation of all the functions found in the dxManager, you can find the source code for this class in the chapter11\part2 directory on the CD-ROM. The dxManager class resides in the dxManager.h and dxManager.cpp files.

Hooking in the DirectX Manager

You access the dxManager class primarily from within the application's WinMain function. The dxManager waits until the main application window is created before trying to start up DirectX. If the dxManager class successfully initializes DirectX using the init function, the application is then allowed to start the application's message loop.

The second dxManager function used by WinMain is shutdown. The shutdown function is called after the game is over and the application window is closing. Called directly after the message loop ends, the shutdown function releases the Direct3D object and device before exiting.

An updated WinMain function is shown here, using functions from the dxManager class. The changes to the default WinMain function are highlighted in bold.

```
/* Get a reference to the DirectX Manager */
static dxManager& dxMgr = dxManager::getInstance();
/***********************************************************************
* WinMain - updated to include the DirectX Manager class
***********************************************************************/
int WINAPI WinMain(HINSTANCE hInstance,
```

```
                              HINSTANCE hPrevInstance,
                              LPTSTR lpCmdLine,
                              int nCmdShow )
{
        // Call the function to init and create the window
        if (!initWindow(hInstance))
        {
                MessageBox(NULL, "Unable to create window", "ERROR", MB_OK);
                return false;
        }


        // Initialize DirectX through the dxManager
        if (!dxMgr.init(wndHandle))
        {
                MessageBox(NULL, "Unable to init DirectX", "ERROR", MB_OK);
                return false;
        }


        // main message loop
        // Enter the message loop
        MSG msg;
        ZeroMemory( &msg, sizeof(msg) );
        while( msg.message!=WM_QUIT )
        {
                // Check for messages
                if( PeekMessage( &msg, NULL, 0U, 0U, PM_REMOVE ) )
                {
                        TranslateMessage( &msg );
                        DispatchMessage( &msg );
                }
        }


        // Shut down the DirectX Manager
        dxMgr.shutdown();

        return (int) msg.wParam;
}
```

You probably noticed immediately the first line of code before WinMain:

```
static dxManager& dxMgr = dxManager::getInstance();
```

This single line of code allows the code within the winmain.cpp source file to gain access to the functions in the dxManager class. The dxManager class is defined as a singleton, meaning that only one instance of this class can exist in the application. You'll have use for the dxManager multiple places in the project. Defining the class as a singleton prevents your application from accidentally creating multiple instances.

note

Singletons are just one instance of C++ design patterns that help make your code more robust.

Coding the Demo

Now that you see what's needed just to get an application and DirectX up and running, it's time to move on to coding the actual project demo.

The Game Application Class

I created the Game application class to serve as a container for the base functionality that each game needs. This class provides you with a single point to initialize your game, as well as a way to update your game objects and render them to the screen. The Game class also provides your game with the needed variables and functions to implement a game timer.

The Game application class provides you with four functions:

- **init**. This function gives you a place to initialize your game objects.
- **shutdown**. The shutdown function provides you with a place to release your objects and the memory they use.
- **update**. Each game object's position and internal properties are updated in this function.
- **render**. The scene is rendered and sent to the screen for display.

As you go further into the project, you'll add more functionality to the Game application class. The Game class definition is shown here.

```
/*****************************************************************************
* Game class
*****************************************************************************/
class Game
{
public:
        Game(void);
        ~Game(void);
```

```
        bool init(HWND wndHandle);
        void shutdown(void);

        int update(void);
        void render(void);

private:
        // timer variables
        LARGE_INTEGER timeStart;
        LARGE_INTEGER timeEnd;
        LARGE_INTEGER timerFreq;
        float           anim_rate;
};
```

Creating the Game Timer

The game timer is an important piece of any game. It helps to keep your animation smooth and your game moving at a constant rate. For the purposes of this project, I'm going to go with the simple timer method that I introduced previously.

The Game class contains four variables that provide a timer to your application:

- **timeStart.** Holds the value of when the timer starts
- **timeEnd.** The value of when the timer is stopped
- **timerFreq.** The frequency of the hardware timer
- **anim_rate.** A value calculated each frame to provide your game with a timer-based animation value

The timer variables work together, providing your game with a steady animation rate. The timeStart variable is filled with the current time at the beginning of each frame. Your game then updates and renders the game objects. Afterward, the timeEnd variable is filled with the new time. The animation rate, stored in the anim_rate variable, is then calculated by determining the difference in time between the timeEnd and timeStart variables. To get the final animation rate, you divide the result by the timer frequency. Each frame, the animation rate is passed to the update function of in-game objects to affect how far they can move around in the world.

The following code demonstrates how to calculate the animation rate.

```
// Determine the animation rate
anim_rate = ( (float)timeEnd.QuadPart -
              (float)timeStart.QuadPart ) /
              timerFreq.QuadPart;
```

Hooking the Game Application into WinMain

Now that the Game application object is defined, you need to add it to the WinMain function. You create the Game application object after the application window appears and you've initialized DirectX.

The following code shows how the Game application object fits into the WinMain function. Again, the changes to the WinMain function are highlighted in bold.

```
/* Get a reference to the DirectX Manager */
static dxManager& dxMgr = dxManager::getInstance();
/******************************************************************************
* WinMain - updated to include the DirectX Manager class
******************************************************************************/
int WINAPI WinMain(HINSTANCE hInstance,
                                        HINSTANCE hPrevInstance,
                                        LPTSTR lpCmdLine,
                                        int nCmdShow )
{
        // Call your function to init and create your window
        if (!initWindow(hInstance))
        {
                MessageBox(NULL, "Unable to create window", "ERROR", MB_OK);
                return false;
        }

        // Initialize DirectX through the dxManager
        if (!dxMgr.init(wndHandle))
        {
                MessageBox(NULL, "Unable to init DirectX", "ERROR", MB_OK);
                return false;
        }

        // Create a pointer to a new Game application object
        Game *pGame = new Game();

        // Initialize the Game application object
        if (!pGame->init(wndHandle))
                return 0;

        // main message loop
        // Enter the message loop
```

```
MSG msg;
ZeroMemory( &msg, sizeof(msg) );
while( msg.message!=WM_QUIT )
{
        // Check for messages
        if( PeekMessage( &msg, NULL, OU, OU, PM_REMOVE ) )
        {
                TranslateMessage( &msg );
                DispatchMessage( &msg );
        }
        else
        {
                // Call the Game application object's update
                // and render functions
                pGame->update();
                pGame->render();
        }
}

// Shut down the Game application object
pGame->shutdown();

// Remove the pGame object
if (pGame)
        delete pGame;

// Shut down the DirectX Manager
dxMgr.shutdown();

return (int) msg.wParam;
}
```

The Game application object is created by calling the constructor of the Game class. In the previous code, a pointer called pGame holds the newly created Game object. After the Game application object comes to life, you must initialize it by calling the init function. Now that the object is up and running, you can call its two most important functions: update and render. You place the update and render functions in an else block following the message loop, which causes them to be called once per frame. The update function handles getting user input, as well as updating the position of objects in the game world. The main task of the render function is drawing each of the in-game objects to the screen.

The render function, shown here, also has the job of updating the animation rate by query-ing the amount of time it takes to render the scene.

```
/*****************************************************************************
* render - Draws all the in-game objects to the screen
*****************************************************************************/
void Game::render(void)
{
        // Get the time before rendering
        QueryPerformanceCounter(&timeStart);

        // Call your render function
        dxMgr.beginRender();

        // End rendering
        dxMgr.endRender();

        // Get the updated time
        QueryPerformanceCounter(&timeEnd);

        // Determine the animation rate
        anim_rate = ( (float)timeEnd.QuadPart -
                        (float)timeStart.QuadPart ) /
                        timerFreq.QuadPart;
}
```

The render function calls the beginRender and endRender functions from the dxManager object to prepare Direct3D for drawing. Between these two calls is where the actual rendering takes place. In the previous code, a for loop iterates through the in-game objects, calling their individual render functions.

Adding Objects to the World

Up until now, you've been building the basic framework you need to support your game. Taking the code that has been presented so far, you can begin any number of game projects.

Now that the basic framework is complete, you can start adding objects to the world. Every object, regardless of its type, has the following properties and functions:

- **position**. Every object needs a position in world space. The position is stored in a vector.
- **model**. The model property represents the actual vertices of the object.
- **create** function. The object is created and initialized with the create function.

■ **render** function. This function performs the actual drawing of the object.

When you're creating your game objects, you can implement each of these properties in each object individually, or you can take advantage of inheritance. Inheritance in C++ allows you to create a parent class from which you can derive additional classes that contain the parent's functionality. Because of the common properties that all in-game objects share, I've chosen to create a parent class called CGameObject upon which all objects in the game are based.

The CGameObject Class

The CGameObject class, which is shown in the next block of code, contains the properties I described earlier. The create and render functions are defined as pure virtual functions, which means that any class that inherits from the CGameObject class must implement these two functions.

In addition, two variables—Model and position—are listed in the protected area of the CGameObject class definition. By creating these variables as protected, you make them accessible to a child class.

```
/****************************************************************************
* CGameObject class
* The parent class for all in-game objects
****************************************************************************/
class CGameObject
{
public:
        CGameObject(void);
        virtual ~CGameObject(void);

        // Abstract methods must be overridden in child classes
        virtual bool create(LPDIRECT3DDEVICE9 device) = 0;
        virtual void render(LPDIRECT3DDEVICE9 device) = 0;

protected:
        CModel *Model;            // a pointer to a model object

        D3DXVECTOR3 position;     // the position of this object in world space
};
```

The CGameObject definition primarily contains data types you've seen before, except for the CModel type. The CModel type is a class I've defined that holds the actual object vertices. By abstracting out this functionality, you can have game objects that contain more than one model.

The CModel Class

The CModel class is essentially a wrapper for a D3DXMESH object. I've chosen to encapsulate the loading and rendering of a D3DXMESH object away from the code needed to position it.

Each object that is created from the CModel class has the built-in functionality you need to both load and render an X file model. Because I restricted the CModel class to performing a single task, I can reuse this class in multiple projects whenever I need to work with X files. Future projects that require model loading will take less time to code because I now have drop-in reusable code.

note

A black box is a way of describing an object in which you are aware of only what data goes in and what data you expect out. How the data is returned is unimportant.

How CModel Is Put Together

The CModel class is essentially used as a black box. I tell the class to load a mesh from disk, and the class performs that action. The rest of the code has no idea how this task is performed, and that's okay. The rest of the game can just assume that CModel will contain a valid D3DXMESH object.

The CModel function contains two functions:

- **loadModel.** This function loads an X file from disk and places it in a D3DXMESH object.
- **render.** This function handles the actual drawing of the vertices and materials contained within a D3DXMESH object.

In addition, the CModel class contains the following private member variables:

- **mesh.** The mesh variable is a pointer to the D3DXMESH object.
- **numMaterials.** This DWORD type variable is responsible for counting the number of materials contained in the mesh.
- **matBuffer.** The matBuffer variable holds the material buffer for the mesh. Each item in the material buffer contains information describing the color, texture, or amount of light that the mesh reflects.
- **m_pMeshTextures.** This variable is an array of DIRECT3DTEXTURE9 objects. Each of these objects describes the texture used for a portion of the mesh.
- **m_pMeshMaterials.** The m_pMeshMaterials variable contains an array of D3DMATERIAL9 objects. Each of these objects describes the material used for a portion of the mesh.

The CModel class definition is shown next.

```
/****************************************************************************
* CModel class
* Contains the needed functions to support a D3DXMESH object
****************************************************************************/
class CModel
{
public:
        CModel(void);
        virtual ~CModel(void);

        // loads an X file from disk
        bool loadModel(LPDIRECT3DDEVICE9 device, std::string filename);

        // renders the mesh
        void render(LPDIRECT3DDEVICE9 pDevice);

private:
        // pointer to a D3DXMESH object
        LPD3DXMESH mesh;

        // holds the number of materials contained within the mesh
        DWORD       numMaterials;

        // the mesh's material buffer
        LPD3DXBUFFER matBuffer;

        // an array of DIRECT3DTEXTURE9 objects
        LPDIRECT3DTEXTURE9* m_pMeshTextures;

        // an array of D3DMATERIAL9 objects
        D3DMATERIAL9* m_pMeshMaterials;
};
```

How CModel Works

Because the CModel class is potentially useful in other projects, I'm going to take the time to describe the implementation of the loadModel and render functions.

The loadModel function consists of all the code you need to load in an X file from disk containing both materials and textures. The loadModel function starts out by calling D3DXLoad-MeshFromX, which is responsible for loading the model. If this call is successful, the materials and textures that are contained in the material buffer are extracted into separate arrays.

The two arrays, shown next, are created based on the number of materials contained in the numMaterials variable.

```
m_pMeshMaterials = new D3DMATERIAL9 [numMaterials];
m_pMeshTextures = new LPDIRECT3DTEXTURE9 [numMaterials];
```

After the arrays are created, a for loop iterates through the material buffer, assigning the materials and textures to their appropriate places in the arrays.

Following is the full source code for the loadModel function.

```
/***************************************************************************
* loadModel
* Performs the loading of an X file model from disk
***************************************************************************/
bool CModel::loadModel(LPDIRECT3DDEVICE9 device, std::string filename)
{
        HRESULT hr;

        hr = D3DXLoadMeshFromX(filename.c_str(),
                        D3DXMESH_SYSTEMMEM,
                        device,
                        NULL,
                        &matBuffer,
                        NULL,
                        &numMaterials,
                        &mesh);

        if FAILED(hr)
                return false;

        D3DXMATERIAL* matMaterials;
        matMaterials = (D3DXMATERIAL*)matBuffer->GetBufferPointer();

        //Create two arrays: to hold the materials and the textures
        m_pMeshMaterials = new D3DMATERIAL9 [numMaterials];
        m_pMeshTextures = new LPDIRECT3DTEXTURE9 [numMaterials];

        // Iterate through the materials
        for (DWORD i = 0; i < numMaterials; i++)
        {
                //Copy the material
                m_pMeshMaterials[i] = matMaterials[i].MatD3D;
```

```
                        //Set the ambient color for the material (D3DX does not do this)
                        m_pMeshMaterials[i].Ambient = m_pMeshMaterials[i].Diffuse;

                        // Make sure the texture name is valid
                        if (matMaterials[i].pTextureFilename != NULL)
                        {
                                // Load the texture
                                hr = D3DXCreateTextureFromFile( device,
                                                               matMaterials[i].pTextureFilename,
                                                               &m_pMeshTextures[i]);
                                If (FAILED (hr))
                                        return false;
                        }
                        // If there is no texture name, then NULL this spot in the list
                        else
                                m_pMeshTextures[i] = NULL;
                }

                // Release the material buffer
                if (matBuffer)
                        matBuffer->Release();

                return true;
}
```

The render function is responsible for drawing the mesh that is contained in the D3DXMESH object.

Each frame, the render function loops through the material and texture arrays, drawing each portion of the mesh using the DrawSubset function. The mesh is separated in the D3DXMESH object based on the material and texture that are applied to each portion. If a mesh contains more than one material, multiple calls to DrawSubset must be made to draw the entire mesh.

The full source code for the render function is shown next.

```
/*************************************************************************
* render
* Renders a mesh contained in a D3DXMESH object
*************************************************************************/
void CModel::render(LPDIRECT3DDEVICE9 pDevice)
{
        for( DWORD i=0; i<numMaterials; i++ )
        {
```

```
                    // Set the material and texture for this subset
                    pDevice->SetMaterial( &m_pMeshMaterials[i] );

                    // Set the texture if a texture is used for this material
                    if (m_pMeshTextures != NULL)
                            pDevice->SetTexture( 0, m_pMeshTextures[i] );

                    // Draw the mesh subset
                    mesh->DrawSubset( i );
            }
}
```

The Game Object List

Now that you know how each of the in-game objects is going to be stored, the only other thing you need to know is how you will access these objects. Because each object in the game is going to inherit from the CGameObject class, you can store the objects in a vector within the Game application object.

```
std::vector <CGameObject*> objects;
```

The vector of CGameObjects, referred to by the objects variable, is responsible for keeping valid pointers to each object in the game. During the Game object's render function, the CGameObjects vector is iterated through and each of the models contained within it is rendered to the screen. The updated render function is shown here.

```
/***************************************************************************
 * render - Draws all the in-game objects to the screen
 ***************************************************************************/
void Game::render(void)
{
        // Get the time before rendering
        QueryPerformanceCounter(&timeStart);

        // Call the render function
        dxMgr.beginRender();

        // Render by looping through all the objects in the list
        for (unsigned int i=0; i<objects.size(); i++)
                objects[i]->render(dxMgr.getD3DDevice());

        // End rendering
        dxMgr.endRender();
```

```
        // Get the updated time
        QueryPerformanceCounter(&timeEnd);

        // Determine the animation rate
        anim_rate = ( (float)timeEnd.QuadPart -
                      (float)timeStart.QuadPart ) /
                      timerFreq.QuadPart;
}
```

Creating the Planet

The first object you're going to create for your game universe is a single planet. The planet, which will reside directly in the center of the universe, will consist of a simple spherical mesh covered with a texture of the earth. You can call this planet Earth if you want to, but it's just a coincidence that the planets will end up looking the same.

The first step to bringing your planet into being is creating the CPlanet class.

The CPlanet Class

The CPlanet class contains everything that your game needs to know to both load and render the planet. Because the CPlanet class is inherited from CGameObject, it automatically has a model and position associated with it. It wouldn't make sense to inherit from the CGameObject class without specifying properties that were unique to the planet, so I've added two additional private variables: size and rotationRate.

note

The planet requires the sphere.x and earth.bmp files from the DirectXSDK\Samples\Media directory.

The CPlanet class uses the size variable to describe how large the planet should be when it's drawn. The rotationRate specifies how quickly the planet makes a complete orbit.

The CPlanet class definition is shown here.

```
/****************************************************************************
* CPlanet class
****************************************************************************/
class CPlanet : CGameObject
{
public:
    CPlanet(void);
    ~CPlanet(void);

    // helper function to set the size of the planet
```

```
        void setSize(float planetSize);

        // overridden methods from the parent class
        bool create(LPDIRECT3DDEVICE9 device);
        void render(LPDIRECT3DDEVICE9 device);

private:
        // the size of the planet
        float size;

        // the rotation rate of the planet
        float rotationRate;
};
```

The create and render functions are declared in the class definition. Because these two functions were declared as pure virtual in the CGameObject class, you have to implement them in the CPlanet class.

The Create Function

The create function initializes the planet object to a default location and loads the X file model. First, set the position vector, placing the planet at the origin of the universe. Because this is where the planet will reside anyway, there is no point in moving it. Next, create the CModel object and send the sphere.x file to the loadModel function. If the loadModel function succeeds, it causes the create function to return TRUE to its caller. Because the sphere.x file also specifies a texture, the CModel class automatically loads it.

Following is the full source code for the create function.

```
/*****************************************************************************
* create
* Handles positioning the object to a default location (origin) and loading
* in the object model.
*****************************************************************************/
bool CPlanet::create(LPDIRECT3DDEVICE9 device)
{
        position.x = 0.0f;
        position.y = 0.0f;
        position.z = 0.0f;

        // Create the model for this planet
        Model = new CModel();

        return Model->loadModel(device, "sphere.x");
}
```

The Render Function

The render function has two jobs: setting up the matrices to correctly position and orient the planet, and rendering the model. The render function starts by translating the planet to its proper position with a call to D3DXMatrixTranslation, which generates the transMatrix variable. Next, you use the D3DXMatrixRotationY function to create the rotation matrix. Finally, you scale the planet to the correct size by using the D3DXMatrixScaling function, where the scaleMatrix is created.

Now that you've created all three matrices, you must generate a final transformation that will place the planet in the correct position in world space. The first step is to multiply the rotation and translation matrices.

```
// Multiply the rotation matrix by the translation
D3DXMatrixMultiply(&transMatrix, &rotateMatrix, &transMatrix);
```

rotateMatrix is multiplied by transMatrix, placing the result back into transMatrix. The transMatrix variable now contains the planet's properly positioned and rotated orientation.

Next, you must apply scaling to properly resize the planet model. Here, multiply scaleMatrix by transMatrix. The result is placed back into the transMatrix variable.

```
// Multiply the translation matrix by the scale
D3DXMatrixMultiply(&transMatrix, &scaleMatrix, &transMatrix);
```

Finally, you have a matrix, contained in the transMatrix variable, that will take the planet model and place it where you want it in world space. The final step is to call the SetTransform function, passing in the transMatrix variable.

```
// Transform the object into world space
device->SetT7ransform(D3DTS_WORLD, &transMatrix);
```

Now that you have set the transform for the planet correctly, you must call the CModel render function to draw the planet.

Following is the full source code listing for the render function.

```
/***********************************************************************
* render
* Sets up the appropriate matrices for positioning and rendering the planet
***********************************************************************/
void CPlanet::render(LPDIRECT3DDEVICE9 device)
{
        D3DXMATRIX transMatrix;           // the translation matrix
        D3DXMATRIX scaleMatrix;           // the scale matrix
        D3DXMATRIX rotateMatrix;          // the rotation matrix

        // Set up the translation matrix
```

```
D3DXMatrixTranslation(&transMatrix, position.x, position.y, position.z);

    // Cause the planet to rotate
    D3DXMatrixRotationY(&rotateMatrix, timeGetTime()/1000.0f);

    // Scale the planet by the size amount
    D3DXMatrixScaling(&scaleMatrix, size, size, size);

    // Multiply the rotation matrix by the translation
    D3DXMatrixMultiply(&transMatrix, &rotateMatrix, &transMatrix);

    // Multiply the translation matrix by the scale
    D3DXMatrixMultiply(&transMatrix, &scaleMatrix, &transMatrix);

    // Transform the object into world space
    device->SetTransform(D3DTS_WORLD, &transMatrix);

    // Render the planet
    Model->render(device);
}
```

Adding the Planet to the Scene

Remember the vector of CGameObjects that I explained earlier? Before you can draw the planet into the scene, you must add the CPlanet object to the list. You can add new objects to the back of a vector's list by calling the push_back function. The code that follows shows how to create and add a CPlanet object to the objects vector.

```
// Create the planet object
CPlanet *pPlanet = new CPlanet();

// Scale the planet to make it larger
pPlanet->setSize(7);

// Create the planet
if (!pPlanet->create(dxMgr.getD3DDevice()))
        return false;

// Add the planet to the in-game objects list
objects.push_back((CGameObject*)pPlanet);
```

First, initialize the pPlanet pointer by creating a new CPlanet object. Next, set the planet's size and load the model by calling the create function. Finally, add the created planet to the objects vector using the push_back function.

At this point, you should have a happily positioned and rotating planet. The planet is shown in Figure 11.3.

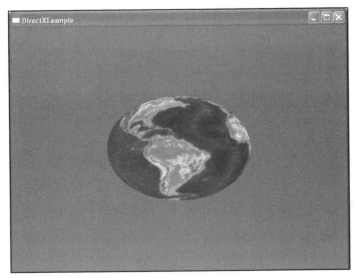

Figure 11.3 A happily rotating planet.

Adding a Spaceship

Although a rotating planet is nice, it isn't much fun by itself. That's why I'm going to show you how to bring in a spaceship. Like the planet, you will load the spaceship from an X file and display it. The biggest difference between the planet and the spaceship is user control. Using DirectInput, I'm going to show you how to move the spaceship within the world using the mouse.

The Game application object considers the spaceship to be just another in-game object. You will add the spaceship to the CGameObjects vector and render it each frame, just like the planet. Because the spaceship is being considered as a standard in-game object, it will inherit from the CGameObjects class.

note

The spaceship requires the bigship1.x file from the DirectXSDK\Samples\Media directory.

You will use the CShip class to represent the spaceship in the game world. As before, the CShip class automatically inherits a position and a CModel object and needs to implement its parent's create and render functions.

In addition, the CShip function implements two other functions:

- **setPosition.** The setPosition function updates the position of the spaceship each frame.
- **move.** The move function receives input from the user and updates the spaceship's position vector.

Two new variables are also added to the CShip class:

- **forwardVector.** This is a D3DVECTOR3 object that holds the current direction the spaceship is traveling. By adjusting the forward vector, you can make the spaceship turn and move in multiple directions.
- **moveRate.** The movement rate determines the speed at which the spaceship moves.

The full definition for the CShip class is shown here.

```
/*****************************************************************************
* CShip class
*****************************************************************************/
class CShip : CGameObject
{
public:
        CShip(void);
        ~CShip(void);
        // overridden functions from the CGameObject class
        bool create(LPDIRECT3DDEVICE9 device);
        void render(LPDIRECT3DDEVICE9 device);

        // The setPosition function repositions the spaceship each frame
        void setPosition(D3DXVECTOR3 newPosition);

        // The move function is used to tell the spaceship the direction
        // it should move
        void move(int direction);

private:
        // The forward vector of the spaceship; this vector describes the
        // direction in which the ship is heading
        D3DXVECTOR3 forwardVector;

        // The movement rate determines how fast the object moves in the scene
        float  moveRate;
};
```

Moving in the Universe

You have both a spinning globe and a spaceship sitting at the origin. The spaceship might be interesting to look at, but the inhabitants of the planet don't want a spaceship sitting on their planet, so it's time to move the ship. Instead of just repositioning the ship in code, you will move the ship interactively using the mouse. I'm going to describe how to do this by introducing you to the `CShip move` function.

The Spaceship Move Function

The `move` function is the main point of interest in the `CShip` class. Using input sent to it from the `Game` application, the `move` function manipulates the internal properties of the spaceship to move it around the scene.

Previously, when you wanted to move an object away from you, you simply subtracted the amount of movement from the object's current Z position value. Moving an object in this manner forces it into absolute directions. I'm going to demonstrate how you can change this to allow for relative movement. Moving an object forward will not necessarily mean moving along the Z axis anymore.

When I created the `CShip` class, I introduced you to a new variable called `forwardVector`. The `forwardVector` variable keeps track of the direction in which the spaceship is facing. When `forwardVector` is initialized, the X and Y values are set to `0.0f`, and the Z value is set to `1.0f`. Because the Z value is set to `1.0f`, the spaceship is pointing along the Z axis. The following code shows how to initialize `forwardVector`.

```
forwardVector.x = 0.0f;
forwardVector.y = 0.0f;
forwardVector.z = 1.0f;
```

Whatever value resides in the `forwardVector` Z value is what the spaceship will consider forward, whereas the value residing in Y will be the spaceship's relative left direction. By manipulating these two values, you can change the ship's direction and allow it to move in a relative forward direction.

For instance, if you wanted to turn the spaceship to the left, you would do so by manipulating the `forwardVector` Y value. To turn the ship 5 units to the left, you would do the following:

```
// The direction of the ship is changed 5 units to the left
forwardVector.y -= 5.0f;
```

The forward vector of the ship would then be pointing in a new direction. Moving along this new vector is a bit more complicated, though. You must update three variables when moving forward.

First, you need to remove the current movement rate from the `forwardVector` X value.

Next, you need to change the current X position of the spaceship by removing the new forwardVector X value and multiplying it by the negative sine of the forwardVector Y value.

Finally, you must update the current Z position of the ship by adding the product of the forwardVector X value and the cosine of the forwardVector Y value.

The code that follows shows how you can make the ship move forward.

```
forwardVector.x = -MOVE_RATE;
position.x -= forwardVector.x * -sin(D3DXToRadian(forwardVector.y));
position.z += forwardVector.x * cos(D3DXToRadian(forwardVector.y));
```

As you can see, the forward vector and the position of the ship must work together to allow for relative movement. The full source code for the move function is shown next.

```
/**************************************************************************
* move
**************************************************************************/
void CShip::move(int direction)
{
        switch (direction)
        {
                case FORWARD:
                        forwardVector.x = -MOVE_RATE;
                        position.x -= forwardVector.x *
                                        -sin(D3DXToRadian(forwardVector.y));
                        position.z += forwardVector.x *
                                        cos(D3DXToRadian(forwardVector.y));
                break;

                case BACKWARD:
                        forwardVector.x = MOVE_RATE;
                        position.x -= forwardVector.x *
                                        -sin(D3DXToRadian(forwardVector.y));
                        position.z += forwardVector.x *
                                        cos(D3DXToRadian(forwardVector.y));
                break;

                case LEFT:
                        forwardVector.y -= 5.0f;
                break;

                case RIGHT:
                        forwardVector.y += 5.0f;
```

```
                break;
        }
}
```

Bringing in DirectInput

DirectInput provides you with a quick and elegant method of gathering user input. Because DirectInput allows for lower-level access to the input hardware, reading input changes from the user is quick.

The amount of code it takes to work with DirectInput can be quite large; therefore, I've enclosed the DirectInput code in the DirectInput manager class.

The DirectInput Manager Class

The DirectInput manager class removes the complexity of input away from the game code, keeping it contained within the class called diManager. The diManager class uses the singleton design pattern to restrict itself to a single instance, which prevents DirectInput from accidentally being initialized more than once.

diManager includes the following main functions:

- **initDirectInput.** Initializes DirectInput and returns TRUE if it's successful
- **shutdown.** Releases DirectInput and frees up its memory usage
- **getInput.** Gathers the device state of the currently selected input device

Because I'll be explaining the mouse device specifically, I've chosen to include three helper functions within the diManager class:

- **isButtonDown.** Returns TRUE or FALSE when queried for a particular mouse button
- **getCurMouseX.** Returns the amount the mouse has moved in the X direction since the last frame
- **getCurMouseY.** Returns the amount the mouse has moved in the Y direction since the last frame

The full diManager class definition is shown next.

```
/*************************************************************************
 * diManager class
 *************************************************************************/
#define BUTTONDOWN(name, key) (name.rgbButtons[key] & 0x80)
class diManager
{
public:
        ~diManager(void);
```

```
             // setting up the diManager as a singleton
             static diManager& getInstance()
             {
                     static diManager pInstance;
                     return pInstance;
             }

             // initializes and cleans up DirectInput
             bool initDirectInput(HINSTANCE hInst, HWND wndHandle);
             void shutdown(void);

             // gathers input from the user and stores it in the mouseState variable
             void getInput(void);

             // returns whether a particular mouse button is pressed
             bool isButtonDown(int which);

             // These functions return the amount the mouse has moved
             // since the last frame
             inline int getCurMouseX(void) { return mouseState.lX; }
             inline int getCurMouseY(void) { return mouseState.lY; }
private:
             diManager(void);

             // the direct input object
             LPDIRECTINPUT8          g_lpDI;
             // the direct input device
             LPDIRECTINPUTDEVICE8  g_lpDIDevice;

             // the current state of the mouse device
             DIMOUSESTATE mouseState;
};
```

Again, because I'll be working specifically with the mouse, I created the mouseState variable to hold the current input from the mouse. Each frame, the getInput function places the current mouse state into this variable.

Adding the DirectInput Manger to the Game

The DirectInput manager is easy to use. Simply call the initDirectInput function at the beginning of your application. If the diManager object is created and initializes successfully, the initDirectInput function returns a value of TRUE. You can place this call in your Winmain.cpp file or anywhere before you try to get user input.

Now that you have a valid diManager object, you are free to query it each frame for input. In the next block of code, I've changed the Game application's update function to show how to use diManager to read from the mouse.

First, you call the getInput function. This queries the current state of the mouse and places the result in the mouseState variable. Next, you use the current input to make your game decisions. In the example code that follows, I've used the mouse movement and button presses to control the spaceship's movement using the move function.

```
/********************************************************************
* update
* This function is called once per frame. It's used to get the user
* input and move the objects in the game accordingly.
********************************************************************/
int Game::update(void)
{
        // Get the current user input
        diMgr.getInput();

        // If the left mouse button is pressed, move forward
        if (diMgr.isButtonDown(0))
                pShip->move(CShip::FORWARD, anim_rate);

        // If the right mouse button is pressed, move backward
        if (diMgr.isButtonDown(1))
                pShip->move(CShip::BACKWARD, anim_rate);

        // If the mouse is moved to the left, turn left
        if (diMgr.getCurMouseX() < 0)
                pShip->move(CShip::LEFT, anim_rate);

        // If the mouse is moved to the right, turn right
        if (diMgr.getCurMouseX() > 0)
                pShip->move(CShip::RIGHT, anim_rate);

        return 1;
}
```

The previous update function responds to the left and right mouse buttons by moving the spaceship forward and backward, respectively. Also, by moving the mouse to the left or right, you can change the direction the spaceship is traveling.

At this point, you've brought together a lot of what you've learned to create a simple 3D demo. Check out the chapter11\part5 directory on the CD-ROM to find all the source code you need to create the spaceship demo.

Releasing Your Creation to the World

Your game is ready and you want to share it with the world. There's just one problem: Your game requires DirectX to be installed. Most Windows PC users already have some version of DirectX on their machines, but not all versions work the same. It's always a good idea to require the installation of the latest version of the DirectX runtime. This chapter covers exactly what's needed to make your game ready for release, as well as installing and running DirectX on a user's machine.

Packaging Your Game for Release

Typically, games are distributed across the Web in either a Zip file format or a self-extracting EXE file.

The Zip file format is the simplest method. All the files and directories within your game are compressed and included in a single file ending in the ZIP extension. When users are preparing to play your game, they will need to first uncompress the ZIP file to gain access to the files compressed within it. The downside of releasing your game using the ZIP file method is that users will need to have a utility already installed on their computers that is capable of opening and uncompressing the ZIP file.

The second type of distribution is the self-extracting EXE file. Although the EXE file uses a similar method to the ZIP file, this type does not require an external utility to uncompress its contents. All the files and directories within your game are again compressed and placed into one file, but instead of having a ZIP extension, the file ends with EXE. The EXE extension tells the system that the file is an executable program and can be run. When the user double-clicks on this executable, the files contained within it are extracted and placed on the user's hard drive.

Most games don't require extensive installation procedures, and packaging them in a ZIP or self-extracting file is quite common. On occasion, though, games need a full installation program, especially if they are being released as a commercial product.

The installation programs present the users with an easy-to-use interface that allows them to change the directory where they would like to install the game and select the features they want to install. When your game gets to be the size of a CD-ROM, an installation program makes it much easier to install and run.

What Tools Are Available to Bundle My Game?

Many programs are available to help you package your game into a ZIP file or self-extracting executable. Following are two of the more common programs:

- WinZip
- WinRAR

Shareware versions of these applications are available on the Internet.

If you want to create a full installation program for your game, you might have to look into professional installation software like the following:

- InstallShield
- Wise Installer
- NSIS: The Nullsoft Scriptable Install System

The DirectX Runtime

The DirectX Runtime is the bundled collection of all the files that DirectX needs to have installed on a machine. Before you can run any software that uses DirectX, you need to install the runtime on that machine. During the installation process, the DLLs that provide all the DirectX functionality are copied to the system. After the DLLs are installed and the machine is rebooted, applications that rely on the DirectX DLLs are able to run.

When you are distributing your game, you have the option of either packaging the DirectX runtime with your software or relying on the end user to find and install it himself.

If you chose to have the user download and install the DirectX runtime, you should provide a link to the Microsoft DirectX Web site with your game. Full instructions for downloading and installing the runtime from Microsoft are available on the Microsoft site.

Shipping the DirectX Runtime with Your Game

Shipping the DirectX runtime with your game is simple. The major downside to shipping the DirectX runtime is its size requirement. If your game is already in the hundreds of megabytes, adding the DirectX runtime is no big deal; however, if your game is small, it might be a hassle to package the runtime along with it.

Shipping the DirectX runtime requires you to package the following files from the DirectX SDK with your game, preferably in a directory called DirectX:

- dxsetup.exe
- Dsetup.dll
- dsetup32.dll
- directx.cab
- bdaxp.cab
- bdant.cab
- bda.cab
- dxnt.cab
- manageddx.cab
- mdxredist.msi

Users navigate to the DirectX directory within your installation and run the dxsetup.exe file. The DirectX installation then proceeds.

You might be asking yourself, "Just where do I get the DirectX runtime?" Well, the DirectX runtime just so happens to be in a directory called Redist within the DirectX SDK folder. When you installed the SDK, the Redist directory was created and all the required files were placed there.

Installing the DirectX Runtime

Now that you have packaged the DirectX runtime with your software, you might want to provide instructions for the end user to install it.

Installing the DirectX runtime happens through a series of wizard dialog boxes that begin when the user double-clicks on the dxsetup.exe file.

Following are the steps necessary to install the DirectX runtime:

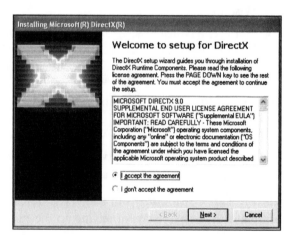

1. Double-click on the dxsetup.exe file. This file launches the setup program that installs DirectX on the user's machine.

2. The license dialog box appears, requesting that the user accept the End User License Agreement from Microsoft. This dialog box is shown in Figure 11.4.

Figure 11.4 The DirectX license dialog box.

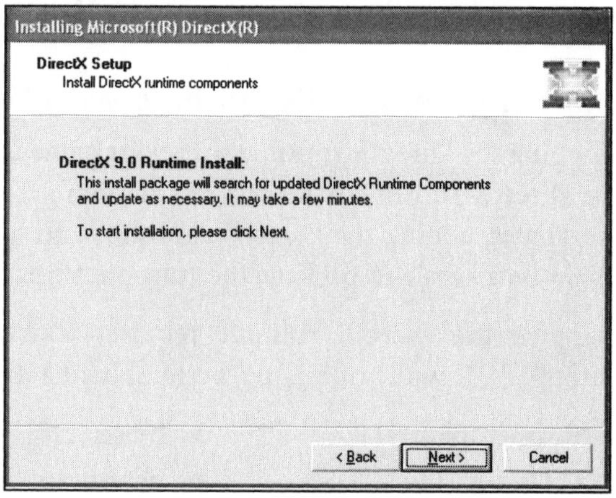

3. The user must select the I Accept the Agreement option button and click on the Next button to proceed with the installation.

4. A confirmation dialog box appears, informing the user that the DirectX runtime is about to be installed. This dialog box is shown in Figure 11.5.

Figure 11.5 The DirectX install confirmation dialog box.

5. Pressing the Next button starts the installation.

6. The necessary files start installing. A progress meter continually updates the installation's progress. Figure 11.6 shows the progress dialog box.

7. After a few m oments, the installation finishes and a final dialog box is displayed. This dialog box is shown in Figure 11.7.

8. The final dialog box requests that the user reboot the machine. This step is necessary because the DirectX install has copied new device drivers to the system.

After the computer reboots, the DirectX installation is complete.

Table 11.1 lists some products that can help you in your game distribution.

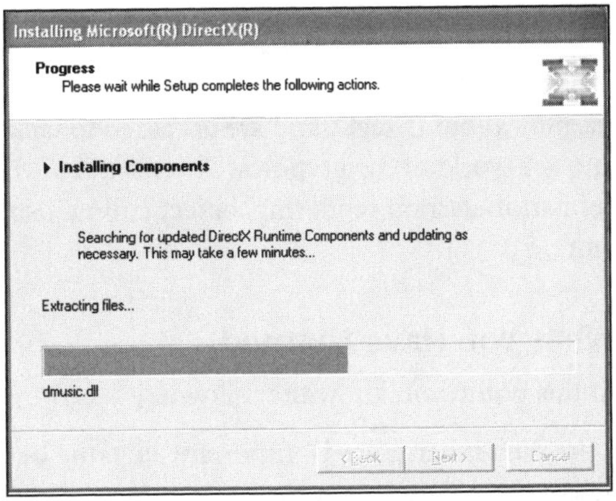

Figure 11.6 The installation progress dialog box.

Figure 11.7 The DirectX runtime is done installing.

Table 11.1 Tools to Help Distribute Your Game

Product Name	Web Site
WinZip	http://www.winzip.com
WinRAR	http://www.rarsoft.com
NSIS	http://nsis.sourceforge.net
InstallShield	http://www.installsheild.com
Wise Installer	http://www.wise.com

Chapter Summary

You've made it to the end of the book! Congratulations! I'm hoping that you've enjoyed learning about DirectX and are prepared to tackle its challenges. I've only opened the door into the world of 3D graphics. There's still a whole range of topics to learn, including 3D animation, terrain rendering, object culling using binary space partitioning, and so much more.

What You Have Learned

At this point, you know the following:

- Why inheritance is important in game development
- How to create a simple game framework
- How to load and manipulate multiple objects in a scene
- How to encapsulate common functionality into classes
- How to create a complete 3D demo with user input

PART IV

APPENDIXES

APPENDIX A

Answers to End-of-Chapter Exercises

Chapter 2

Review Questions

1. You must create the IDirect3D9 object first. It allows you to create the additional Direct3D components that you need.

2. The GetAdapterCount function queries the host machine and returns the number of video adapters in the system.

3. 8 bits for red, 8 bits for green, 8 bits for blue, and 8 bits for an alpha component.

4. D3DDEVTYPE_HAL is the device type that specifies that hardware acceleration should be used.

5. The Clear function clears the back buffer to a specific color.

On Your Own

1. You need to change the Clear function from the blue value of D3DCOLOR_XRGB(0,0,255) to a value of D3DCOLOR_XRGB(0,255,0) to clear the screen to green. The updated line of code is shown here:

   ```
   pd3dDevice->Clear( 0, NULL, D3DCLEAR_TARGET, D3DCOLOR_XRGB(0,0,255), 1.0f, 0 );
   ```

2. You must change the second parameter to the GetAdapterModeCount function from the value D3DFMT_X8R8G8B8 to another chosen format. For instance, if you want to check for adapters that support a 16-bit graphics mode, you can pass the value D3DFMT_R5G6B5 to the GetAdapterModeCount function. An updated call to GetAdapterModeCount is shown here:

   ```
   UINT numModes = pD3D->GetAdapterModeCount(D3DADAPTER_DEFAULT, D3DFMT_R5G6B5);
   ```

Chapter 3

Review Questions

1. You use the `CreateOffscreenPlainSurface` function to create offscreen surfaces. These surfaces commonly hold graphics data that has been loaded from disk.

2. The `StretchRect` function copies a rectangular area of image data between surfaces. You can use this function in 2D rendering to copy sprites from an offscreen surface to the back buffer.

3. Most commonly, offscreen surfaces store images that will be used during the game, such as backgrounds, character sprites, or world objects.

4. You should clear the back buffer at the start of each frame to eliminate any drawing that took place in the previous frame. Occasionally, you'll want to skip clearing the back buffer if the scene you're drawing will fill the entire buffer.

5. The `QueryPerformanceCounter` function is a millisecond timer. It has a higher timing resolution than `GetTickCount`.

On Your Own

1. The `StretchRect` function has two parameters that determine the size of the source and destination rectangles. The code that follows creates two variables of type `RECT`: one for the source rectangle and one for the destination. The source rectangle is created as a 64 × 64 area. The destination rectangle has an area of only 32 × 32. When the `srcRect` and `destRect` variables are passed to the `StretchRect` function, they affect how the image is copied between sources. Because the source rectangle was larger than the destination, the image data being copied is scaled to fit.

```
RECT srcRect;
RECT destRect;

// Set the source rectangle
srcRect.top = 0;
srcRect.left = 0;
srcRect.right = 64;
srcRect.bottom = 64;

// Set the destination rectangle
destRect.top = 0;
destRect.left = 0;
destRect.right = 32;
destRect.bottom = 32;
// Call the StretchRect function to copy from the srcSurface to the back buffer
pd3dDevice->StretchRect(srcSurface,
                        srcRect,
```

```
            getBackBuffer(),
            destRect,
            D3DTEXF_NONE);
```

2. Scrolling a text message consists of changing the location of the destination rectangle that is being sent to the StretchRect function. The following code creates a destX variable that positions the destination rectangle. Each frame, this value is decremented by 1, causing the image to be copied one pixel to the left from its previous position. When the image scrolls off the left side of the screen, you can reset it to the right side of the screen by resetting the destX value.

```
void Render(void)
{
    // This is the X position of the destination rectangle
    static int destX = 128;

    // src and dest rectangles
    RECT src, dest;

    // Set the source rectangle
    src.top = 0;
    src.left = 0;
    src.right = src.left + 64;
    src.bottom = src.top + 64;

    // Set the destination rectangle
    dest.top = 0;
    dest.left = destX;
    dest.right = dest.left + 64;
    dest.bottom = dest.top + 64;

    if( NULL == pd3dDevice )
        return;

    // Clear the back buffer to a blue color
    pd3dDevice->Clear( 0,
                        NULL,
                        D3DCLEAR_TARGET,
                        D3DCOLOR_XRGB(255,255,255),
                        1.0f,
                        0 );

    // Call StretchRect to copy the image to the screen
    pd3dDevice->StretchRect(srcSurface,
                        srcRect,
```

```
                              getBackBuffer(),
                              destRect,
                              D3DTEXF_NONE);

        pd3dDevice->Present( NULL, NULL, NULL, NULL );

        // Decrement the X position
        destX-;

        // If the image goes off the screen, reset it to the far side of the screen
        if (destX < -64)
            destX = 640;
    }
```

Chapter 4

Review Questions

1. A point is defined by three vertices: X, Y, and Z. Each vertex refers to the point's location on each of the three axes.

2. You use the Z axis when determining the depth of objects within a 3D scene.

3. The SetFVF function sets the Flexible Vertex Format that will be used when rendering the vertex data from a vertex buffer.

4. The line strip primitive type consists of a series of connected lines.

5. Seven vertices are needed to create a triangle strip consisting of five triangles. The first triangle requires three vertices, whereas each additional triangle needs only a single vertex to be created.

On Your Own

1. The first step in creating a line list series is declaring the vertices for the lines. You then copy the vertices into a vertex buffer. Finally, you render the lines using DrawPrimitive.

```
// a structure for the custom vertex type
struct CUSTOMVERTEX
{
    FLOAT x, y, z, rhw;     // the untransformed, 3D position for the vertex
    DWORD color;          // the vertex color
};

// your custom FVF, which describes your custom vertex structure
#define D3DFVF_CUSTOMVERTEX (D3DFVF_XYZRHW|D3DFVF_DIFFUSE)
```

```
CUSTOMVERTEX g_Vertices[] =
{
    // line 1
    { 50.0f,   50.0f, 0.5f, 1.0f, D3DCOLOR_ARGB(0,255,0,0), },
    { 150.0f,  50.0f, 0.5f, 1.0f, D3DCOLOR_ARGB(0,255,0,0), },

    // line 2
    { 25.0f,   75.0f, 0.5f, 1.0f, D3DCOLOR_ARGB(0,255,0,0), },
    { 150.0f,  75.0f, 0.5f, 1.0f, D3DCOLOR_ARGB(0,255,0,0), },

    // line 3
    { 50.0f,   100.0f, 0.5f, 1.0f, D3DCOLOR_ARGB(0,255,0,0), },
    { 150.0f,  100.0f, 0.5f, 1.0f, D3DCOLOR_ARGB(0,255,0,0), },

    // line 4
    { 50.0f,   150.0f, 0.5f, 1.0f, D3DCOLOR_ARGB(0,255,0,0), },
    { 150.0f,  150.0f, 0.5f, 1.0f, D3DCOLOR_ARGB(0,255,0,0), },
};

// Create the vertex buffer
g_pVB = createVertexBuffer(8*sizeof(CUSTOMVERTEX), D3DFVF_CUSTOMVERTEX);

// Render the four lines using the D3DPT_LINELIST primitive
void render(LPDIRECT3DVERTEXBUFFER9 buffer)
{
        pd3dDevice->SetStreamSource( 0, buffer, 0, sizeof(CUSTOMVERTEX) );
        pd3dDevice->SetFVF( D3DFVF_CUSTOMVERTEX );
        pd3dDevice->DrawPrimitive( D3DPT_LINELIST, 0, 1 );
        pd3dDevice->DrawPrimitive( D3DPT_LINELIST, 2, 1 );
        pd3dDevice->DrawPrimitive( D3DPT_LINELIST, 4, 1 );
}
```

2. You can create a series of triangles by generating a triangle list. Each triangle consists of three vertices defined in the g_Vertices array. After you create the vertices and copy them into the vertex buffer, you draw them by using the DrawPrimitive function.

```
// a structure for your custom vertex type
struct CUSTOMVERTEX
{
    FLOAT x, y, z, rhw;    // the untransformed, 3D position for the vertex
    DWORD color;           // the vertex color
};

// the custom FVF, which describes your custom vertex structure
```

```
#define D3DFVF_CUSTOMVERTEX (D3DFVF_XYZRHW|D3DFVF_DIFFUSE)

CUSTOMVERTEX g_Vertices[] =
{
    // triangle 1
    { 50.0f,   50.0f, 1.0f, 1.0f, D3DCOLOR_ARGB(0,255,0,0), },
    { 100.0f,  75.0f, 1.0f, 1.0f, D3DCOLOR_ARGB(0,255,0,0), },
    { 25.0f,   75.0f, 1.0f, 1.0f, D3DCOLOR_ARGB(0,255,0,0), },

    // triangle 2
    { 150.0f,  50.0f, 1.0f, 1.0f, D3DCOLOR_ARGB(0,255,0,0), },
    { 200.0f,  75.0f, 1.0f, 1.0f, D3DCOLOR_ARGB(0,255,0,0), },
    { 125.0f,  75.0f, 1.0f, 1.0f, D3DCOLOR_ARGB(0,255,0,0), },

    // triangle 3
    { 50.0f,   150.0f, 1.0f, 1.0f, D3DCOLOR_ARGB(0,255,0,0), },
    { 100.0f,  175.0f, 1.0f, 1.0f, D3DCOLOR_ARGB(0,255,0,0), },
    { 25.0f,   175.0f, 1.0f, 1.0f, D3DCOLOR_ARGB(0,255,0,0), },
};

// Create the vertex buffer
g_pVB = createVertexBuffer(9*sizeof(CUSTOMVERTEX), D3DFVF_CUSTOMVERTEX);

// Render the four lines using the D3DPT_LINELIST primitive
void render(LPDIRECT3DVERTEXBUFFER9 buffer)
{
        pd3dDevice->SetStreamSource( 0, buffer, 0, sizeof(CUSTOMVERTEX) );
        pd3dDevice->SetFVF( D3DFVF_CUSTOMVERTEX );
        pd3dDevice->DrawPrimitive( D3DPT_TRIANGLELIST, 0, 1 );
        pd3dDevice->DrawPrimitive( D3DPT_TRIANGLELIST, 3, 1 );
        pd3dDevice->DrawPrimitive( D3DPT_TRIANGLELIST, 6, 1 );
}
```

Chapter 5

Review Questions

1. An index buffer stores the indices for an object.

2. A matrix is a multidimensional array of values. In a 3D world, a matrix that consists of 4 rows and 4 columns transforms an object from one space to another.

3. The world transformation, the view transformation, and the projection transformation.

4. The identity matrix sets a projection or an object back to the origin.

5. The aspect ratio of a virtual camera affects the projection transformation.

On Your Own

1. Translating an object along an axis is simple if you use the helper functions that D3DX provides. The D3DXMatrixTranslation function creates a translation matrix that you can multiply by a rotation matrix. The resulting output matrix is the product of rotating and translating an object.

```
D3DXMATRIX translationMatrix;
D3DXMATRIX rotationMatrix;
D3DXMATRIX outMatrix;

// Rotate the object by 90 degrees on the X axis
D3DXMatrixRotationX(&rotationMatrix, D3DXToRadian(90));

// Translate the object 5 units along the X axis
D3DXMatrixTranslation(&translationMatrix, 5.0f, 0.0f, 0.0f);

// Multiply the rotation matrix by the translation matrix, storing the result
// in the outMatrix
D3DXMatrixMultiply(&outMatrix, &rotationMatrix, &translationMatrix);
```

2. You can rotate an object constantly around an axis by continually increasing the angle being passed to the D3DXMatrixRotationY function. In the following example, the object is set to rotate using the timeGetTime function.

```
void render(void)
{
    // the matrix that stores the current matrix for an object
    D3DXMATRIX        MeshMat;
    // the matrix that stores the object's rotation
    D3DXMATRIX        meshRotate;

    // Clear the back buffer to a black color
    pd3dDevice->Clear( 0,
                       NULL,
                       D3DCLEAR_TARGET,
                       D3DCOLOR_XRGB(255,255,255),
                       1.0f,
                       0 );

    pd3dDevice->BeginScene();

    pd3dDevice->SetStreamSource( 0, vertexBuffer, 0, sizeof(CUSTOMVERTEX) );
    pd3dDevice->SetFVF( D3DFVF_CUSTOMVERTEX );

    // Set meshMat to identity; this resets the matrix
```

```
D3DXMatrixIdentity(&meshMat);

// Set the rotation along the Y axis
D3DXMatrixRotationY(&meshRotate, timeGetTime()/1000.0f);

// Multiply the meshMat and the meshRotate matrix
D3DXMatrixMultiply(&meshMat, &meshMat, &meshRotate);

// Transform the object in world space
pd3dDevice->SetTransform(D3DTS_WORLD, &meshMat);

pd3dDevice->DrawPrimitive( D3DPT_TRIANGLESTRIP,  0, 2 );

pd3dDevice->EndScene();

// Present the back buffer contents to the display
pd3dDevice->Present( NULL, NULL, NULL, NULL );
}
```

Chapter 6

Review Questions

1. The fill mode affects how objects are rendered. The wireframe fill mode draws all the objects as a series of lines. The solid fill mode renders each object as a solid series of triangles.

2. Direct3D has four types of lighting: ambient, directional, point, and spot lighting.

3. A directional light is a light source that has a direction but not a position in space.

4. The D3DXCreateTextureFromFile function supports loading of the following types of files: bitmap, Windows DIB, Targa, JPEG, PNG, and DDS.

5. When you change the texture coordinates to a value greater than 1.0f, the texture is repeated across a polygon's surface.

On Your Own

1. To cause the teapot to reflect only diffuse lighting, you must create a material structure that contains diffuse values. In addition, you must set the ambient values in the structure to 0.0f. The following code demonstrates a material structure that does this.

```
// Create the material that the mesh will use
D3DMATERIAL9            mtrl;

// Clear out the material structure
```

```
ZeroMemory(&mtrl, sizeof(D3DMATERIAL9));

// Set the diffuse properties for the material
mtrl.Diffuse.r = 1.0f;
mtrl.Diffuse.g = 0.5f;
mtrl.Diffuse.b = 0.5f;

// Set the ambient properties for the material
// Turn off these properties
mtrl.Ambient.r = 0.0f;
mtrl.Ambient.g = 0.0f;
mtrl.Ambient.b = 0.0f;
mtrl.Power = 8.0f;
```

2. Because you'll be using two textures, the first step is to create an additional IDirect3DTexture9 object. After you have two texture objects, you need to load the textures you will be using. You'll notice in the code that follows that I have two calls to the D3DXCreateTextureFromFile function. This function loads each texture and assigns it to the appropriate texture object. The most important step in drawing an object with multiple textures is changing the texture during rendering by using the SetTexture function.

In the following code, the SetTexture function sets the current texture to the first texture object for three triangle strips and then switches to the second texture for the remainder of the triangles.

```
// texture info
LPDIRECT3DTEXTURE9      g_pTexture    = NULL;
LPDIRECT3DTEXTURE9      g_pTexture2   = NULL;

// Load the multiple textures and assign them to the texture objects
D3DXCreateTextureFromFile( pd3dDevice, "test.bmp", &g_pTexture );
D3DXCreateTextureFromFile( pd3dDevice, "test2.bmp", &g_pTexture2);

// Tell Direct3D to use the first texture for three of the triangle strips
pd3dDevice->SetTexture( 0, g_pTexture );
pd3dDevice->DrawPrimitive( D3DPT_TRIANGLESTRIP,  0, 2 );
pd3dDevice->DrawPrimitive( D3DPT_TRIANGLESTRIP,  4, 2 );
pd3dDevice->DrawPrimitive( D3DPT_TRIANGLESTRIP,  8, 2 );

// Switch over to the second texture to render the rest of the triangle strips
pd3dDevice->SetTexture( 0, g_pTexture2 );
pd3dDevice->DrawPrimitive( D3DPT_TRIANGLESTRIP, 12, 2 );
pd3dDevice->DrawPrimitive( D3DPT_TRIANGLESTRIP, 16, 2 );
pd3dDevice->DrawPrimitive( D3DPT_TRIANGLESTRIP, 20, 2 );
```

Chapter 7

Review Questions

1. You can use both the `D3DXCreateMesh` and `D3DXCreateMeshFVF` functions to create a mesh object.

2. The `OptimizeInplace` function does not require the creation of an additional mesh object.

3. A mesh's attribute table allows the mesh to contain one or more materials.

4. `GetNumVertices` returns the number of objects in a mesh.

5. `DXFILEFORMAT_BINARY` creates a binary X file, `DXFILEFORMAT_TEXT` creates a text version of an X file, and the final flag, `DXFILEFORMAT_COMPRESSED`, causes the X file to be compressed.

On Your Own

1. Previously, you loaded a single mesh by using the `D3DXLoadMeshFromX` function. To load more than one X file mesh, you create multiple `D3DXMESH` objects and use `D3DXLoadMeshFromX`. The code that follows shows how you can use this technique to display more than one model.

   The first step in loading more than one model is to provide an easy way to call the `D3DXLoadMeshFromX` function and assign the model to a `D3DXMESH` object. The `loadMesh` function that follows performs this task.

   Next, you create two `D3DXMESH` objects and assign them to the result of the `loadMesh` function. At this point, you should have two valid `D3DXMESH` objects. The final step is rendering the two meshes by using the `DrawSubset` function.

```
/*****************************************************************************
* loadMesh
*****************************************************************************/
LPD3DXMESH loadMesh(LPDIRECT3DDEVICE9 pd3dDevice, std::string filename)
{
    HRESULT hr;
    LPD3DXMESH tempMesh = NULL;
    DWORD numMaterials = 0;

    // Load the mesh from the specified file
    hr = D3DXLoadMeshFromX( filename.c_str(),
                            D3DXMESH_SYSTEMMEM,
                            pd3dDevice,
                            &NULL,
                            &NULL,
                            NULL,
```

```
                               &numMaterials,
                               &tempMesh );

        if( FAILED(hr) )
            return NULL;

        return tempMesh;
    }


    // These are the variables that will hold the loaded meshes
    LPD3DXMESH mesh1;
    LPD3DXMESH mesh2;


    // Load the first mesh
    mesh1 = dxMgr->loadMesh("mesh1.x");
    if (!mesh1)
    {
        MessageBox(wndHandle, "can't load xfile", "ERROR", MB_OK);
        return false;
    }


    // Load the second mesh
    mesh2 = dxMgr->loadMesh("mesh2.x");
    if (!mesh2)
    {
        MessageBox(wndHandle, "can't load xfile", "ERROR", MB_OK);
        return false;
    }


    /****************************************************************************
    * render
    ****************************************************************************/
    void render(void)
    {
        mesh1->DrawSubset(0);
        mesh2->DrawSubset(0);
    }
```

2. You optimize a mesh through the Optimize function. The code that follows shows how to use Optimize to create a function whose job it is to optimize and return a mesh.

```
    /****************************************************************************
    * optimizeThisMesh
    ****************************************************************************/
```

```
LPD3DXMESH optimizeThisMesh(LPD3DXMESH inMesh)
{
        LPD3DMESH outMesh = NULL;

        inMesh->Optimize(D3DXMESHOPT_ATTRSORT, 0, NULL, NULL, &outMesh);

        return outMesh;
}
```

Chapter 8

Review Questions

1. The basic properties of a particle are position, color, and movement.

2. By adding together a particle's current position and its movement rate, you can make the particle move around a scene.

3. An emitter initializes the properties of each particle it creates.

4. The D3DPT_POINTLIST type is used when rendering particles as point sprites.

5. You can render point sprites more quickly than billboards within Direct3D because point sprites are treated as single points.

On Your Own

1. When you were shown how to create a particle previously, each particle lived forever. That causes a lot of problems when the particles go off the screen. Because the particles never die, they are rendered continuously even though they can't be seen.

   To make sure that a particle can die, you must add two variables to the particle structure: m_alive and lifetime. The m_alive variable is a boolean value that is TRUE if the particle is alive or FALSE if it is not. The lifetime variable is an integer that holds the number of frames that the particle has been alive.

   In each time through the render loop, your code must check to see if each particle is alive. If the particle is alive, its lifetime counter is incremented and the particle is rendered. If the particle is dead, it is skipped and the next particle in the list is checked. The code that follows shows how to kill off a particle after just 300 frames.

```
typedef struct
{
        D3DXVECTOR3 m_vCurPos;
        D3DXVECTOR3 m_vCurVel;
        D3DCOLOR    m_vColor;
        bool m_alive;
        int lifetime;
```

```
    } Particle;

    // Define the single particle
    Particle oneParticle;

    // Set the particle's current position
    oneParticle.m_vCurPos = D3DXVECTOR3(0.0f,0.0f,0.0f);

    // Generate a random value for each part of the direction/velocity vector
    float vecX = ((float)rand() / RAND_MAX);
    float vecY = ((float)rand() / RAND_MAX);
    float vecZ = ((float)rand() / RAND_MAX);
    oneParticle.m_vCurVel = D3DXVECTOR3(vecX,vecY,vecZ);

    // This particle is white
    oneParticle.m_vColor = D3DCOLOR_RGBA( 255, 255, 255, 255);

    // Set this particle to alive
    oneParticle.m_alive = true;

    // Set the lifetime to 0
    oneParticle.lifetime = 0;

    /***************************************************************************
    * renderParticle
    ***************************************************************************/
    void renderParticle(void)
    {
        // Check whether this particle is alive
        if (oneParticle.m_alive)
        {
            // The particle is alive; check to see if it reached its life
            // limit of 300 frames
            if (lifetime == 300)
                // If the particle has reached the end of its life, set the
                // m_alive variable to FALSE
                oneParticle.m_alive = false;
            else
                // Increment the lifetime counter; this particle is still alive
                oneParticle.lifetime++;

            // Render the particle
        }
    }
```

2. If you want a particle emitter that constantly releases particles, you would think that you could just increase the number of particles that the emitter has available. Although this would make sense, your computer doesn't have the power or the memory to meet this requirement. The easiest way to accomplish this task is through particle recycling. Particle recycling involves reusing particles that have exhausted their lifetime. Each frame, a particle gets closer to the end of its lifetime. When the particle's death is reached, its m_bAlive flag is set to FALSE, and it's available to be born again from the emitter.

The recycle function that follows shows how to cause a particle to be reborn.

```
void Emitter::recycle(void)
{
    // Loop through the number of particles and recycle the dead ones
    for (int i=0; i<numParticles; i++)
    {
        if (!m_particles[i].m_bAlive)
        {
            m_particles[i].reset();
            m_particles[i].m_vColor = D3DCOLOR_ARGB(0,255,0,0);
            m_particles[i].m_vCurPos = m_vCurPos;

            // Generate a random value for each direction/velocity vector
            float vecX = ((float)rand() / RAND_MAX);
            float vecY = ((float)rand() / RAND_MAX);
            float vecZ = ((float)rand() / RAND_MAX);
            m_particles[i].m_vCurVel = D3DXVECTOR3(vecX,vecY,vecZ);
        }
    }
}
```

Chapter 9

Review Questions

1. You use DirectInput to get input from a device, such as the keyboard, mouse, joysticks, and game pads.

2. The DirectInput8Create function creates a DirectInput object that can access all the functionality of DirectInput.

3. Enumeration is the process of searching and detecting devices that are installed on a system.

4. The GetDeviceState function needs a buffer of 256 characters.

5. c_dfDIMouse is the format that the SetDataFormat function uses to access the mouse input device.

On Your Own

1. Removing the Windows cursor while using the mouse is a simple matter of restricting mouse access to your application only. When you set the cooperative level of the mouse to DISCL_EXCLUSIVE, the Windows cursor is removed.

```
HRESULT hr = SetCooperativeLevel(wndHandle, DISCL_EXCLUSIVE);
```

2. Reading from a game pad or joystick buttons is just as simple as reading their direction. Each time through the game loop, you capture the state of the device and place it into the js structure below. Afterward, you can check this structure for the state of each button. The code that follows shows how to capture the state of the device and check each button for use.

```
DIJOYSTATE2 js;            // DInput joystick state

// Get the input's device state
if( FAILED( hr = g_pJoystick->GetDeviceState( sizeof(DIJOYSTATE2), &js ) ) )
        return hr;

// Loop through the buttons that are available in the DIJOYSTATE2 structure
for( int i = 0; i < 128; i++ )
{
        // If this button is done, print a message
        if ( js.rgbButtons[i] & 0x80 )
        printf("button #[%d] is pressed\n", i);
}
```

Chapter 10

Review Questions

1. You use the DirectSoundEnumerate function when you want to get a list of the sound devices that are installed on your machine. You normally use DirectSoundEnumerate when you don't want to use the default sound device.

2. The lpGuid contains the GUID of the sound device, lpcstrDescription gives you a text description of the device, and lpcstrModule gives you the text description of the sound driver being used.

3. The format of a secondary buffer does need to match the sound data that is contained within it.

4. The primary buffer is where the final mixed sound data from all the secondary buffers is stored before being played.

5. DSDEVID_DefaultPlayback is passed to DirectSoundCreate8 to specify that the default sound device is to be used.

On Your Own

1. You change the volume of a sound through the SetVolume function, which is available to you through the DIRECTSOUNDBUFFER interface. When you change the value that is passed to SetVolume during the game loop, you can decrease or increase the volume of the sound.

```
int curVolume = 0;        // variable to hold the current volume
int volChange = 1000;     // the amount to change the volume by each frame
{
        // main game loop
        curVolume+= volChange;

        // Allow the volume to range from 0 to -10000
        if ((curVolume <= 10000) || (curVolume >= 0))
                volChange *= -1;

        // Set the current volume
        DSBuffer->SetVolume(curVolume);
        // End game loop
}
```

2. Panning a sound between speakers involves the use of the SetPan function. By changing the value passed to the SetPan function, you can increase or decrease the volume in the left or right speakers, giving the impression that the sound is moving from one speaker to the other.

```
// The current pan value, 0, sets both speakers to equal volume
int panVolume = 0;
// This is the amount to pan each frame
int panChange = 500;
{
        // main game loop
        if ((panVolume <= DSBPAN_LEFT) || (panVolume >= DSBPAN_RIGHT))
                panChange *= -1;

        // Increment the panVolume by the panChange value
        panVolume += panChange;

        // Change the pan volume
        DSBuffer->SetPan(panVolume);
        // End main loop
}
```

APPENDIX B

USING THE CD-ROM

T he included CD-ROM contains all the source code from the examples in this book. The DirectX SDK from Microsoft is also included.

What's on the CD-ROM

The code samples are located in the folder corresponding to the approprriate chapter number. For example, you can find all code samples used in Chapter 3, "Surfaces, Sprites, and Salmon," in the chapter3 directory on the CD-ROM.

The code samples within these directories are split into separate folders and are labeled example1, example2, and so on.

Within the example folders are the complete source code listings, the Visual Studio .NET 2003 project files, and a debug folder that includes a ready-to-run executable of that particular sample.

You can run the executables from the CD-ROM, but if you want to recompile the source code, you must copy the example folders to your hard drive. You also might need to remove the Read-Only attribute from the files after they are copied to your hard drive.

Installing the DirectX SDK

To get started programming for DirectX, you must first install the DirectX SDK on your machine. The DirectX SDK is the software development kit from Microsoft that includes all the header files, libraries, and samples you need to write software for DirectX.

The DirectX SDK takes up approximately 300 MB on your hard drive, so make sure you have enough room before running the installation.

You can find the installation program for the DirectX SDK in the DXSDK directory on the included CD-ROM. Figure B.1 shows the files you should find in this directory.

You begin the SDK installation by clicking the install.exe icon. The dialog box shown in Figure B.2 should appear.

Figure B.1 The contents of the DXSDK directory on the CD-ROM.

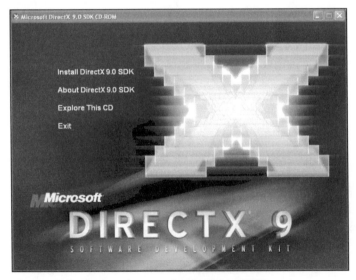

Figure B.2 The launch screen for the DirectX SDK.

Select the option Install DirectX 9.0 SDK.

The installer launches and presents you with the dialog box shown in Figure B.3. Click the Next button to continue with the installation.

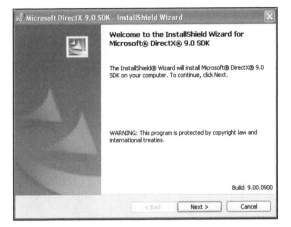

Figure B.3 The installation welcome dialog box.

Next you are presented with the End-User License Agreement (EULA) from Microsoft. You must accept this license agreement to install the SDK. The license dialog box is shown in Figure B.4. Click the Next button to continue.

The next dialog box, Custom Setup, presents you with multiple choices for the install. You want to install the entire SDK, so leave the default options as they are. If you would like to change the directory that the SDK will be installed into, click the Change button and enter the new directory path.

Click the Next button to continue. The Custom Setup dialog box is shown in Figure B.5.

One more option is required: the type of DirectX runtime that you would like to be installed.

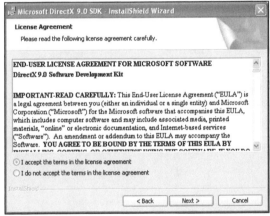

Figure B.4 The End-User License Agreement dialog box.

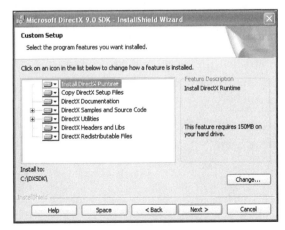

Figure B.5 The Custom Setup dialog box.

Because you will be developing DirectX applications, it's best to choose the Debug runtime. Although the performance of this runtime is not as fast as the retail version, it does help when you're trying to track down a difficult bug.

The runtime selection dialog box is shown in Figure B.6. After you click the Next button again, the installation of the DirectX SDK begins.

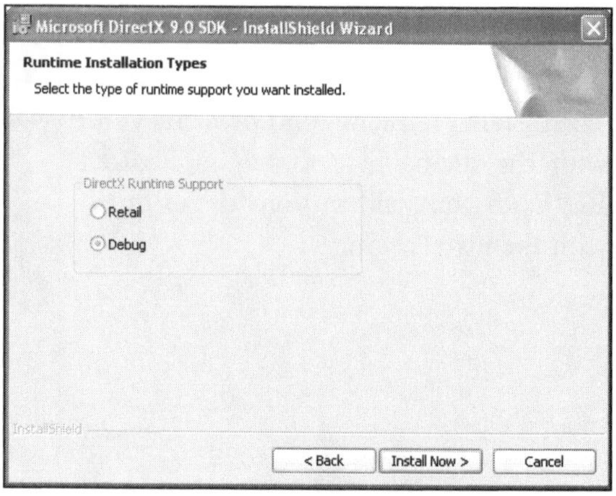

Figure B.6 The runtime selection dialog box.

The progress dialog box should appear. This dialog box continually updates you as to the progress of the installation. This dialog box is shown in Figure B.7.

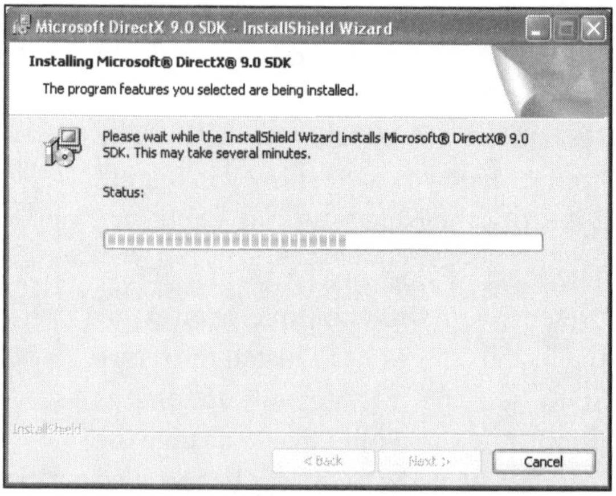

Figure B.7 The installation progress dialog box.

The installation continues for a few minutes, so don't be worried if it's taking some time. A dialog box informs you when the installation is complete. Figure B.8 shows the completion dialog box.

Clicking the Finish button ends the installation.

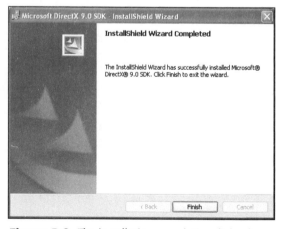

Figure B.8 The installation completion dialog box.

2D animation—The process of displaying still frames in quick succession to create the illusion of motion.

alpha blending—A graphical technique used to make 3D surfaces appear transparent.

ambient lighting—Lighting that is uniform and does not appear to come from any particular direction.

Application Programming Interface (API)—A set of functions that an application uses to carry out tasks.

back buffer—An area of memory to which graphics can be drawn before being displayed on the screen.

Basic Input Output System (BIOS)—The lowest level of software in a computer that handles setting up the hardware for use by the operating system.

billboard—A normally four-sided polygon often used in particle systems. A billboard always faces toward the camera.

bitmap—A series of pixels that represent a graphical image.

Component Object Model (COM)—An architecture developed by Microsoft to create component-based software.

constant force—A force that retains a consistent direction and pressure during its duration.

cooperative level—The level of access permitted to a hardware device within DirectX.

coordinate systems—The way of defining positions within 3D space.

culling—The act of removing objects or vertices from a scene before it is rendered.

Device Driver Kit (DDK)—A set of development code libraries used for the creation of device drivers.

Direct3D—A portion of DirectX that provides functions for creating, manipulating, and viewing 3D data.

Direct3D device—An interface of DirectX that represents the graphics adapter.

DirectDraw—A DirectX component that handles 2D surfaces and images.

DirectInput—A DirectX component that gathers and receives input data from various devices.

directional lighting—Light that travels in a straight line from its source.

DirectMusic—The DirectX component used to play dynamic sounds.

DirectPlay—The DirectX component that provides networking and multiplayer support.

DirectSetup—The DirectX component that provides an easy way to install the DirectX runtime on a client machine.

DirectSound—The component of DirectX that handles the manipulation and playing of sounds.

DirectX—A set of APIs used in the development of game and multimedia applications on the Windows platform.

DirectX Graphics—The component of DirectX that handles graphics output.

DirectX Runtime—The DLL component that provides the functionality of DirectX.

Disk Operating System (DOS)—The low-level program that tells the system how to operate. DOS as an operating system is no longer in wide use.

display adapter—The video output hardware.

enumeration—The process of programmatically searching a system for a particular type of hardware device based on search criteria.

feedback effect—A series of vibrations sent to a force feedback device.

force feedback—The addition of motors within input devices that provide the user with vibration.

frame—A single still image that is usually part of an animation.

front buffer—The area of memory that represents the viewable area of a display screen.

Globally Unique Identifier (GUID)—A number that is used to identify a software component.

Graphical User Interface (GUI)—A user interface that represents the system through a series of icons, pictures, or menus.

Hardware Abstraction Layer (HAL)—A layer of software that provides a standard way to access different hardware without knowing the specifics of the device.

Hardware Emulation layer (HEL)—A layer of software that provides missing functionality of a hardware device.

index buffer—Memory buffers that contain index data, which are offsets into a list of vertices.

matrix—An ordered array of numbers.

mesh—An interconnected set of polygons that represent an object in 3D space.

message loop—The process within a Windows application of retrieving and dispatching system messages.

message queue—The area within the Windows operating system that holds events and messages created by applications.

multitexturing—Applying more than one texture to a given set of vertices.

normal—A directional vector at a right angle to a plane.

offscreen surface—An area of memory into which graphical data can be loaded and manipulated without being displayed.

page flipping—The swapping of the front and one or more offscreen buffers.

particle—A normally four-sided polygon used to represent small objects such as dirt, smoke, or sparks within a game.

periodic effect—A force feedback effect that occurs on a given time interval.

perspective—A type of projection that displays objects that are farther away from the camera in 3D space as smaller than objects that are closer to the camera.

point sprite—A way of representing particles within Direct3D.

polling—Periodically checking an input device like a joystick for input.

primary buffer—A DirectSound buffer into which sounds from secondary buffers are mixed for output.

primitive—A standard 3D object upon which meshes are created.

projection—The process of transforming 3D space into a 2D viewable form.

ramp force—A force feedback effect that gradually increases in intensity over time.

refresh rate—The rate at which the screen is updated.

return code—A value returned from a function that determines whether the function was successful.

secondary buffer—An area of memory that loads sound data within DirectSound.

self-extracting file—An executable file that contains compressed data, with the ability to uncompress this data without an external helper application.

sound buffer—An area of memory that holds sound data.

sprite—A graphic that is used to represent 2D characters or items within a game.

static buffer—An area of memory that holds sound data within DirectSound. The static buffer is commonly used when the entire sound can be loaded.

streaming buffer—An area of memory that holds a portion of sound data. The streaming buffer is used when all the sound data is too large to fit in memory at one time.

surface—A linear piece of memory that stores graphic data. The surface is represented as a rectangular area into which graphics can be held.

texture coordinates—A set of coordinates on a polygon that defines the portion of the texture map to apply.

texture mapping—Applying an image to a polygon to give it the illusion of a real-world object.

timer—An internal counting mechanism that keeps a constant rate of time for animations.

tranformation—Converting a 3D object from one coordinate system to another.

triangle fan—A series of triangles that share a single vertex in a fan pattern.

triangle strip—A series of triangles that are connected, where only a single vertex is needed to specify an addition triangle.

Universal Serial Bus (USB)—A standard port that enables users to connect a wide variety of devices, such as mice, cameras, and game pads.

vector—A straight line segment in 3D space consisting of both direction and magnitude. The length of a vector is defined as its magnitude, whereas its orientation represents its direction.

vertex—A single point of a polygon consisting of an X, Y, and Z coordinate defining its position in 3D space.

vertex buffer—A buffer containing vertex data.

video resolution—The width, height, and bit depth of a particular video mode.

viewport—A rectangular area that defines where in a target surface a scene should be rendered.

windowed application—An application that runs within a window on the desktop.

Windows—An operating system from Microsoft that provides the user with a Graphical User Interface (GUI).

WinMain—The entry point function for Windows applications.

X file—The native DirectX 3D object format.

Z-Buffer—An array used to store the Z coordinate of polygons plotted in 3D space. Direct3D uses the Z value of each polygon to determine which 3D objects are in front of others.

INDEX

Symbols

3D models. *See also* **3D space**
    cubes, rending, 91–92
    index buffers, 92–96
    overview, 87–88
    vertex buffers, 88–90
3D space. *See also* **3D models**
    coordinate systems, 66–68
    depth, 65
    discussed, 65
    planet creation, 277–279, 290–291
    primitive types, 82–85
    spaceship creation, 281–282
    vertex buffers
        copying vertices to, 76
        creating, 71–72
        Flexible Vertex Format, 72–74
        loading data into, 74–78
        locking, 74–75
        rendering, 79–80
        scenes, rendering, 81–82
        stream source, setting, 78–79
        unlocking, 76–78
        vertex shader, setting, 79
    vertices, 68–70

A

A variable, alpha color component, 70
access
    acquiring, 209
    nonexclusive, 207
Acquire function, 209, 228–229
Adapter parameter, CreateDevice function, 18
adapters
    display modes for, 30–31
    information, gathering, 29–30
    querying, 32–33
Add New Item command (Project menu), 11
Add New Item dialog box, 11

addItemToList function, 32
addTexture function, 190
alpha color component, A variable, 70
ambient lighting
    creating, 129–130
    overview, 124
    reflection, 134
Angle parameter, 106
animation
    anim_rate variable, 60, 267
    sprites, 53–57
    timers, 57–61
API (Application Programming Interface), 6
Application Settings tab (Application Wizard dialog box), 10–11
application window
    initializing, 11–15
    initWindow function, 259–261
    WinMain function, 258–259
    WndProc function, 261
Application Wizard dialog box
    Application Settings tab, 10–11
    Overview tab, 10
architecture, DirectX, 6–7
arrays
    attribTable, 160
    IndexData, 94
attenuation, lighting, 128
AttribId variable, 160
attribTable array, 160
attribute table, meshes, 158–162
AutoDepthStencilFormat parameter, 19
axis objects, 223

B

B variable, blue color component, 70
back buffers
    discussed, 19–20, 36
    page flipping, 20

License Agreement/Notice of Limited Warranty